The anonymous Christian – a relativised Christianity?
An Evaluation of Hans Urs von Balthasar's criticisms of Karl Rahner's theory of the anonymous Christian

European University Studies

Europäische Hochschulschriften
Publications Universitaires Européennes

Series XXIII

Theology

Reihe XXIII Série XXIII
Theologie
Théologie

Vol./Bd. 485

PETER LANG

Frankfurt am Main · Berlin · Bern · New York · Paris · Wien

Eamonn Conway

The anonymous Christian – a relativised Christianity?

An Evaluation of Hans Urs von Balthasar's criticisms of Karl Rahner's theory of the anonymous Christian

PETER LANG
Frankfurt am Main · Berlin · Bern · New York · Paris · Wien

Die Deutsche Bibliothek - CIP-Einheitsaufnahme

Conway, Eamonn:

The anonymous Christian - a relativised Christianity? : An
evaluation of Hans Urs von Balthasar's criticisms of Karl
Rahner's theory of the anonymous Christian / Eamonn
Conway. - Frankfurt am Main ; Berlin ; Bern ; New York ; Paris ;
Wien : Lang, 1993
    (European university studies : Ser. 23, Theology ; Vol. 485)
    Zugl.: Maynooth, Pontifical Univ., Diss., 1991
    ISBN 3-631-46209-3

NE: Europäische Hochschulschriften / 23

ISSN 0721-3409
ISBN 3-631-46209-3

© Verlag Peter Lang GmbH, Frankfurt am Main 1993

Printed in Germany 1 2 3 4 5 6 7

Foreword

Hans Urs von Balthasar and Karl Rahner have each written more books than most people could hope to read in a lifetime, and have reflected profoundly on all the major theological issues. Yet having studied the theological method of both scholars I find it hard to see how either Rahner or Balthasar could be truly understood without referring one to the other.

Taken together, Rahner and Balthasar bring out the catholicity which is the very treasure of Catholic theology - a treasure which would remain hidden if either of its essential elements - unity or diversity - became eclipsed. This is why the word "only" in the context of theological method evokes suspicion.

Rahner and Balthasar, each with his own personality and each drawing inspiration from the tradition in his own unique way, continue to contribute differently to the contemporary challenge of handing on the one Christian faith. The diversity of methods in Rahner's and Balthasar's theology is embraced within an even greater unity of personal faith. Both men's lives represent a <u>kenosis</u> at the service of the Gospel. Their own personal experience of God, which evoked such a generous response from each of them, is their common legacy to us. Though theological methods differ, it is only on the surface, for both teach us that the only way to "do" theology is through prayer. The result of prayer is hope, which we can never keep to ourselves.

May the virtue of Christian hope, mediated in abundance through the work of Balthasar and Rahner, send us out to others with courage, confidence, enthusiasm and love.

Eamonn Conway, All Hallows, 1993

Acknowledgement

With grateful acknowledgement to Thomas Norris, Pontifical University, Maynooth, and to Peter Hünermann, Catholic Faculty of Theology, University of Tübingen, for their direction and support throughout my postgraduate studies. Any effort to explore the mystery of God's love is enabled by others, engaged in with others, and is for others. Thank you to my family, friends and colleagues.

TABLE OF CONTENTS

ACKNOWLEDGEMENT
FOREWORD

INTRODUCTION

CHAPTER 1. AN INTRODUCTION TO THE ANONYMOUS CHRISTIAN

CHAPTER 2. CRITICISMS FROM 1939 TO VATICAN TWO

CHAPTER 3. CRITICISMS FROM AFTER VATICAN TWO TO 1988

Introduction

The purpose of this work

The most serious problem facing the contemporary Church is that of proclaiming credibly that Jesus Christ is the Saviour of the world. The Church teaches that God, through Christ, wishes everyone to be saved and reach full knowledge of the truth (1Tim. 2:4)[1]. The Church is challenged today to maintain optimism regarding the possibility of the salvation of all humankind and to give this optimism a credible theological basis, while at the same time maintaining the unique and indispensable role of Jesus Christ and the Church in the mediation of salvation to all humankind.

The Second Vatican Council spoke optimistically about the salvation of those who, through no fault of their own, do not know the Gospel or the Church and do not even have explicit knowledge of God. It acknowledged that such people could indeed be moved by grace and achieve eternal salvation through following the dictates of their conscience.[2]

Even prior to the Second Vatican Council, Karl Rahner recognised the importance, particularly in a secularised Europe, of providing a theological account of how people not baptised Christians or professing to be atheists can be saved. He realised that a contemporary Christian cannot be expected to believe that

> the overwhelming mass of his brothers, not only those before the appearance of Christ right back to the most distant past...but also those of the present and of the future before us, are unquestionably and in principle excluded from the fulfilment of their lives and condemned to eternal meaninglessness.[3]

Convinced from the very beginning that God's will is to save all people, Rahner puts anthropology and transcendental philosophy at the disposal of theology and, through an examination of the structures of human being and knowing, he sets out to show how it is possible within these structures for God to communicate himself to the human being. He also sets out to show how it is possible and necessary for the

---

[1] "All this holds true not for Christians only but also for all men of goodwill in whose hearts grace is active invisibly. For since Christ died for all, and since all men are in fact called to one and the same destiny, which is divine, we must hold that the Holy Spirit offers to all the possibility of being made partners, in a way known to God, in the paschal mystery" (<u>Gaudium et Spes</u>, n.22).

[2] "Those who, through no fault of their own, do not know the Gospel of Christ or his Church, but who nevertheless seek God with a sincere heart, and, moved by grace, try in their actions to do his will as they know it through the dictates of their conscience - those too achieve eternal salvation. Nor shall divine providence deny the assistance necessary for salvation to those who, without any fault of theirs, have not yet arrived at an explicit knowledge of God, and who, not without grace, strive to lead a good life" (<u>Lumen Gentium</u>, n.16).

[3] <u>Theological investigations</u> 6, 391.

human being to respond to God's gracious self-offer, either positively or negatively. A positive response corresponds to the necessary act of faith required of an individual for salvation.

Rahner's theory of the anonymous Christian provides one possible theological basis for the Second Vatican Council's teaching on the salvation of non-Christians. According to Rahner, the anonymous Christian is someone who has accepted God's gracious self-offer transcendentally in and through an implicit act of faith. However this implicit act of faith has not been correctly expressed at the categorical level through baptism and membership of the Church. This is for various reasons for which the anonymous Christian is not culpable.

Christians consider it essential to account theologically for the salvation of the kind of people of whom the Second Vatican Council spoke, while at the same time proclaiming unequivocally that all salvation comes through Jesus Christ, and that the Church is the sacrament of God's salvation. Over a period of fifty years Hans Urs von Balthasar voiced criticism of Karl Rahner's approach to theology. The theory of the anonymous Christian became a particular focal point of his criticism. Balthasar's main fear was that Rahner seems to account for the salvation of non-Christians only through an unacceptable relativisation of Jesus Christ and the Church. The purpose of this work is to outline Rahner's teaching on the anonymous Christian and to evaluate Balthasar's criticisms.

This, the last decade of the century, has been declared a decade of renewed effort at evangelisation. When we reflect on the contemporary faith milieu, particularly in Western Europe, we realise that it is vital to be able to account credibly and in theological terms for the possibility of the salvation of non-Christians and of non-believers and of the increasing number of people who do not identify themselves explicitly with Christianity and the Church, while at the same time proclaiming clearly and unambiguously the unique and indispensable mission of the Church in the world. Such a theological account is essential if efforts at evangelisation are to be placed on a sure footing. It is hoped that having examined Rahner's theory of the anonymous Christian in the light of Balthasar's criticisms, we will be in a better position to provide the kind of theological basis such efforts require.

A note on method

The aim of the first chapter is to introduce the theory of the anonymous Christian. The theory of the anonymous Christian lies at the very heart of Rahner's theology. It is an unavoidable consequence of his teaching on the relationship which exists between nature and grace. However, Rahner's understanding of the relationship between nature and grace evolved out of his earliest studies in transcendental Thomism and modern philosophy. To understand the theory of the anonymous Christian and Balthasar's criticisms adequately it is necessary to understand his earliest philosophical works. The reader will understand that it is impossible to give an adequate account of these here in a work which focuses primarily on Balthasar's criticisms and that some familarity with the work of Karl Rahner, and especially with his sources and method, will have to be presumed. In the first chapter we intend simply to define the theory of the anonymous Christian, situate it within the context of Rahner's theological method as a whole, and give an account of how Rahner believed that the theory should be employed.

The next two chapters will catalogue chronologically Hans Urs von Balthasar's criticisms of the anonymous Christian up to and after the Second Vatican Council.

In Chapters Four and Five, Balthasar's criticisms are evaluated in the light of Rahner's theology as a whole. Chapter Four assesses Balthasar's accusation of a methodological error in Rahner's theology, which would invalidate the theory of the anonymous Christian. Chapter Five evaluates Balthasar's main criticism: that Rahner's teaching on grace leads to a relativisation of biblical revelation and the Church. The final chapter, Chapter Six, points to the value of Balthasar's criticisms and attempts to suggest the relevance and importance of the teaching of the anonymous Christian for the contemporary Church.

Chapter 1
An Introduction to the Anonymous Christian

Introduction

This chapter introduces Rahner's theory of the anonymous Christian, summarises its
remote and immediate theological background, sketches how and why it developed
and outlines some of its consequences. When we subsequently confront the doctrine
of the anonymous Christian with Balthasar's criticisms, many of the points introduced
in this chapter will be taken up and further developed in the course of a response and
an evaluation.

The Church has always been concerned to account for the possibility of salvation for
those who are not baptised. Today this question is perhaps more urgent than ever in
a pluralistic society, given the change in consciousness brought about by
contemporary mass media, world-wide communication, and international travel
facilities. In a world which is becoming ever smaller, we are frequently confronted
with people whose religious world-view and understanding of faith is different from
our own. In addition, we have today the related problem of accounting for the
activity of God's grace among people baptised Christian but for whom membership
of the Church is no longer meaningful, or even a matter of relevance or interest.

These issues are very real for a Church in danger even in Europe of becoming a
diaspora, and at an early stage Rahner realised that they needed to be treated
theologically as a matter of priority. In one of his essays, written before the Second
Vatican Council, Rahner put this problem in perspective:

> I see thousands upon thousands around me - I see whole cultures, whole epochs of history
> around me, before and after me - who are not explicitly Christian. I see the approach of
> times in which Christianity will no longer be a matter of course in Europe and in the whole
> world. I know all that, but ultimately it cannot really trouble me. Why not? Because I see
> everywhere a nameless Christianity, and because I do not see my own explicit Christianity
> as one among others which contradict it. I see nothing other in my Christianity than the
> explicit home-coming of everything in the way of truth and love which exists or could exist
> anywhere else. I neither hold non-Christians to be more stupid than I am nor as having less
> good will than I have. If I were to fall into an empty and cowardly scepticism on account
> of the variety of philosophies of life, would I then have a better chance of attaining to the
> truth than if I remain a Christian? The answer must be in the negative, for even scepticism
> and agnosticism are only two opinions among others - in fact, the most cowardly and empty
> of all. They do not provide a way of escape from the multiplicity of philosophies of life
> in the world. Even "refraining from making any decision regarding a philosophy of life"
> is a decision - and the worst at that.[1]

Rahner realised that in the contemporary milieu, which the Christian can attempt to ignore only at
his peril, some framework was required in which to understand faith if it was not to "fall into an
empty and cowardly scepticism" or worse, if it was not to collapse into agnosticism.

---

[1] Theological investigations 5, 9.

Historical background to the anonymous Christian

Karl Rahner was not, of course, the first to address the problem of accounting theologically for the salvation of non-Christians, nor was he the first to use the term "anonymous Christian" to describe people justified but not baptised.[2]

We can recall first of all, for example, the statement of Justin (before 165 A.D.):

> And those who lived according to Logos are Christians even if they were considered Atheists; like among the Greeks Socrates, Heraclit, and others; and among the Barbarians Abraham, Ananias, Azarias, Misael, Elias and so many others.[3]

This is endorsed two centuries later by Augustine (354-430):

> What is now called Christian religion was there in the past and was never unknown from the beginning of humanity up to Christ's coming in flesh. Since then one began to call Christian the true religion that was already there before.[4]

Then there is the medieval doctrine of the votum baptismi which is the background to the Holy Office's famous letter in 1949 condemning Fr. Leonard Feeney's restrictive interpretation of the traditional formula, extra ecclesiam nulla salus. In this letter to the Archbishop of Boston the Holy Office spoke of the possibility of the votum implicitum baptismi.[5]

According to van der Heijden, Pierre-Lambert Goossens (1827-1906), later Archbishop of Malignes, was the first to use the expression anonymous in this context. Around the same time as the First Vatican Council, the term occurred in the work of the Belgian theologian Auguste Dechamps (1810-1883).

The French philosopher Maurice Blondel (1861-1949) developed a similar terminology. Recognising that neo-scholasticism was a reaction to the problems posed by modernity, but not a solution, Blondel set out to show that Christianity had a meaning which corresponded to the inner logic of human existence. He felt that through a circumincessio between the questions arising out of human experience and the Christian message, the internal credibility of faith could be clearly demonstrated.[6] Blondel argued that people who wish to live life authentically are "determined" to "will" themselves freely. This brings them to an "option" whereby they either accept

---

[2] I am indebted here to M. Boutin, Anonymous Christianity: a paradigm for interreligious encounter, Journal of Ecumenical Studies 20: 4, Fall 1983, and B. van der Heijden's dissertation work published as Karl Rahner: Darstellung und Kritik seiner Grundpositionen, Einsiedeln: Johannes Verlag, 1973. The reader is also referred to W. Kern, Ausserhalb der Kirche kein Heil?, Freiburg: Herder, 1979 (especially Chapter III).

[3] Justin, Apologia I, 46. In: M. Boutin, art. cit., 609.

[4] Augustine, Retractationes I, XIII 3. In: M. Boutin, art. cit., 609.

[5] Cf. M. Boutin, loc. cit.

[6] Cf. H. Bouillard, Blondel und das Christentum, esp. 93, 103, 123-130, 139ff.

or reject God. Brought to the brink of faith by philosophy, they must ask themselves if the claims of Christian revelation are not well-founded. If one accepts revelation, then the "undetermined supernatural", i.e. a thirst for the absolute which is present in all of us and which is recognised by abnegation, becomes determined by Christianity.[7] Writing in the Annales de philosophie chrétienne in 1907, Blondel specifically refers to the "anonymous presence" of an immanent supernatural in every human being.[8]

Karl Rahner was not directly influenced by Maurice Blondel, though he was acquainted with Blondel's writings through his friend Robert Scherer who translated Blondel's works into German.[9] However, Rahner was influenced by Henri de Lubac,[10] and de Lubac was familiar with Blondel's philosophy. De Lubac addressed the problem of the salvation of non-Christians, but being a patristic scholar, he went much further back than Blondel and modern philosophy in order to do so. This is not

---

[7]Blondel's attempts to elaborate a philosophy which would be independent of theology, yet open out spontaneously towards Christianity, were matched by studies in theology and scripture by Loisy, Laberthonnière, Tyrell and von Hugel. Though this so-called "school" was labelled "modernist" and was considered to be condemned by Pius X both in Lamentabili, 1907 and Pascendi, 1910, it has been argued that modernism as a composite movement never really existed. Blondel himself was never publicly condemned. Cf. R. Haight, The unfolding of modernism in France: Blondel, Laberthonnière, Le Roy, Theological Studies 35, 1974, 633-666. Cf. further G. Connolly, Blondel, spiritual experience and fundamental theology today, Science et Esprit 36 (3), 1984, 323-339. Connolly sets out to show that what Ignatius, as presented by Rahner (Theological investigations 16, 24-34), intimated with regard to experience of the spirit, "Maurice Blondel spelled out in magisterial fashion".

[8]Annales de philosophie chrétienne, March 1907, 585. On p.582 Blondel acknowledged the influence of Cardinal Dechamps in leading him to consider that the supernatural present in our consciousness is not graspable in itself, ut est, but rather in its inner activity, ut agit.

[9]Im Gespräch, 1, 33.

[10]De Lubac's position on the grace-nature problem was of particular significance for Rahner. Both Rahner and de Lubac (and the Nouvelle Théologie school) were attempting to reinterpret Aquinas, but while modern philosophy was also of some importance for de Lubac, he was much more influenced by the patristic tradition. Rahner and de Lubac developed opposing positions. In Surnaturel, published in 1946, de Lubac relates Augustine's inquietum cor hominis to the nearly forgotten desiderium naturale of Thomas Aquinas, which he believed could mediate between nature and grace without depriving the latter of its gratuitous character. He considered the potentia oboedientialis as incapable of providing such a mediation because it is not like other human potentialities. In Hearers of the word, Rahner, reading Aquinas from the perspective of his metaphysical anthropology, had already expressed his scepticism concerning Thomas's desiderium naturale. He also remained unconvinced that de Lubac's position avoided collapsing into intrinsicism (Cf. Theological investigations 1, 296-317). Against de Lubac and under the influence of Heidegger, Rahner later developed out of Aquinas's potentia oboedientialis the supernatural existential as the solution to the nature-grace problem. Cf. further K. Rahner, Potentia oboedientialis, Sacramentum mundi V, 65.

to say that de Lubac was not also influenced by modern philosophy.[11] In his book Catholicism, published in 1938 (shortly after the completion of Rahner's Spirit in the world)[12], de Lubac argues that according to the Fathers and according to the principles of St. Thomas Aquinas, the grace of Christ is universal - not lacking in one soul of good will. According to de Lubac we must believe that there is not one unbeliever for whom a supernatural conversion should not be possible.[13] De Lubac goes on to discuss the implications of an implicit Christianity for the Church as a whole.[14]

At the same time as these later developments were taking place in Catholic theology, Karl Barth and Paul Tillich were also reflecting on the problem within Protestant circles. In Church Dogmatics Barth stated that the Christian community must reckon not only with those who are "actually" Christians, but also with those who are "virtual" or "potential" Christians or Christiani in spe.[15] Tillich spoke of a "latent

---

[11]On this point cf. G. Vass, The mystery of man and the foundations of a theological system: understanding Karl Rahner, Volume 2, 63.

[12]Cf. in particular chapter VII "Le Salut par l'Église". References are made to the Paris, 1947 edition. Hans Urs von Balthasar, a life-long friend of de Lubac, translated Catholicisme into German and it was published as Katholizismus als Gemeinschaft by Benziger, Einsiedeln, in 1943. It was de Lubac who opened the world of the Fathers, and especially of Origen to Balthasar. J.R. Sachs, in his dissertation on Balthasar's pneumatology and spirituality, (Katholisch-Theologische Fakultät, Tübingen 1984) would even go so far as to say that it was de Lubac who gave the young Balthasar a sense of the whole mystery of God's revelation. De Lubac's influence on Balthasar's own approach to the question of universal salvation is certainly evident in Balthasar's Dare we hope "that all men be saved"? De Lubac was also an admirer of Balthasar's. Cf. de Lubac's article, A witness of Christ in the Church: Hans Urs von Balthasar, Communio 12, 1975, 229-250.

[13]"Il n'est pas un homme, pas un "infidèle" dont la conversion surnaturelle à Dieu ne soit possible dès le seuil de sa vie raisonnable" (Catholicisme, 181).

[14]"Si un christianisme implicite suffit au salut de qui n'en connait point d'autre, pourquoi nous mettre en quete du christianisme explicite? Bref, si tout homme peut etre sauvé par un surnaturel anonymement possédé, comment établirons-nous qu'il a le devoir de reconnaitre expressément ce surnaturel dans la profession de foi chrétienne et dans la soumission à l'Église catholique?" (Catholicisme, 183). De Lubac answers that it is enough to know that the Church is, according to divine will and the institution of Christ, the normal means of salvation.

[15]"(Die christliche Gemeinde) hat es in allen, in jedem Menschen, an den sie gewiesen ist, gewiß noch nicht aktuell, wohl aber schon virtuell, potentiell, mit einem Christen, mit einem christianus designatus, einem christianus in spe zu tun: mit einem zur Erkenntnis und Betätigung seiner Gliedschaft am Liebe Jesu Christi bestimmen Geschöpf...wie müßte sie den Inhalt ihres Auftrags verkennen und verleugnen, wenn sie dessen Adressaten anders als eben so sehen und verstehen wollte!" (K. Barth, Kirchliche Dogmatik IV/3, 927).

Church" and of a "Christian humanism outside the Christian Church".[16]

Rahner first began to address specifically the question of the salvation of non-Christians and non-practising Christians in an article published in 1950, which set out to deal with "pagan Christians" and "Christian pagans".[17] Some may be walking in darkness because of the shadow which Christians have cast, he warns, and he reminds Christians of their responsibility to show such people that the way to God which Christians walk is "safer and shorter".

In an article which precedes both the Second Vatican Council and his specific development of the supernatural existential and the anonymous Christian, Rahner addresses the problems faced by Christians among unbelieving relations.[18] He describes the contemporary faith situation and attempts to apply the teaching of the Church to this situation in a pastorally meaningful way.

The "dark, confused and bitter question" which Rahner intends to address is the apparent lack of Christian faith in a loved one with the consequent anxiety about this person's attainment of salvation. For to be a Catholic is to profess God's grace in the Church as necessary for salvation. Is our faith in this case only to be a source of anxiety or can it also be a source of hope? Rahner points out firstly that, while in no way should we become complacent about faith, in the future it will be quite "normal" to have unbelievers among one's relatives and friends. Secondly, he suggests the need to respect the opinions of non-believers and to maintain relationships with them. Thirdly, with regard to the eternal salvation of our "non-believing" loved ones, Rahner says that we should not judge. He points out that even in the case of so-called good Catholics, who die "fortified with all the sacraments of the Church", we do not claim absolute certainty about their eternal destiny:

> ...we are called to hope - for ourselves and for others. But this word of confident hope, which on the notifications of death sometimes acquires far too self-assured a tone, as though everything were not unmerited grace and incomprehensible compassion, is no forestalling of the judgement of God. All, including the good Christians, enter silently into the darkness

---

[16]Cf. P. Tillich, Begegnungen. Paul Tillich über sich selbst und andere, Gesammelte Werke Vol. 12, Stuttgart, 1971. For a summary of Barth's and Tillich's treatment of this theme cf. U. Kühn, Christentum außerhalb der Kirche? zum interkonfessionellen Gespräch über das Verständnis der Welt. In: J. Lell, ed. Erneuerung der einen Kirche. Arbeiten aus der Kirchengeschichte und Konfessionskunde, Göttingen, 1966.

[17]K. Rahner, Die heidnischen Christen und die Christlichen Heiden - Matt. 8, 1-13. In: Glaube, der die Erde liebt: Christliche Besinnung im Alltag der Welt, Freiburg: Herder, 1966. An English translation of this article was published in K. Rahner, Everyday Faith, New York: Herder & Herder, 1968.

[18]Theological Investigations 3, 355-372.

of God, and no mortal eye follows them there on their way, no earthly ear listens to the judgement of their eternity. But this uncertainty for all can be contained within the hope for all.[19]

That someone should die apparently in the peace of the visible Church is an additional reason for us to hope in that particular case, but "we must hope for the saving mercy of God for all others too".[20] Stressing that all who are saved are saved only through the grace of Christ, we must at least leave open the possibility that what has in the past been referred to as "brilliant vices" in the lives of the pagans, are in fact supernatural virtues.[21]

Rahner also considers the problem of the salvation of those baptised but who no longer see themselves as Christians. His main point here is that, even in the light of Hebrews 6:4ff[22], and the teaching of the First Vatican Council,[23] we should not judge how effectively these people were originally evangelised.

This article is Rahner's first attempt to reconcile the Church's teaching on the necessity of faith for salvation with the equally important teaching that we should hope for the salvation of all and avoid judging others, aware as we are that we stand under judgement ourselves. Thus he attempts initially to present the Church's pronouncements in a meaningful way for people who encounter apparent disbelief and

---

[19]Theological Investigations 3, 361-362. Compare Rahner's presentation here with the remarkably similar position of Hans Urs von Balthasar, Dare we hope "that all men be saved"?, 23-25. Reflecting deeply on the teaching of the Fathers, Balthasar lambastes those who, at various times in the Church's history, including the present time, claim to know "too much" about the judgement of God. Both theologians emphasise the double obligation for Christians, who stand under judgement themselves, not to judge others but, trusting in God's mercy and judgement which should not be separated or opposed to each other, to hope for the salvation of all.

[20]Theological Investigations 3, 362. Already one can see the beginnings of what will emerge as the greatest problem for theology in the wake of the doctrine of the anonymous Christian: the relativisation of the Christian faith. Later we will have to address this question as to how a Christian's hope differs from that of a non-Christian.

[21]This is in fact a preliminary reference to what Rahner will later develop as the supernatural existential.

[22]"As for those people who were once brought into the light, and tasted the gift from heaven, and received a share of the Holy Spirit, and appreciated the good message of God and the powers of the world to come and yet in spite of this have fallen away - it is impossible for them to be renewed a second time." Cf. further 2 John 9; 2 Peter 2:20.

[23]Rahner interprets the teaching of the First Vatican Council as saying "that Catholics who have once accepted the faith under the magisterium of the Church could have no justified grounds for giving it up or for calling it into doubt by withholding the assent of faith" (Theological Investigations 3, 367).

atheism in their loved ones.

Rahner's first explicit use of the term anonymous in the context of Christianity occurs in the course of a short essay entitled "Poetry and the Christian" published in 1960, almost two years before the Second Vatican Council:

> There is such a thing as anonymous Christianity. There are men who think that they are not Christians, but who are in the grace of God. And hence there is an anonymous humanism inspired by grace, which thinks that it is no more than human. We Christians can understand it, better than it does itself. When we affirm as a doctrine of faith that human morality even in the natural sphere needs the grace of God to be steadfast in its great task, we recognise as Christians that such humanism, wherever it displays its true visage and wherever it exists, even outside professed Christianity, is a gift of the grace of God and a tribute to the redemption, even though it as yet knows nothing of this. Why then should we not love it? To pass it by indifferently would be to despise the grace of God.[24]

The supernatural existential, however, is Rahner's most important theological concept, and it provides the basis for, and in Rahner's own opinion, has its most important expression in his theory of the anonymous Christian.[25]

Theological background: the supernatural existential

When Rahner began to teach theology, the French-based Nouvelle Théologie school was attempting to overcome the extrinsicism inherent in the traditional understanding of the relationship between grace and nature. Extrinsicism presented grace merely as a superstructure freely imposed by God upon human nature. The relationship between nature and grace was understood as being no more intense than freedom from contradiction.[26] At best nature was understood to tolerate or to be non-repugnant towards grace. The reason for this neo-scholastic approach was to protect the gratuitousness of grace. If grace was presented as being entirely beyond consciousness and in itself inaccessible then it could only be made known through faith. Nature was understood, according to this perspective, as what we come to

---

[24]Theological investigations 4, 366. In an essay entitled "The Theology of power" (Theological investigations 4, 391-409) written in the same year, Rahner refers briefly (p.403) to "a Christianity which remains as it were anonymous" ("...wo das tatsächlich vollzogene Christentum gewissermassen anonym bleibt"). M. Boutin (art. cit., 605) notes that because of its more tentative nature, this could be an earlier reference. In another article written in 1960, on "The sacramental basis for the role of the layman in the Church" (Theological investigations 8, 51-74), reference is made to the baptised Christian being sent to anonymous Christians (p.63). Also in 1960, when addressing the topic "On truthfulness" at a conference in Passau, Rahner referred to "anonymous Christianity...a real Christianity which has so far simply failed to be recognised for what it really is..." (Theological investigations 7, 255).

[25]Cf. K. - H. Weger, Karl Rahner: an introduction to his theology, 113.

[26]Cf. Theological Investigations 1, 298.

know of ourselves independently of revelation. In these somewhat negative terms the potentia oboedientialis was defined.[27] Left to itself nature would achieve some natural end, in accordance with Aquinas's doctrine reditio completa in seipsum, but would never come to an immediate intuition of God.

The path to this extrinsicist understanding of grace has its roots in the New Testament where St. Paul, anxious to guard the gratuitousness of God's salvific activity in Christ, rejected any possible misunderstanding that salvation could in some way be merited or earned through the Law. Later Augustine had to protect the gratuitousness of grace against Pelagius and stressed human sinfulness in order to highlight the necessity of God's free loving activity. It is with Augustine that grace began to emerge as a technical term. Aquinas found himself in a dilemma when he attempted to bring together Aristotle's concept of nature, that is that the nature of all beings is their essence in so far as they develop according to their intrinsic potentialities, with the Platonic-Augustinian world-view then prevalent. Human nature was understood to aim at the God-given beatific vision as its goal. What intrinsic potentiality in the human being could be considered to correspond to this process? Developing Aristotle's view of human nature, Aquinas argued that in some way the beatific vision had to be in accordance with human nature. While with Augustine it had to be maintained that even though God is the object of human desire he is always beyond the human being, nevertheless the human being had still to be understood as having the capacity to receive God's grace. The human being is made in God's image, therefore humans had to possess a desiderium naturale visionis beatificae, i.e. an innate desire for the beatific vision. Further, human beings cannot be conceived of without this desire. The problem is that if this human desire is not to be considered to be in vain then God would be bound to give himself and the gratuitousness of grace would be infringed.

Aquinas resolved this dilemma by conceiving of a double human fulfilment: fulfilment in this life and in the next, and he interpreted the desiderium naturale as an obediential potency.

In post-Thomistic theology the desiderium naturale was more or less abandoned and the potentia oboedientialis became little more than a non-repugnance of grace. Meanwhile in order to further protect the gratuitousness of grace it was stressed that human nature even without God's grace had to have the capacity for a fully human life. At the First Vatican Council this understanding of human nature found expression in terms of a natural and supernatural way of knowing God and natura

---

[27]Cf. Theological Investigations 4, 165-188.

pura developed further and became part of the official Church teaching.
While in no way intending to rob grace of its intrinsic gratuitous dimension, the
Nouvelle Théologie school was anything but content with what was now seen as a
double-decker or dualistic understanding of the relationship between grace and nature.
In 1946 Henri de Lubac published Surnaturel. De Lubac attempted to show how
Aquinas's desiderium naturale could act as a mediator between grace and nature
without encroaching upon the gratuitous dimension of grace. De Lubac's patristic
scholarship led him back behind Aquinas, and taking Augustine's inquietum cor
hominis also into account he concluded that the human spirit had as a constitutive
element, a desire for God. In this de Lubac was also undoubtedly influenced by
Maréchal and his concept of a dynamic human subjectivity.
In Humani Generis Pope Pius XII questioned the ability of these moves to overcome
extrinsicism to avoid destroying the gratuitous character of grace. De Lubac realised
that this could only be achieved if we understood the desiderium naturale itself to be
a gift of God. But did this then lead to intrinsicism? If God gives the desire, is he
not also obliged to give the fulfilment of this desire?
Rahner was in full agreement with the criticisms of extrinsicism made by the
Nouvelle Théologie. He also accepted fully the teaching of Humani Generis.[28]
Because of his work in Spirit in the world[29] and Hearers of the word[30], Rahner

---

[28]Theological Investigations 1, 297.

[29]Spirit in the world was Rahner's philosophical dissertation, completed in 1936 and first
published in 1939. In 1934 Rahner was sent to Freiburg, his home town, to study philosophy.
Martin Heidegger had been in Freiburg since 1928. Rahner would have liked to prepare his doctoral
dissertation under Heidegger's direction but because at that point Heidegger was still a supporter of
Nazism, this was considered to be unacceptable. Martin Honecker became the director of Rahner's
dissertation dealing with Aquinas's metaphysics of knowledge. At the same time Rahner participated
in Heidegger's seminars. To understand Karl Rahner, it is important to understand who and what
influenced him at this critical time in his career. Even at this early stage Rahner's motivation was
strongly pastoral and he believed sincerely that both theology and philosophy must enable people to
make sense of their lives. Neo-scholasticism, which following Leo XIII's Aeterni Patris strove to
determine the philosophy and theology to be taught in Catholic schools, did not succeed in this
regard. In Holland, Rahner had received an initial theological training along scholastic lines. At
Freiburg, he was joined by his fellow-Jesuit J.B. Lotz, and participated in what came to be known
as the Catholic Heidegger School with people like G. Siewerth, B. Welte and M. Müller. At this
time, as Vorgrimler points out, theologians like Przywara and Guardini were just beginning to
introduce a new spirit of openness into theology, a spirit which had been all but extinguished by what
Rahner refers to as "Pian monolithism" which had reduced the role of the theologian to one of
defending the dogmas of the Church. But these theologians had not yet had an opportunity to take
a serious look at individual theological problems. Operating from within a scholastic framework,
Rahner believed that one could go back behind the neo-scholastic interpretation of Thomism to the
work of Aquinas himself. Nevertheless, Rahner did not want his work merely to be a repetition of
Aquinas's thought. Rahner, Müller, Siewerth and Lotz were among those who recognised the

found himself in a good position to enter this debate.
In Hearers of the word, Rahner was somewhat sceptical of the ability of the
Thomistic desiderium naturale to act as a mediator between grace and nature. In any
case, subsequent attempts to renovate this concept had run into difficulties and he
realised that it would now be difficult to present the desiderium naturale so that it
would appear completely innocent of any intrinsicist leanings. With de Lubac he
agreed that the desire for a saving God is a fact of existential experience. In Hearers
of the word Rahner had already portrayed the potentia oboedientialis as an a priori
self-transcendent dynamism of man towards the whole breadth of an horizon, towards
the totality of being which also includes God's being.[31] Now going further, he
presented the obediential potency as a dynamism which strives towards the
supernatural goal of God's vision. He argued that human openness to the word of
God and his grace cannot be portrayed merely as a non-repugnance, merely as a
passive receptivity.

---

necessary tools for a process of retrieval in the work of Martin Heidegger though Heidegger himself
was not an Aquinas scholar. It is important to form a judgement on the extent to which Heidegger
actually influenced Rahner, and particularly determined Rahner's treatment of Aquinas's excessus
and his development of the central notion of the "pre-grasp" or "pre-apprehension" (Vorgriff).
Rahner distinguishes between Heidegger's teachings (spezielle Lehre), and his style (ein Styl zu
denken und zu forschen), the latter which he accepts as having influenced him. But to what extent
can such a distinction in the work of Heidegger be valid and meaningful? Whereas Vorgrimler claims
that Rahner was certainly less influenced by Heidegger than his colleagues were, Eicher (Die
anthropologische Wende) has shown that the work of the early Heidegger was critical and decisive
for Rahner. Particularly important for Rahner were Heidegger's attempts to develop a
Fundamentalontologie grounded in metaphysics. Both Spirit in the world and Hearers of the word
are heavily influenced by the Heideggerian Denkenstil, and definitely much more so than the few
explicit references to Martin Heidegger would lead one to believe. Martin Honecker rejected
Rahner's dissertation on the grounds that, because of the Heideggerian influence, it was not an
accurate interpretation of Aquinas. Despite all of this it is clearly wrong to claim that Rahner's
starting-point is in Heidegger. Significantly, Heidegger himself did not recognise Rahner as an
authentic interpreter of his thought.

[30]Hörer des Wortes first appeared in 1940. A second German edition, revised by J.B. Metz was
published in 1963. There are considerable differences between the first and second German editions
which have been attributed to the influence of Metz. The French translation by L. Holbach
(L'homme à l'écoute du verbe, Paris 1968) is useful in that it presents the two editions in parallel
columns for comparison. On the seriousness of the differences between the two editions cf. T.
Mannerman, Eine falsche Interpretationstradition von K. Rahner's Hörer des Wortes, Zeitschrift für
Katholische Theologie, 92 (1970), 204-209; E. Vacek, Development within Rahner's theology, Irish
Theological Quarterly 42, 1975, 36-49. Two English translations of Hörer des Wortes have been
consulted: that of John Donceel contained in G. McCool ed., A Rahner reader (1975), and that of
Ronald Walls's translation of Hearers of the word, 1969. The basic text used is Metz's revised
(1963) German edition.

[31]Hearers of the word, 69.

An 'existential' is, according to Heidegger (and it is in this sense that Rahner employs the term), a permanent determination penetrating all elements of human existence, which reveals its meaning and structures, characterising the human being before he engages in any free action.[32] One clear example of an existential is the awareness of the inevitability of death. Rahner gives as other examples of existentials: being threatened, sinfulness, ambiguity, openness to the incalculable, the capacity to become absorbed.

Rahner introduced the term supernatural existential in 1950. He defined the supernatural existential as a permanent influence by God enhancing the human being's obediential potency, revealing to him the ultimate meaning of human existence (God) and inviting him to commit himself to this meaning.[33] The supernatural existential is distinctive in that it is an a priori which is constitutive of human historicality and not of a human being's essence as a spirit. Otherwise it would define man's nature as a spirit and would be due to him as such.

The supernatural existential presupposes an obediential potency, which is no longer merely a non-repugnance of grace, but an inalienable and transcendental dynamism towards the absolute. It also presupposes, as an important hypothetical human state, the state of pure nature (natura pura), which is necessary to affirm the gratuitous unexactedness of grace. A merely theoretical assumption rather than an assertion of a state which was once realised in history, "pure nature" describes nature as unaffected by grace, even though we have no experience of this. According to Rahner there was never a human being who was "ungraced" as such. Pure nature is a remainder concept (Restbegriff). In our actual experience we know nothing of what comes from nature alone.

The human being is free to accept or reject God's gracious self-offer, but the supernatural existential, being a permanent disposition or determination of his ontological state, continues to exercise an influence which implies that the human being must adopt a stance which is ultimately for or against God. If it is against

---

[32]Cf. M. Heidegger, Being and time, 44.

[33]"Eine dauernde, bleibende Verfasstheit einer endlichen Geistperson, die die Ermöglichung und ontologische Vorherbestimmung eines personalen Handelns ist (das also, was in der freien Tat an der Person ins Spiel kommt)" (Über das Verhältnis des Naturgesetzes zur übernaturlichen Gnadenordnung, Orient 20, 1956, 9). According to Aquinas, the supernatural brings a new, a priori, formal object with it which liés beyond the reach of a natural act of the human spirit. With Aquinas, Rahner is anxious to stress that God's self-offer transforms human consciousness. Cf. Theological investigations 16, 56-57. Cf. further the article entitled "Culture" in K. Rahner and H. Vorgrimler, Concise theological dictionary, London: Burns and Oates, 1981. In Theological investigations 5, 191, Rahner refers to Christ as "the decisive existential factor of man's life".

God, then it is also against his own ontological state. God wishes to communicate himself to us. Everything exists towards this end. Therefore God creates us in such a way that we can receive his love and accept it in such a way as is totally free and unexacted, unmerited and wonderful. Defined from this perspective, the human being is therefore "the event of the free, unmerited and forgiving self-communication of God". Rahner offers this definition in the fourth chapter of his <u>Foundations of Christian faith</u>. The previous three chapters have dealt with the human being as a hearer of a potential word of God, as someone who finds himself in the presence of the absolute mystery (a summary of his work in <u>Hearers of the word</u> and <u>Spirit in the world</u>), and as a being "radically threatened by guilt". These are, according to Rahner, the presuppositions upon which this definition is built.

By "self-communication" Rahner intends to stress that God is not saying something about himself: he is giving <u>himself</u>. Further, we are to understand this in terms of a personal self-giving, and not as merely something "objectivistic or reified".[34] The only possible reason for this self-communication of God is that we should come to possess God in love. If God's offer is to be understood as loving, then it must be freely offered and freely received. God must offer himself to humanity in such a way that he does not cease to be God. We must receive him in such a way that we do not cease to be human. Even in his total self-communication, "God remains God, the first and ultimate measure which can be measured by nothing else...the mystery which alone is self-evident...the holy One who is really only accessible in worship".[35]

The only way in which this can happen is if somehow the acceptance of God's self-communication is borne by God himself. In this way God establishes something different from himself without becoming subject to the difference and can communicate himself without losing himself in the communication. Only in this way can grace retain its gratuitous character without becoming extrinsic. Concretely this means that the human creature is initially constituted as a possible addressee of a divine self-communication. Creation is ordered to God's total self-communication. Only in this total self-communication does it find total fulfilment:

> man is himself through that which he is not, and because that which he is, inescapably and inalienably, is given to him as the presupposition and as the condition of possibility for that which in all truth is given to him as his own in absolute, free and unmerited love: God in

---

[34]<u>Foundations of Christian faith</u>, 116.

[35]<u>Foundations of Christian faith</u>, 119-120.

his self-communication.[36]

Confession of belief in the total self-giving of God is the distinctive characteristic of Christianity. The Christian faith professes belief in the total immediacy of God. Up until this, Rahner's exposition of grace has taken as its starting point the Christian message. But he is anxious to show that this is in fact the deepest possible expression of human self-understanding. Too often the impression is given that God's absolute self-communication addresses man from without - a definite result of extrinsicism. Rahner claims that the statement "man is the event of God's absolute self-communication"[37] is an ontological statement, i.e. it expresses something about the transcendental subject in the depths of his experience. It expresses something about every transcendental subject. This is not to imply that the supernatural existential becomes "natural" because it is present in every human being. The love of God is not diluted or something less of a miracle because it is present to all at least as an offer. In fact it must be present to all at least in the mode of an offer.

Therefore God not only gives himself as "gift". He also gives himself as the condition making acceptance of the gift possible. Only in this way can God be accepted without being reduced to an object of our finiteness. This implies that God's self-communication must always be present in us "as the prior condition of possibility for its acceptance".[38] Now, while transcendental human experience always remains ambivalent and is never fully or satisfactorily expressed, the supernatural existential helps us to understand how God is experienced as the ever distant one, who draws close in unparalleled proximity to us without destroying our freedom to accept him or reject him.

The anonymous Christian and anonymous Christianity

The concept of the anonymous Christian is a direct and inevitable consequence of the supernatural existential. To summarise briefly what has been said above: the human being is a being of unlimited openness towards the limitless being of God, i.e. the human being is a spirit capable of hearing the word, and through God's grace, expecting it with no right to demand it. Since God must be understood to have been effective in his self-communication, we must presume that there is a supernatural existential present in each person, a presumption which accords with a metaphysical

---

[36]Foundations of Christian faith, 124.

[37]Foundations of Christian faith, 126.

[38]Foundations of Christian faith, 128.

anthropology. We cannot presume that a supernatural existential is only present in some, if God's grace is considered to be universal. The supernatural existential accounts for God's presence in the human being in such a way that God does not cease to be God and that the human being does not cease to be human. It expresses God's presence as an offer, enabling the human being to accept God's self-communication or reject it.[39] However, because the supernatural existential is a human existential, the decisions of "yes" and "no" are not to be considered as alike or equal, because existentials determine human nature and lend it a particular character. Now a decision in favour of God's offer is also a decision corresponding with the human being's deepest orientation. A decision against God's self-communication involves the human being not only in a contradiction with God but also with his deepest self, for once the supernatural existential is present, the human being is no longer in a state of "pure unimpaired nature".[40] Therefore those who decide against God's self-communication find themselves in contradiction not only with God but also with themselves. We must admit this as a real possibility if we are to profess God's self-giving as a loving self-communication, which leaves the beloved free to accept or reject. Were grace to be an imposition, then it would simply not be grace, but a consumption of human nature by the divine. Despite our hoping that all are saved, if salvation is to have any meaning at all we must admit of the possibility that one can refuse salvation.[41]

If the possibility of refusing God's gracious self-offer is real, however, so is the possibility of accepting it. Moreover, though the Christian must refrain from judging

---

[39]God's self-offer should not be thought of as a single event, or as something which happens occasionally or even intermittently in one's life. It should be understood rather as "an abiding possibility of human freedom" (Theological investigations 16, 56).

[40]For Rahner, Aquinas's concept of natura pura is an important one, and this is a source of difference of opinion between him and the Nouvelle Théologie. Rahner claims that grace is present in every human being, in the form of an offer freely accepted or freely rejected. There is in fact no human being who exists in a state of "pure nature", which for Rahner means a human being who has not experienced God's self-offer, i.e. who has not experienced grace. Nevertheless, if we are to preserve the total gratuitousness of grace, natura pura is an indispensable remainder concept (Restbegriff) which describes the human being were he not to have experienced God's grace. Cf. Theological investigations 4, 184-185.

[41]Cf. Balthasar's reference to this particular emphasis in Rahner's theology in Dare we hope "that all men be saved"?, 32. Balthasar also quotes (p.165) the German Church's catechism: "Neither Holy Scripture nor the Church's tradition of faith asserts with certainty of any man that he is actually in hell. Hell is held before our eyes as a real possibility, one connected with the offer of conversion and life" (The Church's confession of faith: a Catholic catechism for adults, 346). Cf. also Rahner's article on Hell in Sacramentum mundi II, 736.

others, he nonetheless must also have unlimited optimism for the salvation of all. Not to profess such optimism is to doubt the success of the Christ-event. Did Christ fail to die for all?[42] But how do we account theologically for this optimism and for the real possibility of God's gracious self-offer being accepted? We cannot claim that people are saved in and through their human condition alone for that is to deny the necessity of grace for salvation. This is precluded as a possibility.

What of those who accept God's self-offer, even though they are unbaptised, even though they may not have related what they have transcendentally experienced and accepted to the name of Jesus Christ? If we are to claim, as we must, that all salvation comes through Jesus Christ, then we must claim that these people, even though they do not realise it, attain salvation through Jesus Christ. The best expression that Rahner could find to describe these people is that of "anonymous Christians":

> The seed has no right not to seek not to grow into a plant. But the fact that it is not yet developed into a plant is no reason for refusing to give the name which we give to the plant destined to grow from it to the seed as well.[43]

Rahner wrote several articles on the anonymous Christian and anonymous Christianity, and the term is mentioned in sixteen volumes of Theological investigations. It is probably the aspect of Rahner's theology which has received the most attention. There are two different but related reasons for this. First: while Rahner did not originally intend it to be a central and dominating concept, it represents his theological method carried to its logical conclusion. In many ways, being the most important development arising out of the supernatural existential, it represents the heart of his theology. Therefore students of Rahner's theology cannot simply ignore it or leave it to one side. Second: for a Church in diaspora, whose members counted among their families and friends many now complacent about faith and even unbelieving, and whose members lived in a situation of world-wide and militant atheism, the concept of the anonymous Christian was of vital importance in providing a theological framework for understanding this new and frightening faith milieu.

The concept of the anonymous Christian has particular implications for the Church's attitude to atheism, for its own missionary activity, for its relationships with non-Christian religions, and finally for the Church's own self-understanding. We will

---

[42]Cf. Theological investigations 6, 391-398. Compare H. U. von Balthasar, Dare we hope "that all men be saved"? 171-176.

[43]Theological investigations 14, 291.

now briefly examine the anonymous Christian in each of these contexts.

The Church and atheism

Rahner developed the concept of the anonymous Christian specifically to facilitate the Church's self-understanding within a secular Europe, experiencing widespread atheism for the first time in history. Just shortly after the Second Vatican Council, Rahner wrote specifically on the implications of anonymous Christianity for the Church's approach to atheism.[44] The thesis of this study is that even an atheist may possess Christianity implicitly.[45] By "implicit Christianity" Rahner means being in a state of justification and grace without being in contact with the explicit preaching of the Gospel.[46]

The main objection to such a thesis is the traditional scepticism in the theology of the schools regarding the possibility of long-term inculpable atheism. Rahner appeals to the teaching of the Second Vatican Council to overcome this objection.[47] Whereas in 1963 Rahner had interpreted the Council's teaching on the possibility of inculpable atheism as leaving the matter open, "that an atheism of this kind can last a long time whether individually or collectively is not stated, but not excluded either"[48], now he goes further, claiming that

> it is safe to say that the Council...actually assumed...that it is possible for a normal adult to hold an explicit atheism for a long period of time - even to life's end without this implying moral blame on the part of such an unbeliever.[49]

---

[44]Cf. Theological investigations 9, 145-164. This article, entitled "Atheism and implicit Christianity" is based on a lecture given during a tour of American universities in 1967.

[45]In 1973, in a supplementary article, Rahner speaks of an atheist as possessing "anonymous faith", i.e. faith without any explicit reference to God or to Christ, but which is nevertheless necessary and effective for salvation. Cf. Theological investigations 16, 52-59.

[46]Cf. W. Kasper, The God of Jesus Christ, 52-53. Here Kasper briefly summarises and criticises Rahner's concept of transcendental theism. Kasper provides a good overview of the problem of atheism and recent theological approaches (pp. 16-64) within which context Rahner's method should be understood.

[47]In this regard Cf. Rahner's later essay in Theological investigations 14, 280-294, esp. 281. The official text-book theology was based in scripture and developed in the context of a world in which God's knowability seemed so clearly and unambiguously given, a world-view which for the first time is now confronted with "world-wide and militant atheism".

[48]Theological investigations 6, 297.

[49]Theological investigations 9, 146-148. Rahner admits that this view is not taught explicitly but considers this omission to be very significant. He refers in particular to Gaudium et spes, nn. 19-21, 22, Lumen gentium 16 and Ad Gentes, n. 7.

At the least, the Council leaves open the possibility of the coexistence of atheism and justification, and the fact that it did not appeal to the traditionally held view is, for Rahner, highly significant. According to Rahner, the Council would seem to be saying two things: not every atheist is necessarily living in a state of sin, and atheists can be justified if they follow their consciences.[50]

The Council does not offer a specifically theological argument to substantiate this teaching. It does not explain clearly how supernatural faith and the grace of justification, both necessary for salvation, can be present in an atheist who has not acted against his conscience as a result of his atheism. In what can be interpreted, however, as a development of the traditional admonition not to judge others, the Council states only that grace works in people in an unseen way and that the possibility of salvation is offered to all "in a manner known only to God".[51]

The task facing theology, then, is to demonstrate how an atheist can possess saving faith. Traditionally the minimum content of faith, as laid down in Hebrews, consisted in belief in the existence of God and in him as guarantor of the moral order. The Council Fathers, however, stressed the need to follow one's conscience. Somehow then, in the following of one's conscience there must be some, albeit implicit, reference to God. Rahner goes further:

> The person who accepts a moral demand from his conscience as absolutely valid for him and embraces it as such in a free act of affirmation - no matter how unreflected - asserts the absolute being of God, whether he knows it or conceptualises it or not, as the very reason why there can be such a thing as an absolute moral demand at all.[52]

This preliminary explanation of how an atheist may be justified needs to be further grounded. Rahner sets out to demonstrate the possibility of coexistence of a conceptually objectified atheism and a non-propositional and existentially realised theism. In doing so, he refers back specifically to his understanding of the nature of human knowing.

In each act of human knowing the subject has subjective knowledge of himself and of his act. In the same act of knowing there is also a known and conceptualised object which is the act's goal: in knowing about oneself and one's knowing act, one knows about something. A distinction always remains between the subject as present

---

[50]By "salvation" the one supernatural goal for all humankind is being referred to. The traditional teaching that non-Christians could attain to some sort of natural as distinct from supernatural salvation has clearly been rendered obsolete by the teaching of the Council.

[51]Gaudium et Spes, 22. Cf. also Ad Gentes, n. 7.

[52]Theological investigations 9, 153.

to itself and the known object. Because of this distinction it is always possible for an act of human knowing to be falsely or inadequately interpreted on the objective level even though subjectively it has been correctly interpreted and is present in its known reality.

Now every instance of intellectual knowledge and freedom on the part of the subject is a transcendental experience, and transcendental experiences are, according to Rahner, always experiences of absolute Being. This implies that on the subjective side every instance of knowledge is a real, even if implicit, knowledge of God.[53] If this knowledge of God is freely accepted then we can speak of transcendental theism. This knowledge of God which is real may remain implicit, i.e. it may not become objectified. What we commonly refer to as (objective) knowledge of God is always an objectification of what we already and always necessarily know of God apart from reflection.

If God is always and necessarily present in human nature, then there are four possibilities. These possibilities arise because the human being possesses both knowledge and freedom. As we examine these four options, Rahner's distinction between transcendental and categorical theism should become clear.

First: the justified theist is justified because he has freely accepted God who is present in his transcendental nature. He is a theist because he has also objectified God's transcendental presence correctly, and at this level also affirmed and accepted God. The justified Christian definitely belongs to this category. It would seem that other justified theists may belong to this category or to the third, depending on how developed their objectively expressed and accepted knowledge of God is.[54] This is a case in which both transcendental and categorical theism are accepted and affirmed.

Second: God, who is necessarily transcendentally present, is rejected. Furthermore, God's presence is recognised at an objective level, but rejected in moral freedom.

---

[53]Rahner is taking for granted here the reader's familiarity with Hearers of the word.

[54]Rahner has concentrated on addressing the question of anonymous Christianity within a European secular worldview. He has given less attention to dealing with the non-Christian within non-Christian religions. Therefore it is not entirely clear how non-Christian (anonymous Christian) theists are to be categorised. A later essay, written in 1973 (Theological investigations 16, 52-59) does not make matters any clearer, for here Rahner deliberately deals only with an "anonymous faith" which he defines as "a faith which on the one hand is effective for salvation...and on the other occurs without an explicit and conscious relationship to the revelation of Jesus Christ contained in the Old and/or New Testament and without any explicit reference to God through an objective idea of God" (emphasis mine). On Rahner's treatment of non-Christian religions Cf. Theological investigations 5, 115-134.

Here we have a case in which both transcendental theism and categorical theism are rejected. An unjustified Christian, one who denies God in his heart through immorality or unbelief, would seem to belong to this category.

Third: God, who is necessarily present at a transcendental level, is freely and positively accepted. This acceptance is expressed in a deliberate decision to be faithful to conscience. There is not necessarily any idea of God at an objective level, or perhaps there is a false and inadequate notion (in this case Rahner mentions polytheism) and this notion may in fact be rejected. This is the case of transcendental theism which is freely accepted and affirmed, and of categorical theism which is rejected. This categorical theism may in fact be replaced by a categorical atheism. Rahner's anonymous Christian belongs to this category: the person who may have a conceptually objectified atheism but at the same time a transcendentally realised and accepted theism.

Fourth: God who is present at the transcendental level is freely rejected. Further, at the objective level there may be no explicit idea of God or a false one, which may also be rejected. In this case we have what Rahner calls "culpable transcendental atheism", in which, as in the second possibility, a definite, free and deliberate decision against God has been made at the transcendental level. Transcendental atheism is always culpable because in this decision, a "no" is freely uttered to God and, Rahner would add, to the whole human enterprise including the person himself. There is no possibility of salvation in such a case.

The third possibility represents the situation of what could be called innocent (as opposed to culpable) atheism, and in reality is only atheism at the conceptual and objective level.

So far, Rahner has shown how an atheist can make the necessary response which implicitly accepts God's transcendent self-offer. When we reflect on the concrete order of salvation, it becomes clear how we can properly speak of this acceptance of transcendental theism even by a categorical atheist, as implicit <u>Christianity</u>.

Because of God's universal will for salvation, we can say that the atheist's transcendental, freely accepted theism is elevated by supernatural will. Rahner interprets the Council texts as definitively ruling out recourse to a distinction between natural and supernatural salvation. This distinction arose in traditional theology to account for the eternal destiny of those who lived according to some "natural morality". It was correctly assumed that justification as such is impossible without revealed faith. It was incorrectly presumed, according to Rahner, that revealed faith could never be present in an atheist. Through an application of the Thomistic thesis that every supernaturally elevated human moral act has a supernatural formal object which cannot be reached by any merely natural intellectual or moral act on the part of the agent, even if in both cases the objective, a posteriori content of the act is the same, it would seem that the communication of a supernatural formal object is in a true sense revelation already. It is constituted such prior to any a posteriori and historical communication of an objective content by means of historical revelation. Therefore Rahner concludes that "the supernatural elevation in grace automatically involves revelation and the possibility of faith".[55] The Church has already admitted the possibility of the offer of supernatural sanctification outside of baptism in certain cases. We have only to assume that this offer is always and everywhere present, and its free acceptance always and everywhere a possibility.

If one's acceptance of one's own transcendentality includes an implicit acceptance of transcendental theism, as Rahner argues, then because of God's universal will for salvation, the result is implicit Christianity.

Rahner draws some conclusions regarding pastoral strategy for addressing the problem of atheism and these are important for us in that they show how Rahner intended his theory to be employed. The principal insight which we have gleaned is that if this atheist is honestly trying to follow his conscience, then he has already implicitly accepted God.

Rahner is sceptical about previous attempts at evangelisation which were based upon the traditional proofs of God's existence. These, he believes, led to false or inadequate notions of God. Rahner suggests instead that one should attempt a kind of "mystagogy". By this he means that if a person is attempting to live life honestly and selflessly, and is caring and responsive to the needs of others, then he already knows something of God. This knowledge of God may not be recognised as that because of some contradicting experience, e.g. a realisation of the evil in the world, a negative religious experience etc. Often we make the mistake of saying too much about God. We often forget that God is expressly defined as being incomprehensible. The emphasis today, Rahner believes, must be on the presence of God as absolute mystery, a mystery which penetrates our whole existence. A successful mystagogy relates theoretical knowledge of God to our existential experience of life so that we come to recognise God's abiding presence in the incomprehensible mystery of our

---

[55]Theological investigations 9, 162-163; cf. also Theological investigations 5, 97-114; K. Rahner and J. Ratzinger, Revelation and tradition, Freiburg, 1966. The relationship between the transcendental and categorical elements in revelation will require further treatment. At this point Rahner seems anxious to stress that there are not two revelations, transcendental and categorical, but rather one single revelation, and that the transcendental element of revelation does not render the categorical element superfluous.

existence.[56]

Speaking in Rome in 1980, almost two decades later, Rahner points out that a significant change in the character of atheism has taken place.[57] We are no longer confronted with the intellectual atheism of the Enlightenment, propagated by the religious criticisms of Feuerbach etc., which was principally the kind of atheism envisioned by the Second Vatican Council. Today atheism is conditioned by life in a rationalistic and technological society which systematically erodes experience of God. Rahner criticises the Church's lack of awareness of the new historical situation within which it finds itself. He reminds the Church that it is the sign and sacrament of universal salvation and encourages dialogue with atheists and atheistic regimes, with a view to coming to a better understanding of the contemporary reasons which lead to a denial of God. He suggests that these include an inadequate notion of God, for which the Church, because of naive and superficial statements, is partly responsible, and the increasing ease in modern society with which the God-question can be avoided.[58] Once again he expounds his doctrine of the anonymous Christian. While still arguing for a mystagogical approach to evangelisation, in the last part of this article Rahner seems to go further than in his previous writings.[59] Atheism contradicts the most fundamental affirmation of Christianity and can have a negative effect on people's consciences. God should hold sway in society and in human theory, therefore the Church has a responsibility to struggle against atheism. To struggle against atheism is to overcome the inadequacies in our own theism, and ecumenism is mentioned as important in this regard.

The missionary activity of the Church and non-Christian religions

Only one of Rahner's articles in Theological investigations deals specifically with the concept of the anonymous Christian in the context of the Church's missionary

---

[56]Cf. Theological investigations 9, 160; Theological investigations 4, 36-73; Theological investigations 7, 3-24; Foundations of Christian faith, 44-89; K. Lehmann, Some ideas from pastoral theology on the proclamation of the Christian message to non-believers today, Concilium 3, 1967, 43-52.

[57]Theological investigations 21, 137-150.

[58]On this point cf.W. Kasper, An introduction to Christian faith, where he acknowledges (p.19) that more and more people today seem to live happily and fulfilled without any explicit reference to or belief in God. Cf. further, J. Ratzinger, Principles of Catholic theology, where he recognises fully (p.15) the "epochal transformation" taking place at the present time.

[59]Theological investigations 21, 146-150.

activity, and three further articles deal with the anonymous Christian and non-Christian religions.[60] First of all, we must remember that Rahner's theological Sitz-im-Leben was first and foremost the threat posed to Christianity and the Church in Europe by secularism, pluralism and atheism. In this context, the theory of the anonymous Christian was intended to contribute to Christianity's self-understanding. Rahner did not intend the theory as an instrument of evangelisation. Clearly, however, the anonymous Christian concept had important consequences for mission. These can be summarised by saying that the missionary who accepted what was meant theologically by the term had to also accept that those he or she wished to evangelise had not only been addressed by the God of Jesus Christ, but had also implicitly made an act accepting or rejecting God's gracious self-offer in Christ. Those whom the missionary encountered could already have made an act of faith, albeit implicitly. Naturally, the missionary who previously believed that his work was necessary if souls were not to be lost, might now feel that his or her task had been robbed of much of its urgency and importance.[61] The anonymous Christian theory demolishes the assumption which was central to the traditional theology of mission and most of the controversy surrounding the anonymous Christian arose in this context.[62] However, as Rahner himself notes, some missionaries felt that the theory enabled them to understand their true task even better. Rahner refers to a Japanese student chaplain, for example, who told him that in his missionary work the theory constituted an indispensable condition precisely because he could then appeal to the anonymous Christian in the pagan and not simply seek to indoctrinate him or her with

---

[60]Anonymous Christianity and the missionary task of the Church, Theological investigations 12, 161-180; Christianity and non-Christian religions, Theological investigations 5, 115-134; Jesus Christ in the non-Christian religions, Theological investigations 17, 39-52; On the importance of the non-Christian religions for salvation, Theological investigations 18, 288-295.

[61]Theological investigations 12, 175.

[62]Cf. for example: Anon., A modern conception of salvation which hampers apostolic zeal according to Fr. Karl Rahner, Christ to the world 8, 1963, 421-428, 543-544; A. Race, Christianity and Other religions: Is inclusivism enough?, Theology 1983, 1,2, 178-186; R. Schreiter, The Anonymous Christian and Christology, Occasional Bulletin of Missionary Research, Jan. 1978, 2-11; W. J. Danker, The Anonymous Christian and Christology: A response (to Schreiter's article), Missiology, Apr. 1978, 235-241; H. Kruse, Die "Anonymen Christen" exegetisch gesehen, Münchener Theologische Zeitschrift 18, 1967, 2-29; P. Hacker, The Christian attitude toward non-Christian religions, Zeitschrift für Missionswissenschaft und Religionswissenschaft 55, 1971, 81-97; G. D'Costa, Karl Rahner's anonymous Christian - a reappraisal, Modern Theology 1: 2, 1985, 131-148. Rahner himself (Theological investigations 14, 280), refers us to Kruse's critical comments and those of L. Elders, Die Taufe der Weltreligionen. Bemerkungen zu einer Theorie Karl Rahners, Theologie und Glaube 55, 1965, 124-131.

a teaching ab externo.[63] But when challenged that to refer to a Buddhist, for example, as an anonymous Christian was not only disrespectful but also arrogant, Rahner's response was twofold.[64] First: he reiterated that the theory was primarily intended to express one important aspect of the Christian's self-understanding within the contemporary faith situation. Rahner is anxious to provide the Christian with a framework for understanding the disbelief which he sees around him, and how God's grace can still be active in what might appear on the surface to be a graceless world.[65] Further, on one occasion Rahner said that he personally would have no objection to being referred to as an anonymous Buddhist:

> From a formal point of view there is no problem, then, in my treating someone as an anonymous Christian, even if he energetically denies my interpretation and rejects it as false or incoherent; Nishitani, the well known Japanese philosopher, the head of the Kyoto school, who is familiar with the notion of the anonymous Christian, once asked me: What would you say to my treating you as an anonymous Zen Buddhist? I replied: Certainly you may and should do so from your point of view; I feel myself honoured by such an interpretation, even if I am obliged to regard you as being in error or if I assume that, correctly understood, to be a genuine Zen Buddhist is identical with being a genuine Christian, in the sense directly and properly intended by such statements. Of course in terms of objective social awareness it is indeed clear that the Buddhist is not a Christian and the Christian is not a Buddhist. Nishitani replied: Then on this point we are entirely at one.[66]

The theory of the anonymous Christian was primarily meant to help Christians make sense of their secularised world and not primarily intended as a tool of dialogue or evangelisation and in the light of the above quotation Rahner must himself accept

---

[63]Theological investigations 14, 292-293.

[64]Particularly objecting to the arrogance involved in addressing someone else as an anonymous Christian, Hans Küng writes:"Die hinter dem terminus 'anonymer Christ' steckenden guten theologisch-pastoralen Intentionen bezüglich der Nichtchristen sind beizubehalten. Der unglückliche und widersprüchliche Terminus aber, der nach außen und innen zweideutig, für Nichtchristen anmaßend und für Christen und besonders für christliche Missionare verwirrend ist, kann ohne Schaden für jene Intentionen aufgegeben werden. Man sage von den Nichtchristen alles Güte, Wahre, Religiöse, was immer möglich ist. Aber man nenne sie, die weder Christen sind noch Christen sein wollen, weder "Christen" noch "anonym", sondern lade sie durch ein ihnen angemessen verkündigtes Evangelium in Wort und Tat ein, völlig unanonym, mit vollem Namen Christi zu werden!" (Anonyme Christen - wozu? Orientierung 39, 1975, 216).

[65]Cf. Theological investigations 6, 396.

[66]Theological investigations 16, 220. Objecting to the sheer confusion which dialogue engaged in on these lines is likely to cause Küng asks: "Wenn Rahner angeblich nichts - ich hätte sehr viel! - gegen die Bezeichnung seiner Person als eines 'anonymen Buddhisten' (durch einen Buddhisten) einzuwenden hat: wie soll man sich wohl einen ehrlich klärenden Dialog vorstellen zwischen einem "anonymen Buddhisten" der in Wirklichkeit Christ, und einem "anonymen Christen", der in Wirklichkeit Buddhist ist, besonders...wenn der eine womöglich auch noch "anonymer Marxist" und der andere "anonymer Kapitalist" ist oder umgekehrt?" (H. Küng, art. cit., 216).

some of the responsibility for the misapplication and misinterpretation of his theory.[67]

Rahner's more consistently held position is that to many anonymous Christians, be they people who profess other faiths or people who claim to be atheists, "these reflections may mean very little, and they are not in the first place directed to them".[68] Rahner also argues that it is legitimate to develop a Catholic dogmatic interpretation of non-Christians and non-Christian religions. That this interpretation would make the "arrogant" claim of knowing non-Christians better than they know themselves is an inevitable consequence of the Church's teaching that all salvation comes through Christ and of the recognition that the Church is not the exclusive community of those to whom salvation is offered:

> Non-Christians may think it presumption for the Christian to judge everything which is sound or restored (by being sanctified) to be the fruit in every man of the grace of his Christ, and to interpret it as anonymous Christianity; they may think it presumption for the Christian to regard the non-Christian as a Christian who has not yet come to himself reflectively. But the Christian cannot renounce this 'presumption' which is really the source of the greatest humility both for himself and for the Church. For it is a profound admission that God is greater than man and the Church. The Church will go out to meet the non-Christian of tomorrow with the attitude expressed by St. Paul when he said: What therefore you do not know and yet worship (and yet <u>worship</u>!) that I proclaim to you (Acts 17:23). On such a basis one can be tolerant, humble and yet firm towards all non-Christian religions.[69]

More will be said about Rahner's understanding of non-Christian religions when we come to contrast his position with that of Balthasar. His position, to summarise briefly, is that if we accept the theory of the anonymous Christian, and if even implicit faith must find some categorical expression, non-Christian religions can be understood as more or less successful categorical interpretations of God's salvific activity in the world. The extent to which these interpretations are successful, or fail because of sin and depravity, can be assessed only from the standpoint of Christianity which provides the ultimate and normative interpretation.

---

[67]In response to a criticism along these lines from E. Jüngel, K. - H. Weger replies: "...it is not a question, in this doctrine of anonymous Christianity, of imposing anything on non-Christians that they would themselves not want to be or even of trying to increase the rapidly diminishing number of Christians by letting others in through the back door. The question of anonymous Christianity is simply and solely a question that applies within the Christian framework itself. It is <u>my</u> question, not that of non-Christians. As a believing Christian, I am bound to ask myself about the situation with regard to the salvation of those whom I see around me and who are no worse or more stupid or more malicious than I am, but who are not Christians and who do not want to be Christians" (<u>op. cit.</u>, 117).

[68]<u>Theological investigations</u> 6, 395.

[69]<u>Theological investigations</u> 5, 134.

The Church and the anonymous Christian

The consequence of the theory of the anonymous Christian which will dominate the remaining chapters of this work is the effect which such a concept has upon the Church's self-understanding. Whereas Rahner intended it to enable the Christian to make sense of Christian faith in a pluralistic world and to identify that which constitutes the essence of being a Christian, Balthasar argues that it robs the Church of its identity, signals the surrender or conversion of the Church to the world and relativises the work of the historic Christ in the process of redemption.

Rahner's own position is that the individual anonymous Christian is essentially related to the Church which provides the objectively correct interpretation of his or her existence on the categorical level. The grace of Christ which the anonymous Christian possesses finds its historical concretisation and embodiment precisely in the Church. As we shall see, Rahner freely admits that the anonymous Christian's categorical expression of his or her faith is defective. Even more than the state of the "named" Christian, who is always engaged in a pilgrimage of faith, the state of the anonymous Christian, far from being considered as stable, should be understood as one which has as its goal explicit Christian expression.[70] Further, we shall see how Rahner argues that both God's gracious self-offer to the anonymous Christian and the anonymous Christian's response to this gracious self-offer are dependent on the incarnation and cross of Jesus Christ. Rahner does not intend any relativisation of the Church. He does intend, however, to locate the historical saving event of the life, death and resurrection of Jesus Christ within the history of salvation as a whole. It will emerge in the course of this work that Rahner's overriding theological concern is to proclaim that God wishes the salvation of the world.

Language and terms

With regard to the questions of atheism, of missionary activity, of non-Christian religions and of named Christianity, Rahner's students and critics made much of anonymous Christianity which Karl Rahner neither intended nor endorsed. Rahner himself can be held at least partly to blame for this: while the kernel of his theory remains the same, in different contexts we find different emphases and different terms

---

[70]Theological investigations 6, 393. Commenting on the Christian approach to atheism Rahner writes: "Christians who for their part believe that the salvation of all humankind is effected by God's grace in Christ who continues to be historically present in the world through the Church; Christians who at the same time possess the confident hope that God's grace can be victorious even in those who in their own reflexive theory interpret themselves as godless and without grace - these Christians cannot help but interpret inculpable atheists in a way that these atheists themselves theoretically reject" (Theological investigations 21, 145). Cf. further Theological investigations 5, 21.

not, is saved through Christ.[87] Only Christian revelation confirms
and unambiguously what humans always experience implicitly in the depth
ng.[88]

the meaning beyond the terms

bout minor concessions regarding language, Rahner is uncompromising
de to what is signified by these terms. He considers the subject matter to
by the Second Vatican Council and therefore not to be a matter for
by Catholic theologians. Rahner invites his critics to reflect on two main
rst: the fact is that there are men and women who, through no fault of
re not explicit Christians.[90] We cannot believe that these people are in
cluded from salvation. We cannot believe in principle that they are not
e justified. It would be contrary to our faith to believe this.[91]
erm "anonymous Christian" claims that the non-Christian if justified, is

___

logical investigations 9, 145.

to me that one reason why Rahner refuses to see anonymous Christianity as
stianity and the Church is because he sees anonymous Christianity as an important
h and of Christianity. To claim that anonymous Christianity relativises the Christian
ner, tantamount to claiming that Christianity relativises itself. Further, as we shall
at the salvation of the non-Christian takes place in and through Christ is also central
rine.

gical investigations 9, 145 and 14, 282.

ms to suggest that we should not presume guilt simply because people have actually
of Christianity. Firstly, it is not appropriate for Christians who, as both Rahner
nt out, stand under judgement themselves, to pass judgement on one another or on
it is very difficult to assess how effectively the Gospel has been proclaimed. It may
that many who reject Christianity as they have experienced it, are rejecting an
oorly presented form of it or even an entirely false presentation of it.

ical investigations 6, 391 (already quoted in the introduction, p. 4): "But can the
ven for a moment that the overwhelming mass of his brothers...are unquestionably
excluded from the fulfilment of their lives and condemned to eternal
He must reject any such suggestion, and his faith is itself in agreement with his
o Theological investigations 14, 282, 283. Compare Balthasar's chapter "The
for all" in Dare we hope "that all men be saved"?, 210-221. Whereas Rahner
hurch historically showed little trust in the universality of salvation (Theological
283) and therefore places greater emphasis on the teaching of the Second Vatican
provides a careful study of scriptural evidence and the teaching of the Second Vatican
neless, as Balthasar explicitly acknowledges (p.211) his view and that of Rahner
being optimistic with regard to the universality of salvation are remarkably

___

being employed.

For example, in Theological investigations 9 Rahner writes:

> Implicit Christianity - it could also be termed "anonymous Christianity" - is what we call
> the condition of a man who lives on the one hand in a state of grace and justification, and
> yet on the other hand has not come into contact with the explicit preaching of the Gospel
> and is consequently not in a position to call himself "Christian".[71]

And from an earlier essay it is clear that Rahner intended to include

> not only those before the appearance of Christ right back to the most distant past (whose
> horizons are being constantly extended by paleontology) but also those of the present and
> of the future before us...[72]

However, in Theological investigations 14 these people are seemingly excluded
because now,

> ...the "anonymous Christian" in our sense of the term is the pagan after the beginning of
> the Christian mission, who lives in the state of Christ's grace through faith, hope, and love,
> yet who has no explicit knowledge of the fact that his life is orientated in grace-given
> salvation to Jesus Christ.[73]

Why this shift of emphasis to those born after the Christ-event? As has already been
pointed out, Rahner has developed his theory primarily in the context of secularised
Europe, to provide the Church with a framework within which to understand
widespread atheism. One of the areas of dispute is whether long-term inculpable
atheism is possible. Rahner wants to make it quite clear that this is what he is
implying.

Another area of confusion relates to Rahner's use of the term "anonymous theist" as
distinct from "anonymous Christian". In his first statement of the concept of the
"anonymous Christian", Rahner is anxious to stress the fact that all salvation comes
only through Christ and that a faith response, even an implicit or unthematic one, is
always a response to Christ:

> If man accepts revelation...whenever he accepts himself completely...he is taking upon
> himself not merely his basic relationship with the silent mystery of the Creator-God...he is
> becoming not merely an "anonymous" theist...In the acceptance of himself man is accepting
> Christ as the absolute perfection and guarantee of his own anonymous movement towards
> God by grace...[74]

Later, in Theological investigations 14, without elucidating any further, he states quite
clearly that the terms "anonymous Christian" and "anonymous theist" do not mean

___

[71] p.145

[72] Theological investigations 6, 391.

[73] p.283.

[74] Theological investigations 6, 394.

the same.[75] Even where there is no apparent development or change in concepts, the change in terms used to express the same concepts can also be confusing. Rahner has particular difficulty relating the concept of the anonymous Christian to Christianity and the Church. Several different terms are used, e.g. "Christianity at the social level"[76], "explicit Christianity"[77], and "official ecclesiastical faith"[78]. And are anonymous Christians to be considered as members of the Church? In Theological investigations 6 Rahner feels that in the light of the extra ecclesiam teaching, the salvation of anonymous Christians can only be understood if

> somehow all men must be capable of being members of the Church; and this capacity must not be understood merely in the sense of an abstract and purely logical capacity, but as a real and historically concrete one.[79]

It is therefore necessary, according to Rahner, to conceive of degrees of membership of Church from the explicitness of baptism to a non-official and anonymous Christianity which can and should be called Christianity in a meaningful sense. Responding to criticism of this position, in Theological investigations 14 Rahner simply says that anonymous Christians stand outside "the social unity of the Church".[80]

In response to criticism from Henri de Lubac in particular, which is endorsed by Balthasar, Rahner is also prepared to re-negotiate his use of the word "Christianity" in the context of "anonymous Christianity".[81] From the very beginning he is aware that the terms "anonymous Christian" and "anonymous Christianity" are not ideal. Yet he finds it difficult to provide better expressions and challenges his critics to do the same. Initially Rahner rejects de Lubac's distinction between "anonymous Christianity" and "anonymous Christian".[82] "Christianity" (Christentum), he admits,

---

[75]p.282. Cf. also Theological investigations 9, 145-164.

[76]Theological investigations 14, 283.

[77]Theological investigations 14, 286.

[78]Theological investigations 6, 394.

[79]p.391.

[80]p.282.

[81]Cf. H. de Lubac, Paradoxe et Mystère de l'Eglise, 153-156. On Balthasar's endorsement of de Lubac's distinction, cf. Cordula oder der Ernstfall, 129; Herder-Korrespondenz 30, 1976, 72-82, esp. 76.

[82]Theological investigations 12, 162-165.

---

can mean both the sum total of Christians an individual as a Christian. He would seem to a the sum total of Christians approximates to the in association with the word "anonymous" it is We are therefore concerned with the use of the t "Christianity" as referring to the "being Christ if explicit Church membership belongs to the v individual as a Christian, then the term "anony because the word "anonymous" is meant to de But what goes for "Christianity" in this ca therefore both terms must either be accepted that the terms are far from ideal he says:

> we can set on one side the distinction betw "anonymous Christianity" as being unimpo in the concrete we must either accept the

reject both.[84]

Writing some three years later (1971) Rahr he writes

> We may concede to de Lubac that with r been called in question there is a certa Christian" and "anonymous Christianity readily be admitted than that of "anony avoid the term "anonymous Christianity Christian" etc. They can count on my

He goes on, however, to claim as enti Christianity" when what is being referred concerned and says that it is in this sen It is perhaps also worth mentioning that is not postulating another ecclesiastica Christianity".[86] The most important po word "Christian" or "Christianity" in the conviction that all grace comes

---

[83]Cf. Theological investigations 12, 2

[84]Theological investigations 12, 163.

[85]Theological investigations 14, 281.

[86]Cf. Theological investigations 14,

---

baptised o irrevocably of their be

Conclusion
Whatever a in his attitu be defined questioning points.[89] Fi their own, a principle exc and cannot b Second, the

---

[87]Cf. Theo

[88]It seems relativising Chr part of the Chur faith is, for Rah see, the claim th to Rahner's doc

[89]Cf. Theo

[90]Rahner se been made aware and Balthasar poi others. Secondly, well be the case impoverished or

[91]Cf. Theolo Christian believe a and in principle meaninglessness? doing so." Cf. al obligation to hope considers that the Investigations. 14, Council, Balthasar this regard. Never on the necessity o similar.

justified through Christ. We must remember that by "anonymous Christian", Rahner is not referring to all those to whom God has offered himself in grace, which in fact for Rahner is every human being - every human being has a supernatural existential. Anonymous Christians are among those who have responded positively and accepted God's self-offer. Albeit implicitly or "unthematically", as Rahner says, anonymous Christians have made the faith response necessary for salvation through Jesus Christ, for there is no other way.

With respect to the charge that the theory of the anonymous Christian relativises the Christian faith, Rahner believes that this charge could also be levelled against the teaching of the Council and therefore

> in the face of the theological optimism of the Council regarding salvation it remains the task of theology to show why the necessity of the gospel, the Church and the sacraments are not thereby devalued...[92]

Arguably, given the nature of the kind of faith milieu which is becoming more and more dominant in Europe, it is theology's most urgent task to provide a credible and theologically sound basis for the Church's optimism regarding universal salvation without at the same time relativising biblical revelation.

---

[92]Theological investigations 6, 398.

Introduction

The aim of this chapter and the next is to present Balthasar's critique of Rahner's anonymous Christian. Following a brief introduction to Balthasar's life and work, his critique will be presented as it has evolved in articles and books over almost fifty years.

Balthasar's critique could have been presented thematically. However, this might not have proved very helpful. First of all, Balthasar's critique can in fact be reduced to one theme: the anonymous Christian is only possible through a subsumption of theology under a philosophical system, thus diverting theology from its central task and in fact "reducing" the historical life, death and resurrection of Jesus Christ to being merely the historical manifestation of God's salvific will from all eternity and not the event of salvation. Second, a thematic approach would fail to bring out the evolutionary nature of Balthasar's critique. It would also underplay the importance of the ecclesio-sociological milieu at the time of writing, which accounts for certain emphases and for the tone of Balthasar's criticisms. Third, it is important for us to understand that Balthasar was reacting to Rahner's theology as it was developing and as it was influencing theology and pastoral practice. A chronological presentation, therefore, represents Balthasar's critique more accurately and comprehensively.

It is important to evaluate Balthasar's critique not only as it evolved but also within the context of Balthasar's theology as a whole. This would require a substantial treatment of Balthasar's trilogy, which Balthasar himself always insisted must always be treated as a unity. God's self-authenticating testimony to God's self in revelation (theological Aesthetik) ignites the historical encounter between the infinite and the finite (Dramatik) which is subsequently meditated upon and ordered into human words and actions (Logik). Here it will be possible to present only a brief summary of Balthasar's theological aesthetics, which should nonetheless enable the reader to compare and contrast Balthasar's starting-point to that of Rahner and provide at least an intimation of the masterpiece which is Balthasar's trilogy as a whole.

An evolutionary approach to Balthasar's criticisms further helps us to appreciate that Balthasar made decisive choices regarding theological method from the very outset. One of these was a rebuff of any renovation of neo-scholasticism. His early criticisms of Spirit in the world and Hearers of the word are best understood as criticisms of a whole school of thought emerging at that time within Catholic theology.[1] His later sharp and polemical criticisms of Rahner which one finds in a number of books and articles written in the immediate aftermath of the Second Vatican Council are perhaps the best known of his censures of Rahner, but interpreted outside the context both of Balthasar's earlier   rejections of renovated neo-scholasticism and his theology as a whole lead to distortions.[2] For example, too much has been made of Balthasar's disappointment at not been invited to participate in the Second Vatican Council.[3]   Considered from the perspective of Balthasar's theology as a whole and of his critique of Rahner in its entirety, Balthasar's post-conciliar criticisms should only be understood as an intensification and crystallization of pre-conciliar criticisms which have gradually evolved out of Balthasar's own theological reflection and dialogue with the Fathers, de Lubac, Barth, Przywara, etc., and are a response to his interpretation of the contemporary social and ecclesial milieu. They are a criticism of what Rahner's (and others') whole theology does, and of what it fails to do.   Though it is important to distinguish between Rahner's theology and the consequences of his theological approach for pastoral practice, Balthasar raises criticisms of both.

Balthasar's development of a totally different theological system, therefore, has to be seen as a deliberate choice to reject a transcendental theological approach which he

---

[1]The so-called Catholic Heidegger School.

[2]In the course of an attempt to reject criticisms of idealistic tendencies in Rahner's theology in his introduction to the 1968 English edition of <u>Spirit in the world</u> (p. xxxii), Fiorenza writes:"These considerations illustrate the degree of misunderstanding contained in the criticism raised against Rahner by Hans Urs von Balthasar, who in the general context of his conservative evaluations and negative criticism of contemporary tendencies within the Church attacks not only current aspects of the biblical, liturgical and ecumenical movements, but also the attempts of Karl Rahner and Johannes Metz to develop a positive relationship to modern philosophy and the secularisation of society and its institutions." Fiorenza refers us to <u>Glaubhaft ist nur Liebe</u> (1963), Wer ist ein Christ? (1965) and <u>Cordula oder der Ernstfall</u> (1966). Fiorenza's position is coherent only if one ignores Balthasar's critique of Rahner as a whole (beginning with his review of <u>Geist in Welt</u>, 1939) and his own theological system.

[3]See H. Vorgrimler (<u>Understanding Karl Rahner</u>, 124). Together with the implication that the theological differences between both men can be related to Balthasar's unsuccessful attempts to acquire a chair in theology (according to Vorgrimler, <u>loc. cit.</u>, Balthasar applied for Guardini's position in Munich, which Rahner got), this perhaps over-simplistic argumentation ignores the fact that Balthasar had serious criticisms of Rahner's theology from the very beginning.   It is disputed whether or not Balthasar ever applied for a chair of theology. Peter Henrici S.J. (Balthasar's nephew), for example, claims that Balthasar never applied for one but had several offered him, including that of Guardini in Munich. Henrici certainly admits that Balthasar's position as confessor to Adrienne von Speyr and his leaving of the Society of Jesus did make difficulties for him in this regard (<u>op. cit.</u> 36-38). Cf. P. Henrici, Erster blick auf Hans Urs von Balthasar. In K. Lehmann and W. Kasper, ed. <u>Hans Urs von Balthasar. Gestalt und Werk</u>, 38.

considers to be inadequate and unsatisfactory. He also considers it unable to meet the challenges posed to the Christian faith today, being rather engulfed by them. A transcendental theology, according to Balthasar, finds no place of intersection with his theological aesthetics: this is not accidental.[4]

While we intend only to examine Balthasar's critique of the anonymous Christian, this concept is so central to Rahner's theology that any criticism of Rahner's theology is in some way a criticism of the anonymous Christian. In addition, the anonymous Christian, being a logical outcome of the transcendental method, indeed this method carried to its conclusion, represents Rahner's theology in a very real way. Thus when Balthasar criticises the anonymous Christian, he is in a very real way criticising Rahner's whole method. In fact, as we shall see, the anonymous Christian (not necessarily exactly as Rahner has developed it but as it has come to be understood) becomes a symbol for Balthasar not only of Rahner's theology but of a whole movement within theology and indeed in the Church as a whole. It becomes a symbol for dialogue with the world but on the world's terms, an openness to the world but at the same time a flight from the central teachings of Christianity.

All Balthasar's critical reflections therefore, from the vague and general to the harshly polemical, must be taken seriously and interpreted within their appropriate context.

An introduction to Hans Urs von Balthasar

Balthasar was born in Lucerne, in 1905. On the completion of his doctorate in Germanistik in 1928 he joined the Society of Jesus and was ordained a priest in 1936. Hans Urs von Balthasar was a contemporary of Karl Rahner. However, from the very outset they progressed along different theological paths. Some of the great influences on Balthasar include Ignatius of Loyola, Henri de Lubac, Eric Przywara, Goethe and Adrienne von Speyr.

Balthasar's Ignatian roots are revealed in his emphasis on the task of the believer as doing all for God's ever-greater glory (ad maiorem Dei gloriam). The stamp of Ignatius may also be detected in Balthasar's emphasis on "thinking with the Church", contemplation in action, ecclesial obedience and the deep inner relationship between the Cross and the Incarnation. In fidelity to the spirit of Ignatius he felt compelled to leave the Society of Jesus to found the Johannesgemeinschaft together with Adrienne von Speyr.

---

[4]In the final chapter it will be pointed out that there are in fact points of intersection between Balthasar's understanding of Christian anthropology and transcendental theology.

Henri de Lubac acquainted Balthasar with the works of the Fathers and especially with the writings of Origen. Balthasar's contemplative theology, like that of so many of the Fathers, grows out of and is nourished by meditation on the scriptures. At a later point we will discuss Balthasar's approach to scripture. Through de Lubac, the Fathers taught Balthasar not only how to pray, but how to relate prayer to life and particularly to theology. From the outset Balthasar saw the potential for a recovery of the unity between spirituality and theology in the Fathers of the Church.

The analogy of being plays a central role in Balthasar's theology - in terms of the relation between Creator and creature, grace and nature, faith and reason. Przywara's philosophical works mediated the notion of analogia entis to Balthasar. But through the work of Barth, Balthasar recognised the limitations of analogy, limitations which he felt compelled to overcome. Balthasar saw Barthian theology as a yardstick by which one could measure Catholic theology. He was determined to take Barth's objections to Catholic theology seriously. Balthasar's Karl Barth: Darstellung und Deutung seiner Theologie, first published in 1951, contains a long discussion particularly of the relationship between analogia entis and analogia fidei. Undoubtedly Balthasar was influenced by Barth insofar as he wished to produce a truly Catholic theology which would not be open to the valid objections which Barth had made. Referring to this particular book which is a remarkable synthesis of Barth's thought, Barth is supposed to have commented that Balthasar understood him better than he understood himself!

Balthasar's post-graduate studies were in Germanistics, and Goethe's concept of Gestalt is central to his theological aesthetics. Gestalt provides him with a structure for mediating the glory of the Lord.

The experiences of Adrienne von Speyr (1902-1967) had a major influence on Balthasar, who saw it as an important part of his ministry to make her writings and her thoughts known to a wider audience. Under Balthasar's direction, von Speyr, a medical doctor, converted to Catholicism in 1940. Balthasar has written a number of books specifically with her. In many others he credits particular insights to her. Her own suffering led Balthasar to a deeper understanding of the suffering of Jesus Christ and the role of the Cross in the saving mystery. In particular, Balthasar attributes his understanding of the theological significance of Holy Saturday to the mystical insights of Adrienne von Speyr. She taught him the deep relationship which exists between suffering and love. The shift which one can detect in Balthasar's theology from an Ignatian to a Johannine influence can be traced back to Adrienne von Speyr:

It was Adrienne von Speyr who pointed out the fulfilling way from Ignatius to

John, and thus laid the foundation for most of what has been published by me since
1940. Her work and mine is neither psychologically nor philosophically separable,
two halves of a whole which, as centre, has but one foundation.[5]
It is clearly evident as a result of this present research that Karl Rahner also
influenced Balthasar. This is not so only in a negative way as, for example, the way
in which two boxers determine each other's performance in the ring. Balthasar's
critique of Rahner shows a familiarity with all his major works, and occasionally
Balthasar builds upon some particular concept of Rahner's.[6] In addition, Balthasar
clearly considered Rahner to be a fine theologian, and they co-operated with one
another on a number of theological projects.[7] But from the very beginning Balthasar
was anxious to move beyond neo-scholasticism, to provide something new which
could not be dragged down or made to succumb to the spirit of the age. At the same
time, he recognised that Rahner and de Lubac, in different ways, were seriously
attempting to renovate theology from within a neo-scholastic base. While sceptical
of the fruitfulness of such an effort, and at times questioning its appropriateness and
even its legitimacy, Balthasar considered Rahner's work to represent the best effort
at a renovation of neo-scholastic theology.[8] While identifying the main limitation of

---

[5]Rechenschaft 1965, 35.

[6]One example of this is in Balthasar's book Dare we hope "that all men be saved?", 32. Rahner
had emphasised several times that salvation is something which in full freedom must be accepted or
rejected by the individual. He had stressed that the rejection of God's free and gratuitous self-
communication must be a real possibility. Hell must be a possibility. Cf. the article on Hölle in
Sacramentum Mundi II, 736; Foundations of Christian faith, 133.

[7]"(Rahner and Balthasar) were never students together, though in the summer of 1939 they did
collaborate on the outline of a dogmatics, which Rahner published in the first volume of Schriften.
They had various literary quarrels with one another, accusing one another of lacking a sense of
humour, yet they held one another in high esteem. At the time of their sixtieth birthdays, which fell
quite close together, they expressed their mutual admiration and respect in a way that went beyond
mere politeness" (P. Henrici, op. cit., 55). In 1976 Balthasar himself wrote, "I consider Karl
Rahner, taken from an overall perspective, to be the strongest theological potential of our time...in
1939 we worked together on a plan for dogmatics which later became Mysterium Salutis...but our
starting points were actually always different. There is a book by Simmel called Kant and Goethe.
Rahner chose Kant, or if you wish, Fichte, the transcendental basis. I have chosen Goethe - as a
Germanistic. The form (Gestalt), the insolubly unique, organic, self-developing form - I am thinking
about Goethe's Metamorphose der Pflanzen - this form, to which even Kant in his Aesthetic does
not come close" (Geist und Feuer, Herder Korrespondenz 30, 1976, 75-76). The original text of
the 1939 dogmatic schema, in Rahner's handwriting with amendments by Balthasar, is now on
display in the Rahner Archives, University of Innsbruck.

[8]In his review of Geist in Welt (Zeitschrift für Katholische Theologie 63, 1939, 375), Balthasar
refers to Rahner's thesis as "vielleicht die tiefsinnigste der neueren Scholastik". In Karl Barth:
Darstellung und Deutung seiner Theologie (p.310), Balthasar approves some of Rahner's criticisms
and development of de Lubac's position on nature and grace.

being employed.

For example, in Theological investigations 9 Rahner writes:

> Implicit Christianity - it could also be termed "anonymous Christianity" - is what we call
> the condition of a man who lives on the one hand in a state of grace and justification, and
> yet on the other hand has not come into contact with the explicit preaching of the Gospel
> and is consequently not in a position to call himself "Christian".[71]

And from an earlier essay it is clear that Rahner intended to include

> not only those before the appearance of Christ right back to the most distant past (whose
> horizons are being constantly extended by paleontology) but also those of the present and
> of the future before us...[72]

However, in Theological investigations 14 these people are seemingly excluded
because now,

> ...the "anonymous Christian" in our sense of the term is the pagan after the beginning of
> the Christian mission, who lives in the state of Christ's grace through faith, hope, and love,
> yet who has no explicit knowledge of the fact that his life is orientated in grace-given
> salvation to Jesus Christ.[73]

Why this shift of emphasis to those born after the Christ-event? As has already been
pointed out, Rahner has developed his theory primarily in the context of secularised
Europe, to provide the Church with a framework within which to understand
widespread atheism. One of the areas of dispute is whether long-term inculpable
atheism is possible. Rahner wants to make it quite clear that this is what he is
implying.

Another area of confusion relates to Rahner's use of the term "anonymous theist" as
distinct from "anonymous Christian". In his first statement of the concept of the
"anonymous Christian", Rahner is anxious to stress the fact that all salvation comes
only through Christ and that a faith response, even an implicit or unthematic one, is
always a response to Christ:

> If man accepts revelation...whenever he accepts himself completely...he is taking upon
> himself not merely his basic relationship with the silent mystery of the Creator-God...he is
> becoming not merely an "anonymous" theist...In the acceptance of himself man is accepting
> Christ as the absolute perfection and guarantee of his own anonymous movement towards
> God by grace...[74]

Later, in Theological investigations 14, without elucidating any further, he states quite
clearly that the terms "anonymous Christian" and "anonymous theist" do not mean

---

[71]p.145

[72]Theological investigations 6, 391.

[73]p.283.

[74]Theological investigations 6, 394.

the same.[75] Even where there is no apparent development or change in concepts, the change in terms used to express the same concepts can also be confusing.

Rahner has particular difficulty relating the concept of the anonymous Christian to Christianity and the Church. Several different terms are used, e.g. "Christianity at the social level"[76], "explicit Christianity"[77], and "official ecclesiastical faith"[78]. And are anonymous Christians to be considered as members of the Church? In Theological investigations 6 Rahner feels that in the light of the extra ecclesiam teaching, the salvation of anonymous Christians can only be understood if

> somehow all men must be capable of being members of the Church; and this capacity must not be understood merely in the sense of an abstract and purely logical capacity, but as a real and historically concrete one.[79]

It is therefore necessary, according to Rahner, to conceive of degrees of membership of Church from the explicitness of baptism to a non-official and anonymous Christianity which can and should be called Christianity in a meaningful sense. Responding to criticism of this position, in Theological investigations 14 Rahner simply says that anonymous Christians stand outside "the social unity of the Church".[80]

In response to criticism from Henri de Lubac in particular, which is endorsed by Balthasar, Rahner is also prepared to re-negotiate his use of the word "Christianity" in the context of "anonymous Christianity".[81] From the very beginning he is aware that the terms "anonymous Christian" and "anonymous Christianity" are not ideal. Yet he finds it difficult to provide better expressions and challenges his critics to do the same. Initially Rahner rejects de Lubac's distinction between "anonymous Christianity" and "anonymous Christian".[82] "Christianity" (Christentum), he admits,

---

[75]p.282. Cf. also Theological investigations 9, 145-164.

[76]Theological investigations 14, 283.

[77]Theological investigations 14, 286.

[78]Theological investigations 6, 394.

[79]p.391.

[80]p.282.

[81]Cf. H. de Lubac, Paradoxe et Mystère de l'Eglise, 153-156. On Balthasar's endorsement of de Lubac's distinction, cf. Cordula oder der Ernstfall, 129; Herder-Korrespondenz 30, 1976, 72-82, esp. 76.

[82]Theological investigations 12, 162-165.

can mean both the sum total of Christians and that which constitutes a specific individual as a Christian. He would seem to accept that "Christianity" referring to the sum total of Christians approximates to the Church, and when he uses the term in association with the word "anonymous" it is not to be interpreted in this sense.[83] We are therefore concerned with the use of the term "anonymous" in conjunction with "Christianity" as referring to the "being Christian" of an individual Christian. Now if explicit Church membership belongs to the very nature of that which constitutes an individual as a Christian, then the term "anonymous Christianity" becomes a nonsense because the word "anonymous" is meant to describe the very exclusion of this aspect. But what goes for "Christianity" in this case would also go for "Christian" and therefore both terms must either be accepted or rejected. Therefore while admitting that the terms are far from ideal he says:

> we can set on one side the distinction between the concepts of "anonymous Christian" and "anonymous Christianity" as being unimportant, and assume that for practical purposes and in the concrete we must either accept the possibility of using both terms or else we must reject both.[84]

Writing some three years later (1971) Rahner appears to have changed his mind, for he writes

> We may concede to de Lubac that with regard to the justification of the terms which have been called in question there is a certain distinction to be drawn between "anonymous Christian" and "anonymous Christianity"; that the term "anonymous Christian" may more readily be admitted than that of "anonymous Christianity". Some therefore may prefer to avoid the term "anonymous Christianity", while being ready to use the term "anonymous Christian" etc. They can count on my agreement on this point.[85]

He goes on, however, to claim as entirely valid the use of the term "anonymous Christianity" when what is being referred to is the "being Christian" of the individual concerned and says that it is in this sense that he will use it.

It is perhaps also worth mentioning that by the term "anonymous Christianity" Rahner is not postulating another ecclesiastical branch alongside "orthodox" and "catholic Christianity".[86] The most important point here is that the justification for using the word "Christian" or "Christianity" in conjunction with the term "anonymous" lies in the conviction that all grace comes through Christ and everyone who is saved,

---

[83]Cf. Theological investigations 12, 281.

[84]Theological investigations 12, 163.

[85]Theological investigations 14, 281.

[86]Cf. Theological investigations 14, 281.

baptised or not, is saved through Christ.[87]   Only Christian revelation confirms irrevocably and unambiguously what humans always experience implicitly in the depth of their being.[88]

Conclusion: the meaning beyond the terms

Whatever about minor concessions regarding language, Rahner is uncompromising in his attitude to what is signified by these terms. He considers the subject matter to be defined by the Second Vatican Council and therefore not to be a matter for questioning by Catholic theologians. Rahner invites his critics to reflect on two main points.[89] First: the fact is that there are men and women who, through no fault of their own, are not explicit Christians.[90] We cannot believe that these people are in principle excluded from salvation. We cannot believe in principle that they are not and cannot be justified. It would be contrary to our faith to believe this.[91]

Second, the term "anonymous Christian" claims that the non-Christian if justified, is

---

[87]Cf. Theological investigations 9, 145.

[88]It seems to me that one reason why Rahner refuses to see anonymous Christianity as relativising Christianity and the Church is because he sees anonymous Christianity as an important part of the Church and of Christianity. To claim that anonymous Christianity relativises the Christian faith is, for Rahner, tantamount to claiming that Christianity relativises itself. Further, as we shall see, the claim that the salvation of the non-Christian takes place in and through Christ is also central to Rahner's doctrine.

[89]Cf. Theological investigations 9, 145 and 14, 282.

[90]Rahner seems to suggest that we should not presume guilt simply because people have actually been made aware of Christianity. Firstly, it is not appropriate for Christians who, as both Rahner and Balthasar point out, stand under judgement themselves, to pass judgement on one another or on others. Secondly, it is very difficult to assess how effectively the Gospel has been proclaimed. It may well be the case that many who reject Christianity as they have experienced it, are rejecting an impoverished or poorly presented form of it or even an entirely false presentation of it.

[91]Cf. Theological investigations 6, 391 (already quoted in the introduction, p. 4): "But can the Christian believe even for a moment that the overwhelming mass of his brothers...are unquestionably and in principle excluded from the fulfilment of their lives and condemned to eternal meaninglessness? He must reject any such suggestion, and his faith is itself in agreement with his doing so." Cf. also Theological investigations 14, 282, 283. Compare Balthasar's chapter "The obligation to hope for all" in Dare we hope "that all men be saved"?, 210-221. Whereas Rahner considers that the Church historically showed little trust in the universality of salvation (Theological Investigations. 14, 283) and therefore places greater emphasis on the teaching of the Second Vatican Council, Balthasar provides a careful study of scriptural evidence and the teaching of the Fathers in this regard. Nevertheless, as Balthasar explicitly acknowledges (p.211) his view and that of Rahner on the necessity of being optimistic with regard to the universality of salvation are remarkably similar.

Rahner's transcendental method as its difficulty in proving the necessity for an explicit historical Christianity, Balthasar nevertheless considered it to be one of three approaches within modern theology which should be taken seriously.[9] But within this approach Balthasar also identified what he considered to be crippling limitations with unfortunate consequences.

Neo-Thomism and the Catholic Heidegger school
Balthasar concluded his Jesuit studies in 1937, just as Rahner was preparing to publish Spirit in the world, and following some time set aside for writing was appointed as a student chaplain in Basel. In 1939 he reviewed Spirit in the world for the Zeitschrift für Katholische Theologie, together with the published dissertation of Johannes B. Lotz, a fellow Jesuit and colleague of Rahner's. Lotz also belonged to the so-called Catholic Heidegger school. In this review Balthasar also refers to an article by Rahner which is the basis of what was later developed in Hearers of the word.[10] Balthasar's review is a comment not only on Rahner's philosophical basis but on the whole direction which this school was taking.[11] His specific comments on Rahner are comments on any system of theology which attempts to marry Kant, Maréchal and Heidegger to Aquinas.[12]

In this review Balthasar presents a summary of Rahner's thesis, together with an account of how he understands it as having evolved. He is particularly anxious to show Rahner's reliance on Maréchal.

> The basis of the problem is (as with Maréchal), the absolute binding of knowledge (Erkenntnis) to the senses; not just as a starting-point but as the only source of

---

[9]Aside from his own method, Balthasar also discusses liberation theology. All three methods, including Rahner's, "desire to be fully Catholic and to help the Christian in the world to witness more effectively. Each system has its own characteristic approach and its specific motivation that leads into Christian practice" (Current trends in Catholic Theology, Communio, Spring 1978, 78).

[10]K. Rahner, Religionsphilosophie und Theologie. In G. Baumgartner, ed., Die Siebenten Salzburger Hochschulwochen, Salzburg, 1937, 24-32.

[11]This is clear from Balthasar's introduction in Zeitschrift für Katholische Theologie 63, 1939, 372.

[12]In the beginning of his review (Zeitschrift für Katholische Theologie 63, 1939, 372), Balthasar mentions a number of other approaches which he considers to be along the same lines e.g. G. Söhngens (Sein und Gegenstand) who attempts to bring Aquinas into a metaphysical dialogue with Nicolai Hartmann, and Andrè Marc who attempts to combine Aquinas with Hegel.

knowledge as regards content (inhaltlichen Wissens).[13]

The role attributed by Rahner to the "agent intellect" encounters the same difficulties as Maréchal's concept of the dynamism of the spirit. Maréchal's failure was that he made the starting-point of metaphysics - an analysis of human subjectivity which reveals a human dynamism towards the absolute - into metaphysics itself. Within this analysis of human subjectivity, Maréchal, in an attempt to overcome the limitations of Kant's emphasis on judgement as merely a synthetic operation, attempted to establish the metaphysical significance of the judgement primarily as a result of a transcendental reduction. To some extent, Balthasar admits, Rahner has overcome these difficulties by laying emphasis on the need for the objective order, for the importance of grasping this order intelligibly and sensibly (it is only in and through the grasping of the individual objects as individual and particular objects that the Vorgriff is revealed). But, asks Balthasar cautiously, can the Vorgriff be effective? Did not Maréchal so concentrate upon this pre-understanding to the extent that he made it empty and meaningless? In Rahner's understanding, does it not also become a somewhat closed-off inner capacity which is so abstractive in its mode of operations that it is excessively formal and abstract? Further, Balthasar is not convinced that it can in fact lead to a concept of absolute being as opposed to a concept of nothingness. Can it not equally be argued that the Vorgriff leads to a grasp of sheer indeterminacy as much as it can be argued that it leads to a grasp of pure being?[14]

In the review under discussion Balthasar does not pursue his criticism of Rahner as much as he will later.[15] Instead, he suggests an amendment which, he believes, renders the reliance on such a philosophical system somewhat superfluous. Here Balthasar anticipates the direction which his own theology will take and points to what will be his overriding concern in the future: that theology be not subsumed under any other system of thought which will direct it away from its centre.

"The one thing necessary" - the theological character of theology
In 1951 Balthasar published his monumental book on Karl Barth. He respected Barth

---

[13]"Der Ansatz der Problematik ist (wie bei Maréchal) die absolute Bindung der Erkenntnis an die Sinnlichkeit; nicht nur als Ausgangspunkt, sondern als einzige Quelle inhaltlichen Wissens" (H. U. von Balthasar, Zeitschrift für Katholische Theologie 63, 1939, 375).

[14]W. Kasper (Jesus the Christ, 51) makes precisely this same criticism of Rahner: "Rahner's approach is still largely within the bounds of the idealistic philosophy of identity and its identification of being and consciousness. Hence he argues directly from the undoubted openness of the human spirit to the infinite to the reality of that infinite."

[15]Balthasar specifically takes up these earlier criticisms in Cordula oder der Ernstfall, 124.

immensely. Balthasar was, of course, concerned about ecumenical dialogue and he considered the "torn garment" to be a constant source of scandal to anyone who loved the Church. But his aim in this book was not primarily ecumenical. He knew that Barth posed very important questions to Roman Catholicism. Therefore he wanted to present Barth's thought and enter into dialogue with him, a dialogue which he felt could only be of immense benefit to Roman Catholic theology. Balthasar considered the insights of Barth to be a yardstick by which one could measure the catholicity of Roman Catholic theology.

Barth's own theology had developed as a via media between two unacceptable extremes: neo-protestantism and Roman Catholicism. What interested Balthasar most was Barth's main concern: to ensure that God's revelation in Christ would not be subsumed under some broad philosophical category and thus betray the faith. Barth targeted Schleiermacher's system, which emphasised religious awareness, as one system guilty of such a betrayal of the faith. But was Roman Catholic theology guilty of a similar betrayal? According to Barth, the Roman Catholic emphasis on the centrality of the analogy of being relativised revelation and its claims. The philosophical presupposition in Roman Catholic thought implied the recognition of a relationship between God and creation. God's revelation in Christ merely fulfilled an already existing framework. Christ's place was already determined in advance, prior to revelation, rather than derived from revelation. This emphasised Christ as the fulfilment of the natural order, but not as its foundation.[16] Balthasar considered Barth's main objection to Roman Catholicism to be the manner in which it compromised its specifically theological character in favour of a principle of natural science. Barth went so far as to say that the analogy of being was the invention of the Anti-Christ. It was why he could not be a Catholic.[17] Balthasar took these objections seriously and from Barth's standpoint he began to reflect on the various developments within Roman Catholic theology. Immediately he noticed that Roman Catholic theology had begun to busy itself with modern thought (e.g. Scheler, Husserl and Heidegger) at the same time as Barth began to move away from it. For Barth, who could be considered to be the founder of existential theology, preoccupation with these forms of modern thought only served to distract from "the one thing necessary". For Balthasar, their rejection by Barth and Barth's persistence

---

[16]Cf. H. U. von Balthasar, Karl Barth: Darstellung und Deutung seiner Theologie 46-47 (hereinafter given as Karl Barth).

[17]"Ich halte die analogia entis für die Erfindung des Antichrist und denke, daß man ihretwegen nicht katholisch werden kann" (K. Barth. In: Karl Barth, 56-57).

in attempting to speak about Jesus Christ in purely theological terms put a question mark on efforts to integrate philosophical categories, be they personalist ideals, phenomenology or, as in Heidegger, the radical historicity of finite existence, into Roman Catholic theology.[18]

It is clear that in this book Balthasar attempted two things. He sought to establish criteria by which to evaluate Roman Catholic theology.[19] He also set himself an agenda.[20]

In this book on Barth, in the course of his presentation of Catholic theology at that time, Balthasar presents a summary of Rahner's work on nature and grace. By 1951 the main framework of Rahner's aim and method in theology had clearly emerged, even if the consequences of such an approach within theology were not fully realised. As both Metz and Fiorenza acknowledge, Spirit in the world provided the unifying principle and presupposition of Rahner's whole theology.[21]   Even aside from the fact that Balthasar had studied Spirit in the world and Hearers of the word, Rahner and he had collaborated on a number of theological issues and were at this time also occasionally in informal contact with each other.[22]

---

[18]"Sie werden sich aber auch der Tatsache mit Existentialismus...beschäftigt haben, Karl Barth unentwegt nur das Eine Notwendige gesucht und betrieben hat, von Jesus Christus zu reden, für jeden verständlich und doch streng theologisch ...Die Unentwegtheit bleibt schon als solche eine stille, eindringliche Frage an die katholische Theologie" (Karl Barth, 50).

[19]"So könnte die entscheidende Frage an eine Dogmatik so gestellt werden, daß man der Weise der Auffassung und der Darstellung überall klar wird, daß das spezifisch theologische Prinzip als Quellgrund von allem gekannt, gewahrt, respektiert wird" (Karl Barth, 56).

[20]Two years after the publication of his book on Barth, Balthasar took up and developed the points made therein regarding the concept of nature in a joint article with Engelbert Gutwenger in Zeitschrift für Katholische Theologie (75, 1953, 452-464).

[21]Cf. their introductory comments to the second English edition. Though Vorgrimler claims that Rahner considered Geist in Welt to be very much a work of youth (Understanding Karl Rahner, 58-61), towards the end of his life Rahner reiterated his belief that his earliest Thomistic insights were correct (Im Gespräch I, 29-30).

[22]Balthasar had reviewed Geist in Welt for the Zeitschrift für Katholische Theologie in 1939. In Karl Barth he refers specifically both to this work and to Hörer des Wortes, which he also critically assesses in Die Gottesfrage des heutigen Menschen, published in 1956. While initially there was apparently much collaboration between Rahner and Balthasar, following the publication of Cordula contact between the two was rarer, though both served together later as members of the International Theological Commission. P. Henrici, (Erster Blick auf Hans Urs von Balthasar, Hans Urs von Balthasar: Gestalt und Werk, 55) comments that while their mutual admiration and respect went far beyond mere politeness, Balthasar and Rahner never understood each other at a really deep level. While endorsing Henrici's comments on the mutual respect which existed between both theologians, Vorgrimler records the last informal meeting between Balthasar and Rahner as having

In this book on Barth, Balthasar presented Rahner in the context of an effort to develop de Lubac's understanding of the relationship between grace and nature. Rahner had made his debut into main-line theological writing with an article which attempted to assess critically and develop the position adopted by de Lubac and the Nouvelle Theologie.[23] It seemed to Balthasar that de Lubac had achieved for Catholic theology what Barth had achieved for Protestant theology, then dominated by Schleiermacher: he had shifted the focus from a philosophical concern with nature (as in Maréchal) to a theological concern with real history.[24] Thus the focus was no longer on the (natural) desiderium but upon the human response to grace.[25] Whereas many misunderstood de Lubac, according to Balthasar, Rahner was one of the few to have responded with an expert and thorough critique. Both Rahner and de Lubac were anxious to avoid extrinsicism. However Rahner also believed that every effort had to be made to prevent grace and nature merely collapsing into one another. Rahner was not convinced that, in concentrating on the desiderium and (correctly) proposing only one (supernatural) goal for humankind de Lubac guarded sufficiently against such a collapse. Rahner therefore proposed the retention of the concept of natura pura as a remainder concept (Restbegriff) to guard against the reduction of grace.[26] In this way one can conceive of the human being as open to the possibility of a supernatural existence i.e. as possessing a supernatural existential,

---

taken place in 1961 and claims that the alienation between both men did not begin on Rahner's side (op. cit., 124).

[23]Cf. Theological investigations 1, 297-346. Rahner acknowledges Balthasar's comments on his definition of nature from the standpoint of grace through the employment of pure nature as a Restbegriff (pp. 296, 304).

[24]Cf. Karl Barth, 308.

[25]Maréchal perceived the human spirit as possessing an intuition for absolute being. This dynamic thrust necessarily presupposes an absolute being towards which it tends. Kant's failure, according to Maréchal, was to attempt to move from the sensible world to the spirit world and from there to God by logical deduction. In metaphysics, which is the science of absolutes, all abstraction must begin from the absolute concrete. Therefore he proposed a reversal of perspective, arguing that we must begin not from the dynamic thrust observable in the human spirit but rather from the necessary (absolute) being which it presupposes. De Lubac imported this reversal of perspective into theology, believing that Maréchal's metaphysics masked a latent theological a priori (desire for the beatific vision) which could serve as a starting-point for theology.

[26]De Lubac had rejected the concept of natura pura on the grounds that it was a useless exercise to talk about "pure nature" and a "purely natural goal" when the only world which existed and which concerned us was a graced world. In any case he deemed such a concept unnecessary if one began one's theological system from the one and only goal which God has actually set for humankind, i.e. the beatific vision.

without having any unconditional claim on such an existence. Balthasar accepted this amendment, indeed he had already proposed something similar himself.[27] But he had two questions which he felt necessary to put to Rahner at this point. Is it possible or meaningful to claim that the ultimate purpose of creation and human nature is God's giving of grace, and at the same time to attempt, really even if only theoretically, to "abstract" nature from grace?[28] How can one abstract from the very centre (die innerste Mitte abziehen)? Balthasar's second question queries the presumption, unsubstantiated according to him, that the remainder concept can be simply identified with the human Spirit-Nature (Geistnatur).[29] The root of the problem, according to Balthasar, is that a futile attempt is being made to reconcile Maréchal's philosophical understanding of the spirit's dynamism towards its own goal, an understanding which is philosophical and not theological, with a theological system (de Lubac's) which takes as its starting-point the one goal which God has set for human nature - the beatific vision.[30] If we really take the beatific vision as our starting-point, argues Balthasar, then we can simplify matters considerably. God's eternal will was to reveal his love to humankind. To this end the world was created. To hypothesise about a world without grace, and to distinguish between nature and grace by employing natura pura as a Restbegriff is tedious, and necessary if we accept the de facto supernatural condition of the existing world order. Such hypothesising indicates, for Balthasar, that we have not really begun to think theologically:

> From the point of view of a creaturely theology Karl Rahner is right not simply to dispense with the concept of pure nature. But from God's point of view it would be difficult to attach any meaning to this concept. God wished one and only one

---

[27]Karl Barth, 308. Earlier (p. 290) Balthasar proposed the concept of "subtraction" which also defines and "sets off" nature from the standpoint of grace: "In jenem dividitur liegt beschlossen, daß Natur in der faktischen Weltordnung jeweils aposteriori, durch Subtraktion, aus einem zunächst gegebenen Ganzen herausgetrennt, abstrahiert muß."

[28]Karl Barth, 311. J.P. Mackey (Life and grace, 31) echoes this criticism: "...this (remainder concept) is not far enough removed from the superstructure way of thinking, especially when we take it in conjunction with his (Rahner's) tendency to say that grace is the innermost thing in man without explaining in any easily intelligible manner how grace is the innermost thing in man, and in further conjunction with his misunderstanding of the role of verbal revelation...".

[29]Karl Barth, 311.

[30]"Will man hier nicht Unvereinbares, nämlich die Versöhnung der Philosophie Maréchals mit der Theologie de Lubacs, wobei vielleicht zu wenig bedacht zu sein scheint, daß Maréchals scheinbar philosophischer Dynamismus in Wahrheit doch theologischer Herkunft ist?" (Karl Barth, 311). Here the criticism made in the 1939 review of Geist in Welt is being echoed once again.

thing: to open up his love to humankind. This is why he created the world. So
from God's standpoint, the question whether or not there could have been a world
without this grace is an idle question. And what bears no weight in God's eyes
should not carry any weight either from the human perspective, even more so when
one takes our humble position into account.[31]

Balthasar was not satisfied that Rahner succeeded in avoiding Barth's criticisms of
Roman Catholic theology. While he does not say so explicitly at this point, he is
clearly developing the opinion that Rahner has failed to preserve the specifically
theological character of theology. In a later section of this same book Balthasar listed
some Roman Catholic theologians whose work seemed to meet Barth's criterion for
an authentic theology, which by his definition must be Christocentric. Rahner was
not included. But the main point being made here is that, from Balthasar's view-point
the concept of the natura pura was of value (and at best, limited value) only to a
"creaturely theology". It was a somewhat plausible solution to a theological problem
which would not arise if the specifically theo-logical, or more precisely, christological character of theology was preserved.

Karl Barth influenced Balthasar in determining criteria for an authentic (Catholic)
theology.   Barth was also decisive in influencing Balthasar's own methodology.
Balthasar was impressed by Barth's key insight: the necessity to avoid theology being
subsumed within some other all-embracing system which in the end can only lead to
a disembowelling of theology - the robbing of theology of its essential
Christocentricity. In Barth's view neo-protestantism had moved farther and farther
away from revelation and nothing remained of Christianity except the name.
Revelation had been relativised.[32] Barth rejected Schleiermacher because

he is the "Niagara" in which the main currents of at least two centuries of

---

[31]"So hat vom Standpunkt einer kreatürlichen Theologie Karl Rahner recht, den ganz formalen
Begriff der reinen Natur nicht einfach fallen zu lassen. Vom Standpunkt Gottes aus aber wird man
ihm schwerlich dieselbe Bedeutung zumessen. Got hat nun einmal, von Ewigkeit her, gerade das
Eine und nur das Eine gewollt: dem Menschen seine Liebe erschließen. Dazu hat er die Welt
geschaffen. So ist, vom göttlichen Standort aus, die Frage, ob es eine Welt auch ohne diese Gnade
hätte geben können, eine müßige Frage. Und was für Gott kein Gewicht hat, das soll auch für die
Menschen, sogar für die Demut des Menschen, kein wirkliches Gewicht erhalten" (Karl Barth, 312).

[32]"Die Ersetzung der Offenbarung Gottes, in welcher die Gnade schlechthin von außen und oben
kommt, um den Menschen zu erwählen, zu retten, zu heiligen und zu erlösen, durch ein steigendes
Interessantwerden der religiösen Subjektivität, durch eine erst verhüllte (im Pietismus), dann offene
Selbsterlösung des 'religiösen' Menschen (im Idealismus vorbereitet und bei Feuerbach vollendet),
die Reduktion des Glaubens auf eine 'höchste Möglichkeit' der Vernunft, der Offenbarung auf eine
'höchste Möglichkeit' der Geschichte, schließlich auch des 'Gottesbewußtseins' Jesu auf eine höchste
Möglichkeit menschlicher Religiosität: dieser ganze Weg mündet nach Barth folgerichtig bei den
'Deutschen Christen', im Neuheidentum überhaupt" (Karl Barth, 44-45).

theological thought necessarily come crashing down...[33]

When one reflects on the work of both Schleiermacher and Rahner a number of similarities in methodology emerge. Firstly, as Vass points out, both Rahner and Schleiermacher were addressing a similar type of Sitz-im-Leben.[34] Schleiermacher's first sermons are directed against religion's so-called "cultured despisers"[35] and we have already seen that Rahner's context is clearly the growing ambivalence and hostility to Christianity and to theism in general in a post-Enlightenment Europe. Both Schleiermacher and Rahner employ philosophy in such a way that it leads to a contact point between human thought and divine revelation. Whereas for Schleiermacher philosophy served to bring out the feeling of absolute dependence (which he refers to as "religious piety"), Rahner focused on the human capacity and responsibility to hear God's Word, should God choose to communicate himself. There are, of course, significant differences between these two thinkers but the methodological similarity is striking.[36] So also is the similarity between the criticisms which Barth made of Schleiermacher and which Balthasar made of Rahner.[37]

Before the Council - A bastion under attack

Immediately after his book on Barth, Balthasar published a small volume entitled Schleifung der Bastionen. In the context of remarks which call upon the Church to address itself with openness and confidence to the world and fulfil its mission of being a light to the world, Balthasar makes it clear that this is to be done on certain and uncompromisable terms, and his remarks are at the very least open to an interpretation that he considers more recent directions taken within neo-scholastic

---

[33]loc. cit.

[34]G. Vass, A theologian in search of a philosophy: understanding Karl Rahner Vol. 1, 21.

[35]Cf. F. Schleiermacher, On religion: speech to its cultured despisers. In: G. Vass, op. cit., 21-23.

[36]For example, "whereas Schleiermacher assumes alongside man's worldly activity of knowing and doing, a kind of third accomplishment (or faculty - as some take it) termed 'feeling' (Gefühl) in which he is, so to say, in touch with God, Rahner will assert that precisely in knowing and doing man transcends himself, he becomes a 'transcendental' subject whose 'transcendental experience' makes him capable of perceiving the word of God" (G. Vass, op. cit., 22).

[37]Balthasar's main criticism of Schleiermacher follows that of Barth: "Everything is determined by the fact that...he subsumes Christology under the heading of the consciousness of being saved, as the condition of its possibility" (Love alone: the way of revelation, 31).

theology as having the undesirable effect of undermining the role of the Church and confusing its mission to the world.[38] Developing the critique begun in his book on Barth, Balthasar attempts to outline the need for theology to return to its centre. While Balthasar does not mention Rahner specifically, I think it is clear that he has Rahner very much in mind. However, the tone of the book reveals his anxiety about a wrong turn which could be taken by the Church as a whole and not just by individual theologians.

Balthasar was reacting to a spirit emerging in the Church which would reach a climax in the convening of the Second Vatican Council by Pope John XXIII. He did not deny that change was necessary in the Church, but was concerned about the nature of that change and how that change would come about. Legitimate change could not come about through a destruction of tradition; the future could not be built upon a destruction of the past.[39] But already Balthasar was critical of any purely secular understanding of "building up the future", and especially of any understanding which was dominated by sociological factors masquerading as theology. Over against existentialist notions of the importance of history (adapting Heideggerian insights from Being and time Rahner had dedicated a chapter of Hearers of the word to the subject of "Spirit and historicality"), genuine holiness, Balthasar recalled, is always the refutation of the idea that the interval of the years has an essential role to play in Christianity.[40] In fact, Balthasar claimed, the opposite is the case: the passing of time always allows us to return to the source of our faith, i.e. the revelation of Christ without need of mediation. Theology must remain Christocentric.[41] Thinking systems other than theology are only at the service of theology to the extent that they enable us to meet the mystery of God. Those who seek to explain revelation in human terms should never forget "si comprehendis non est Deus". Theological systems must guard against claiming to know too much.

Schleifung der Bastionen is significant in that for the first time Balthasar confronts

---

[38]Schleifung der Bastionen, von der Kirche in dieser Zeit, Einsiedeln: Johannesverlag, 1952. An abbreviation of this book was also translated into French (Raser les Bastions, Dieu Vivant 25, 1953, 17-32).

[39]Schleifung der Bastionen, 12.

[40]op. cit., 16

[41]"...die drei Mittelpunkte einer christlichen Theologie sind ohne Zweifel die Lehre von Gott dem Dreieinigen, von Gott dem Wort, das in Christus fleischlich vernehmbar wurde, von Gott dem Geist, der in der Kirche und in ihren Gliedern die Offenbarung der Liebe auslegt" (Schleifung der Bastionen, 17).

directly what he perceives as the negative effects which existentialist thought has had not only on theology but also on the life of the Church. Even if Rahner himself is not confronted directly, it is clear that at this time Rahner was the torch-bearer in theology's attempts to dialogue with existentialism. That Rahner was on Balthasar's mind at the time may be gleaned from an article written shortly after Schleifung der Bastionen which focuses on what is in reality the fundamental theological problem: the relationship between nature and grace.[42] In this article Balthasar replies to an earlier article by Rahner on the subject and reiterates his objections to Rahner's concept of the relationship between grace and nature which he had already outlined in his book on Barth.

Balthasar had also entered into dialogue with Rahner on the nature and the mission of the laity in the Church. The contents of this debate are relevant to us in that, from Balthasar's perspective, they have the same origin.[43] The key issue was the relationship of the Church to the world. The Church should be a leaven within the world, making visible God's glory already shining in the world. The main task of the Church is its task to evangelise the secular world, a task which is the responsibility of the laity. But to be able to carry out its task the laity must really be "salt" and "leaven". Provida Mater (1947) laid down the role of the secular institute in the life of the Church, but Balthasar could see no living example of an institute actually fulfilling its responsibility.[44]

When Rahner's first two volumes of Schriften zur Theologie appeared, Balthasar gave them a reasonably favourable review.[45] Following a brief discourse on the difficulty of thinking theologically today, Balthasar outlines what he identifies as three tensions running through these two volumes of Rahner's: between the theologian's personal courage and his responsibility to the magisterium of the Church; between the theologian's own thought system and his duty to teach as a Catholic cleric; between

---

[42]Der Begriff der Natur in der Theologie, Eine Diskussion zwischen Hans Urs von Balthasar, Zürich, und Engelbert Gutwenger, S.J., Innsbruck, Zeitschrift für Katholische Theologie 75, 1953, 452-464.

[43]In 1948 he had published Der Laie und der Ordenstand, which was to be the constitution of the Johannesgemeinschaft.

[44]He specifically attacked Opus Dei in an article, Friedlichen Fragen an das Opus Dei, (Der christliche Sonntag 16, No. 15, 1964, 117f). They, in reply, clarified that they did not consider themselves to be a secular institute. Cf. P. Henrici, op. cit, 40.

[45]H. U. von Balthasar, Grösse und Last der Theologie heute, Einige grundsätzliche Gedanken zu zwei Aufsatzbänden Karl Rahners, Wort und Wahrheit 10, 1955, 531-533.

the theologian's personal encounter with the Word of God and the ever more tremendous tradition of the Church with its approved and laid down dogmatic principles. The background to such specific mention being given to these points is the climate of suspicion surrounding the Nouvelle Theologie and the fear that this school was not sufficiently protective of the gratuitousness of grace.[46] Balthasar clearly felt that Rome was overreacting in the present situation and felt compassion for Rahner.[47] In his review Balthasar commented:

> Rahner talks only when he has discovered something. One could add that the point from which his work shines forth is an entirely comprehensive and entirely open philosophy - outlines of which Rahner had already given in his book Geist in Welt - a philosophy which is precise and which allows him to grasp all questions, to transform them and in a new fruitfulness to let them go again. This philosophy finds its centre in Thomas Aquinas, its breadth in Augustine, and its actuality in the posing of the questions of modern German philosophy of idealism and of phenomenology to Heidegger.[48]

Balthasar classified Rahner's method as a "taking with" (mitnehmende).[49] By this he meant Rahner's attempt to reconcile all elements: Aquinas, neo-scholasticism,

---

[46]In the 1950s "unpopular theologians, above all in France, had been silenced by Rome. Where they were members of orders, the measures were particularly far-reaching: some were even banished to other countries" (H. Vorgrimler, op. cit, 92). Rahner was not specifically under question at this time, but nevertheless Balthasar felt that the genuineness of Rahner's efforts to address serious questions needed to be pointed out. That his intention in this review was to defend Rahner against possible critics is stated clearly by Balthasar later in his own defence, when in the aftermath of Cordula oder der Ernstfall he is taken to task for the vociferous nature of his own criticism of Rahner. Referring to the 1955 article in Wort und Wahrheit, Balthasar replies: "Ich habe aus meiner Bewunderung für die spekulative Kraft und den Mut Rahners nie ein Hehl gemacht und ihm in schweren Stunden nach Kräften die Stange gehalten..." (Cordula oder der Ernstfall, Nachwort zur dritten Auflage, 124).
In 1962, as he was completing his fifth volume of Schriften, Rahner was placed under preliminary censorship by the Prefect of the Holy Office, Cardinal A. Ottaviani, who explained it "by saying that they wanted to protect Rahner from friends who misunderstood him, and that was a privilege. Rahner replied that he would gladly forego this privilege" (H. Vorgrimler, op. cit., 93).

[47]After Rahner's first volume of Schriften appeared Balthasar wrote: "This is surely the only book upon which to ground hope in this area today. Seldom has the flame of theological Eros climbed so high or so steeply. The closer he comes to finding himself, the more seriously must he be taken and seriously and reverently (ehrfürchtigter) listened to. I am looking forward to the future volumes. I only hope that the the Romans, with their scalp-hunters (Skalpjägerei), do not get him first" (H. U. von Balthasar. In: P. Henrici, op. cit., 55).

[48]H. U. von Balthasar, Grösse und Last der Theologie heute, Wort und Wahrheit 10, 1955, 533.

[49]loc. cit.

Kant, German idealism and Heidegger. He also warned of the consequences.[50] The main consequence of a philosophical starting-point seemed to him to be the inevitable relativisation of biblical revelation, even though admittedly Rahner himself was anxious to develop a theology of the life of Jesus and give salvation history and ecclesiastical history their proper place in theology.[51]

In 1956 Balthasar published a book dealing specifically with the the relationship between Christianity and anthropology.[52] Die Gottesfrage des heutigen Menschen is made up of a number of lectures given at various German universities from 1950-1952, at a time when Balthasar, who had left the Society of Jesus to found the Johannesgemeinschaft and was not incardinated anywhere, was in grave need of financial support for his newly founded Johannesverlag (publishing firm). The first part of this book is a description of the religious situation then. While not wishing to be pessimistic, Balthasar concludes that this situation seemed to be

> a dismantling, a certain impoverishment, not to say wretchedness, and an emptiness
> and estrangement regarding old and treasured customs and views.[53]

Balthasar holds the confusion of natural religion with Christianity partially responsible for this impoverishment. Through the shift from a cosmological to an anthropological world-view a new framework for expressing the human being's experience of God had been developed, a framework which had reached its clearest expression in Rahner's Hearers of the word.[54] While he accepts that natural religion in its highest

---

[50]"Er wird mit der Nase darauf gestoßen, daß er wieder einmal etwas vergessen hat, was Thomas schon wußte, daß er zufällig übersehen hat, was für unerwartete, kühne deduktionen aus seinen so harmlosen Voraussetzungen sich ergeben, was für hohe Türme sich mit seinen von ihm eigenhändig gebackenen Ziegelsteinen bauen lassen..." (Wort und Wahrheit 10, 1955, 533).

[51]"...daß die herkunft von der philosophischen Vision oft ein wenig die Frische und Unmittelbarkeit des Bibelwortes in der Gedankenführung vermissen läßt, scheint mir der gewichtigste Einwand, obwohl Rahner ja selbst in seinem Dogmatikentwurf kategorisch nach einer Theologie des Lebens Jesu und der ganzen Heilsgeschichte auf ihn hin und sogar der Kirchengeschichte ruft" (loc. cit.).

[52]Die Gottesfrage des heutigen Menschen, Wien: Herold, 1956 (English translations: Science, religion and Christianity, London: Burns and Oates, 1958; The God question and modern man, New York: Seabury, 1967).

[53]Die Gottesfrage des heutigen Menschen, 136.

[54]op. cit., 109. In Glaubhaft ist nur Liebe, 1963 (first published in English as Love alone: the way of revelation in 1968), Balthasar specifically contrasts the cosmological and anthropological world-views and lists what he sees as their limitations which make them unable to present Christianity adequately. In this context Balthasar offers his own framework: love alone. God must be allowed to be his own exegete if all reductions are to be avoided.

form may present the human being as a potential hearer of the Word, he insists that
it must be stressed that God does not "naturally" (naturhaft) reveal himself, i.e. not
in any worldly sense. In support of this argument Balthasar quotes from an article
by Rahner in which Rahner argues for the necessity of the anthropological approach,
while at the same time stressing its limitations.[55]

In this article Rahner claimed that "today...we can make no image of God that is not
carved from the wood of this world", but that this need not be interpreted as a form
of atheism or as an anthropomorphism.[56] That this image does not fit, that it cannot
be clearly drawn, that the world appears to be devoid of meaning and even profane
does not mean that atheism results. All these experiences "are fundamentally only
the experience that God does not belong to the concept of the world". While we are
witnessing the collapse of a cosmic world-view, in which God's presence was
experienced in nature, into a predominantly anthropological world-view, this can,
Balthasar agreed, lead us to a more adequate idea of God. The Fathers have already
prepared us for the proper articulation of the relationship between God's immanence
and transcendence. Today above all we must remember that

> the great "articulation" is between theology (God in himself, exalted above all) and
> economy (God, from his infinite superiority, in his grace condescending for us).
> But the economy or syncatabasis (concession by grace, descending below oneself
> by way of adaption) can only be measured in its full character of being a grace if,
> at every moment of it and in all its manifestations, it always remains clear who it
> is that condescends and adapts himself, who is making such concessions to the
> creature as to deign to meet it and be known by it. So a true "economy" is only
> possible if it is consistently balanced by "theology".[57]

The present faith situation provides a new opportunity for discovering the
transcendent presence of God, but this presence can only be experienced in faith and
for the deepening of one's faith. Balthasar warned, one

> ought not to treat the doctrine of the incomprehensibility of God like an object once
> possessed but long forgotten in a cupboard, which is now unearthed and dusted for
> this particular purpose of talking with, say, Jaspers or Buber or Heidegger. This
> awful thing has happened to modern man, that God in nature has died for him.[58]

There can be no separation of the transcendent God and the God of Jesus Christ.
What we symbolise on Good Friday by the stripping of Church altars is what is
happening to the Church as a whole today, suggested Balthasar. The Church is being

---

[55]K. Rahner, Wissenschaft als Konfession?, Wort und Wahrheit 9, 154, 811-813.

[56]K. Rahner. In: H. U. von Balthasar, Die Gottesfrage des heutigen Menschen, 142.

[57]op. cit., 146-147.

[58]op. cit., 149.

stripped to its bare essentials - and we must not forget the truly essential, that the transcendent God became flesh and died on a cross for our sins. Even if we cannot experience this God in our world, or even if we have in the past clung to false concepts of this crucified God, the crucified God remains as the basis of our faith. Balthasar is clearly warning us here against any development of a transcendent notion of God which, though useful in dialogue with non-believers, is divorced from the historical life, death and resurrection of Jesus Christ.

The glory of the Lord

In addition to the numerous shorter books and articles which Balthasar continued to publish, in 1961 the first volume of Herrlichkeit appeared. Herrlichkeit, Theodramatik and Theologik go together to make up his major work, which, in the words of Rahner, is "really breathtaking"[59]. Herrlichkeit alone runs to seven volumes in its English version.

I have already pointed out that it is impossible here to present an adequate account of Balthasar's whole theological system. However, because Balthasar's own theology is arguably an implicit critique of the anthropological starting-point, a brief examination of his own starting-point is useful. It is also worth noting that throughout the trilogy there are occasions when Balthasar explicitly takes the anthropological approach to task, so much so, that one could possibly argue that his whole approach to theology is, in fact, a reaction against such a system.

Traditionally, Christianity has been presented in three (complementary) categories, each convertible one to the other: truth, goodness and beauty. Classical truth was concerned with the attuning of the mind to reality, based upon the principle of the knowability of being as such. Revelation was then understood as the communication of the ultimate truth about humankind. This truth lives on in the Church among the community of believers who attempt to attune their lives to the truth about God from generation to generation.

The "good" consists in that which best accords with our deepest desires for self-actualization. God created the world and saw that it was "good"; Jesus came with the "Good" News that we are redeemed, which can be understood as the climactic victory of "good" over evil. The Christian community tries to embody and re-present this goodness.

However, the truth and the goodness of what is communicated to us in Jesus Christ is so immense that it cannot serve the mystery of love adequately. We discover a

---

[59]K. Rahner, Hans Urs von Balthasar, Civitas 20, 1964, 602.

third category if we ask ourselves why we are drawn to the God-man, even though he was apparently without beauty or majesty (Isaiah 52:15). Why are we attracted towards the one who, though in the form of God, relinquished it to take the form of a slave (Phil. 2:6)? Beauty is a mystery - it fascinates us, it demands our attention. It lures us into contemplation because when we see something truly beautiful, we perceive an attuning to some inner harmony. We experience a powerful radiance which attracts us irresistibly. Beauty is a mystery of form.[60] It is the gracious appearance of being in concrete form.

Balthasar maintains that we can employ the category of beauty in an analogous way to help us speak theologically about the reality of God's self-revelation. Further, he claims that all epoch-making theology has done so. This is achieved not by simply drawing an analogy between natural worldly beauty and revelation, which would only provide us with an aesthetic theology. What Balthasar has in mind is entirely different: a theological aesthetics.

The first step in developing a theological aesthetics involves relating the two moments of the beautiful, "form" (Gestalt) and "splendour" (Glanz). In contrast to Protestant aesthetics where "splendour" is completely contained in "form"[61], Balthasar, drawing upon his earlier Germanistik studies, adapts Goethe's conception of "form" by which it can be understood as a sign of "splendour". "Form" signifies "splendour" which lies in a fullness beyond our vision.

When we perceive a beautiful "form", it has an effect on us. When we try to discover why, we find ourselves needing to bring concepts such as truth and value to bear upon our perception of beauty. We realise then that a particular "form" strikes us as beautiful because it manifests "the truth and goodness of the depths of reality".[62] It signifies a splendour which lies beyond itself and which is greater and more whole. It is important to understand that "form" is not merely a sign-post to "splendour": it is itself the real presence of that which it signifies.

But the aesthetics outlined above is not yet a theological aesthetics. This step involves confronting aesthetics with Christian revelation.[63] Revelation is so wondrous that the faculties of "hearing" and "seeing" cannot do it justice. Revelation

---

[60]Cf. The Glory of the Lord 1, Seeing the form, 23ff.

[61]Cf. The Glory of the Lord 1, 57-69.

[62]The Glory of the Lord 1, 118.

[63]The Glory of the Lord 1, 79-116.

must be perceived: its truth must be taken to oneself (per capere, wahrnehmen). We must allow ourselves to be "caught up" in the wonder of what God has done for us:

> In the wonder of the incarnation your eternal Word has brought to the eyes of faith
> a new and radiant vision of your glory. In him we see our God made visible and
> so are caught up in love of the God we cannot see.[64]

Understanding Jesus Christ as the "form" of God, we can now take a fresh look at the writings of e.g. Plato, Aristotle, pseudo-Dionysius the Areopagite, St. John of the Cross and others for a more informed understanding of the true richness and breadth of this approach to revelation.

However, a theological aesthetics must be related to theology as a whole if it is to be useful. The concern of fundamental theology corresponds to the perception of the "form" of God's self-revelation, which is the first moment in Balthasar's theological aesthetics. The second part of his aesthetics - "splendour" concerns itself with the manifesting of God's glory, which is the task of dogmatic theology. If the first part is a theory of vision, the second is a theory of rapture. Theology as a whole tells the story of God's "venturing forth" to us and our "venturing forth" to him - a double and reciprocal ekstasis[65]. These two branches of theology should never be separated from each other, and Balthasar mentions in particular his disagreement with a purely apologetical theology.

The main benefit of Balthasar's approach to theology is that it re-situates God's glory at the very heart of Christianity. It guarantees a Christocentric Christology and soteriology. Examining the Old and New Testaments carefully, Balthasar discovers how significant and decisive it is to refer to Christ as doxa.[66]

John alone employs the term doxa with reference to the earthly Jesus, still only visible through the eyes of faith (pistis). He emphasises that glory is recognised only through suffering. Whereas Matthew and Mark confine references to Christ as doxa

---

[64]Preface of Christmas 1 (ICEL translation). In the Latin version, as Balthasar points out, the word "faith" is not used.

[65]The Glory of the Lord 1, 126.

[66]In the Old Testament, the kabhod YHWH referred to manifestations of God (theophanies) which were the key moments in salvation history and in which God revealed himself through meteorological phenomena as the God who at the same time lies hidden. The root kbd literally means "to be heavy", with honour, reputation or standing within the community. The Greek word doxa gives us the root of words such as orthodoxy and had the related meaning of "my opinion" or "my reputation" - other people's opinion of me. In the New Testament and the Septuagint doxa described the heavenly brilliance and manifestation of God insofar as God revealed himself and insofar as people were able to comprehend. Because of the glory of God which has been revealed in Christ, the New Testament can be more optimistic than the Old Testament that people will not only behold the doxa of God, but that they will share in it.

to the parousia, Luke extends this to include the nativity story and his account of the resurrection.

The letters of Paul develop an understanding of the glorification of the risen, post-Easter Christ. Since his resurrection, Jesus is the "Lord of doxa" (1 Cor. 2:8). The Corinthians are slow to grasp this and St. Paul is impatient with them. The conflict among themselves not only weakens their witness to "Jesus Christ and him crucified": it shows that they have not really understood what has been achieved by "the Lord of glory" (1 Cor. 2:8). In the midst of a stubborn and unspiritual people the Corinthians must understand themselves to be a "letter from Christ". Whereas in the Old Testament hardheartedness (sklerokardia) led to a fading of God's splendour and glory, the doxa manifest in Christ, the brightness and splendour surrounding God's ultimate self-revelation, will never fade. It is to be continued in the Church. This can only happen if disciples live lives worthy of their vocation (Eph. 4:1).

Balthasar returns to his theological aesthetics and explores the implications for Christology, the doctrine of the Trinity and ecclesiology.[67]   When we explore these three, even very briefly, it becomes quite clear why "anonymous Christianity" is, for Balthasar, a contradiction in terms.

Jesus' unique experience of God "furnishes the form that conditions all other experiences". Jesus is unique in mission (he is not just another prophet) and in origin (not just "sent by" but "comes from" and "returns to"). As the only one who comes from God, Jesus is the theophany itself. He does not simply relate something he knew of God before he came - with him there is no before or after. Balthasar understands "the coming from" of Jesus to represent a unique Christological movement.   This Christological movement speaks to us both about God and ourselves.

Through the Christological movement, we are invited to associate ourselves intimately with Jesus who has associated himself intimately with us, and through him and with him and in him to return to the Father, to whom Christ is united in love through the Holy Spirit. Through his life, death and resurrection, Christ brings us back to the Father to whom, as the Word made flesh, he witnesses with his whole self.

Those who wish to be intimately associated with Christ must also bear witness. In aesthetical terms, just as Christ is the form of God, his disciples are also called to be "mediating" or "forming" forms i.e. they are called to be realities which continue to present to us the saving presence of Christ. Balthasar considers Sacred Scripture, Mary, the saints, and the Church also to be "forms".

---

[67]Cf. The Glory of the Lord 1, 321-331.

The Church is the unity of those who are prepared to let the saving will of God transform their lives. The Church's task is to be the greatest possible radiance of God's grace in the world by virtue of the closest possible following of Christ, even, if necessary, to the point of martyrdom. This is why Balthasar is so anxious that the Church, in the face of widespread disbelief, should not become complacent or, worse, self-satisfied. The doctrine of the anonymous Christian is unacceptable because of its consequences for the name-bearing Christian's understanding of the Christian life.

Chapter 3
Criticisms from after Vatican Two to 1988

Introduction

As soon as the Council documents appeared, Balthasar began to comment on them. In an interview ten years after the Council, Balthasar gave his overall impressions of it, and these provide us with a context in which to interpret his writings during the 1960s and early 1970s:

> ...the Council wrote much, in my opinion too much. 763 pages in the small compendium from Rahner and Vorgrimler. Therein lie many disparities, very many revisions, very many things of different value (Verschiedenwertiges), some splendid, some amateur (Dilettantische) e.g. Gaudium et Spes. What should actually be taken on board from it? I think what is really fundamental, which forces itself, e.g. Dei Verbum has become accepted theologically and what is essential in Lumen Gentium. Now to today: is it true that the Church has once again entrenched herself? I am not so sure. But she has fully forgotten that she must reflect upon her own reality if she is to be able to be missionary: distinguer pour unir...The Church seems to me to be a little like a watering-can with a hole in it. When the gardener comes to the flower-bed which he wishes to water, there is nothing left within. The Church reflects too little on the treasure in the field. She has sold much. But has she really got the treasure in return? She has descended into the valley of democracy. But can she still be the city on the hill-top?[1]

Rahner's doctrine of the anonymous Christian, and the anthropological approach to theology upon which it was based, represented one clear example for Balthasar of the Church having "sold all". We must understand this if we are to understand the harshness and severity with which Balthasar attacked Rahner's theology in the years immediately following the Council. Balthasar had worked for an understanding of the Church as open to the world, as having a mission to the world. But what was happening after the Council was that the Church seemed to be adapting herself to the world - selling herself short, becoming "modern" in the worst sense.[2] The anonymous Christian concept became a symbol of the Church surrendering herself, of her reneging on the essentials - prayer, suffering, faithful obedience, humility.

Love alone: the way of revelation

Glaubhaft ist nur Liebe, published in 1963, was intended to balance the negative

---

[1]Geist und Feuer, Herder Korrespondenz 30, 1976, 78. The consistency between Balthasar's pre-conciliar and post-conciliar assessments of the Church's self-presentation to the world is striking.

[2]"The Church, they say, to appear credible, must be in tune with the times. If taken seriously, that would mean that Christ was in tune with the times when he carried out his mission and died on the Cross, a scandal to the Jews and folly to the Gentiles. Of course, the scandal took place in tune with the times - at the favourable time of the Father, in the fullness of time...Modern is something Christ never was, and, God willing, never will be" (Wer ist ein Christ?, Einsiedeln: Johannesverlag, 1965, 30).

assessment of the state of theology outlined in previous writings and to serve as a summary introduction to Balthasar's own theological aesthetics which was in the process of being published in his Herrlichkeit series.   The aim of Glaubhaft ist nur Liebe (translated into English as Love alone: the way of revelation) is to establish positively what is specific and unique about Christian faith, and in the course of fulfilling this aim, Balthasar also provides us with a clear presentation of his critique of Rahner's anthropological starting-point.

> If the first (cosmological) approach suffers the limitations of a past age, this second (anthropological) is methodologically in error: the framework of God's message to man in Christ cannot be tied to the world in general, nor to man in particular; God's message is theological, or better theo-pragmatic. It is an act of God on man; an act done for and on behalf of man - and only then to man, and in him. It is of this act that we must say: it is credible only as love...[3]

This directs Balthasar to his chief theological insight and to the heart of his own theological aesthetics: God is and must be allowed to be his own exegete.[4]

The first two chapters of Love alone: the way of revelation list the inadequacies of the cosmological and anthropological frameworks for presenting the Christian faith.

When humankind began to search for self-understanding, this naturally led to a contemplation of the cosmos.   As the human capacity for self-understanding developed, there was a switch from a merely magical attitude to the world to an understanding that life was determined not by arbitrary numinous powers but by unchangeable laws.   Philosophy developed as a system of thought aimed at discovering these laws so that humankind could become attuned to itself.   But there were different philosophies representing different, fragmentary and conflicting understandings of the world.   The cosmological method developed by the Fathers presented Christianity as the fulfilment of a fragmented understanding of the universe. The scattered fragments of God's presence, in which the whole classical world was suffused, were presented as being united in Christ.   In Christ the universe "achieved unity, depth and redeemed freedom."[5] But Christianity was not only the fulfilment of fragmented insights.   It was also a call to conversion, because fragmented insights which other religions presented tended to claim absolute validity, and heresies

---

[3]Love alone: the way of revelation (English translation of Glaubhaft ist nur Liebe), London: Sheed and Ward, 1968, 8-9.

[4]Cf. Love alone: the way of revelation, 46.

[5]op. cit, 11. Cf. also L. O' Donovan, God's glory in time, Communio XII, 1975, 255; M. Proterra, Hans Urs von Balthasar: theologian, Communio XII, 1975, 275.

generally arise when partial truths claim to represent the whole. Christianity claimed to represent the whole truth, the highest form of truth the world can bear. The philosophical view of the universe was fulfilled by the theological. The true philosopher sought wisdom. In Christ wisdom became flesh. A conversion to Christ was a conversion to the whole truth.

Balthasar was critical of this understanding because in his view it represents a reduction. The world became the weighing-scale by which revelation was to be measured. But surely no created thing, even creation itself, can be the measure of the Creator, argued Balthasar: no form that belongs to the world as such can ever provide the light in which the whole truth of the world might be seen.

It is important for us to understand this cosmological method, because the anthropological method is merely its re-appearance on a higher plane; the same principle of reduction, according to Balthasar, now reintroduced in an anthropological sense.[6] In the Renaissance period an understanding of humanity in partnership with God developed. If previously the world had been the measure of the divine, then humanity had come to fill the vacuum when the cosmos lost its religious significance. Christianity sought to express itself in this situation, the writings of Pascal representing the first attempt at an "existential apologetic", according to Balthasar. Torn between greatness and abject misery the human condition was portrayed as tragic until order became restored in Christ.

What role does God play in all modern philosophical thought since Descartes and Kant? His position becomes merely functional:

> God is not interesting for his own sake. God is brought in to bolster up the human subject and guarantee his search for security. Already the notion of God is relativised. Something pernicious is beginning to happen here.[7]

Balthasar traces the development of the anthropological reduction through Kant and Fichte and names Feuerbach as Kant's logical successor. Having discussed the failure of Schleiermacher to avoid reductionism - he ends up subsuming Christology under the heading of the consciousness of being saved, as the condition of its possibility - Balthasar goes on to discuss the comparative developments in Catholic theology: the modernist movement. Modernism considered that all objective, dogmatic propositions

---

[6]Love alone: the way of revelation, 25.

[7]J. O'Donnell, The mystery of the triune God, 8. O' Donnell is following Balthasar and E. Jüngel, God as the mystery of the world, in their understanding that the anthropological starting-point in theology represents a reduction. Cf. also W. Kasper, The God of Jesus Christ, 16-20, where he makes the same points as O' Donnell and considers this reduction to have sown the seeds of modern atheism.

depended for their meaning and significance upon their ability to fulfil and complete the individual.[8] The philosophical methods of Maurice Blondel and Joseph Maréchal were not modernist, admits Balthasar, but they did "debouch into an anthropological justification of revelation".[9] While the dynamism of the intellect (Maréchal) drives the individual on to search for an infinite, divine being to fulfil his intellect's capacitas entis, this results in the content of dogma being measured by the effect which it has on the individual. But this is attempting "to measure the depths of grace by the abyss of human need and sin".[10]

All but one form of the anthropological reduction end with the individual possessing both the world and God in his or her self-understanding. But it is equally if more subtly a reduction to think that God can be encountered in "the other", in "my neighbour". This reduces Christian revelation to a system based on the principle of dialogue.

In the course of outlining his own system, Balthasar gives us one more very important insight into his understanding of the anthropological reduction. He refers to it as "bilateral".[11] What he means by this is made clear by way of contrast with his own system which he defines as "unilateral":

> But before the individual can encounter the love of God at a particular moment in history, he must have experienced another, primary, archetypal meeting, which is one of the conditions for the appearance of divine love on earth. This sort of meeting is one in which we understand the unilateral gesture of God's love for man, and understanding includes appropriate reception and answer. Were the answer not in some sort adequate, Love would not have been revealed - for it cannot be revealed in terms of being - it must at the same time achieve spiritual consciousness. But if the answer were not included in God's unilateral gesture, which presupposes its own action in giving grace, the relationship would be bilateral from the first and we should find ourselves back in the anthropological scheme.

God's love had to prepare the individual for its own coming. Otherwise the gratuitousness of God's self-giving would be compromised and the relationship would be bilateral from the beginning.[12]

---

[8]Love alone: the way of revelation, 33.

[9]op. cit., 34.

[10]op. cit., 35.

[11]op. cit., 62.

[12]"Christianity is destroyed if it allows itself to be reduced to transcendental presuppositions of a man's self-understanding whether in thought or in life, in knowledge or in action" (Love alone: the way of revelation, 43).

Balthasar's argument that the anthropological system is reductionistic can be summarised as follows: the anthropological system presents the human being as a co-initiator in the human-divine relationship which is then considered to be bilateral, thus compromising the gratuitousness of God's self-giving and resulting in the individual's experience of Christ being limited by his pre-understanding (Vorverständnis).[13]

In Love alone: the way of revelation, Balthasar does not explicitly identify Rahner with this anthropological system. However, it is clear that he has Rahner foremost in mind. On a number of occasions Balthasar has referred to Rahner as the heir to Kant and Maréchal and the anthropological system's "best-known representative".[14] And in Cordula oder der Ernstfall, published just three years later, Balthasar specifically attacks Rahner's system, characterising it as reducing one's love of God to one's love of neighbour, and as basing Christian revelation on a principle of dialogue. In Love alone: the way of revelation, Balthasar considered this to be the most subtle of all forms of the anthropological reduction.[15]

The Church and the world

The Church's mission to the world was Balthasar's chief theological preoccupation and his primary spiritual concern also - in Balthasar the two are one. It was this that led to what he described as his having to "leave all" a second time to follow the Lord - abandoning the Jesuits to found the Johannesgemeinschaft.[16] After the Council his fears that the Church misunderstood its mission continued to grow. He was particularly anxious about the terms upon which the Church entered into dialogue with conflicting world-views. In an article written in 1965 Balthasar set out to show the inadequacy of all philosophical systems as bearers of the Christian message.[17]

---

[13]In our evaluation of Balthasar's critique we will examine more closely how he considers love to be perceived and precisely what he means by a pre-understanding (Vorverständnis).

[14]Cf. for example, Geist und Feuer, Herder Korrespondenz 30, 1976, 76; Current trends in Catholic theology, Communio 5, 1978, 78. Balthasar also had Rahner's students and especially J. B. Metz in mind. For a brief discussion of the similarities and differences between Rahner and Metz, cf. Metz's foreword to Spirit in the world (second English edition), xiii-xviii. In his introduction to the same work (p.xxxii), Fiorenza refers to Balthasar's criticism (in Love alone: the way of revelation) of "the attempts of Karl Rahner and Johannes Metz to develop a positive relationship to modern philosophy and the secularisation of society and its institutions".

[15]Love alone: the way of revelation, 38-40.

[16]Cf. Erster Blick auf Adrienne von Speyr, Einsiedeln: Johannesverlag , 38.

[17]Meeting God in today's world, Concilium 6, 1, 1965, 23-39.

It is evident both from the issue which is tackled in this article and from the manner
in which it is dealt with that Balthasar was criticising Rahner's transcendental
theology. Even Balthasar's very first point, that the relationship between the Church
and the world is totally unique and cannot be compared to the dialogue between two
people or two institutions, makes this quite clear. For some time Rahner had been
lecturing and writing on the importance of dialogue between the Church and atheism,
and Marxist ideology in particular. It was in the context of Christianity being
confronted with widespread atheism for the first time that Rahner developed the
doctrine of the anonymous Christian. Though the concept of the anonymous Christian
was not intended as a tool for evangelisation, Rahner saw his own anthropological
framework as providing a common language or a bridge towards dialogue.[18] The
purpose of Balthasar's Concilium article is to show that philosophy cannot provide
a common language for dialogue between atheism and Christianity, and to show that
in fact no intellectual bridge can span this abyss.

The cause of the current faith crisis, according to Balthasar, is the inability to
experience God in the world. This is not because God has changed - God cannot
change his ontological relationship to the world - but because humanity has. We no
longer look upon the objects of this world in such a way that they point us to what
is absolute. The objects of this world have become ends in themselves. This has
resulted in the futile analysis of God in the same way as one would analyze worldly
things. This is the tragedy of German idealism - and Balthasar mentions specifically
Fichte and Hegel - that an identity is postulated between the human and the divine
self. Balthasar sees this position as the logical outcome of modern philosophical
thought and says it should be accepted as such. Indeed, the demise of philosophical
thought should have been accepted a long time ago, because Christianity dispenses
with the need for a metaphysical knowledge of God. Such knowledge is impossible
if one has already been encountered by the revealed God.[19] Therefore metaphysical
knowledge of God and biblical knowledge of God must be set one over against the
other. Christianity has done so at every major moment in its history. The great saints,
Ignatius, Benedict, Francis, Augustine and the Greek Fathers, for example, all

---

[18]Balthasar's article presently under discussion can be taken as a direct response to a lecture
given by Rahner in 1964, entitled "Ideology and Christianity". The text appeared alongside
Balthasar's article in the same issue of Concilium and is reprinted in Theological investigations 6,
43-59. In 1964 Rahner also gave a broadcast review of A. Röper's book Die anonymen Christen
which had appeared in 1963. The text of this interview is also reproduced in Theological
investigations 6, 390-398.

[19]Cf. H. U. von Balthasar, Meeting God in today's world, Concilium 6, 1, 1965, 28.

recognised the limitations of metaphysical knowledge of God. The darker moments in Christianity's history have in fact been caused by the failure to recognise this limitation. A recalling of these past errors "may... lead Christianity out of its present state of uncertainty and pusillanimity".[20]

The main limitation of philosophy is its inability to establish that the individual can possess eternal value:

> ...what room does Fichte allow for a real meeting between an "I" and a "thou"? What is not the "I" is the "non-I", which has been projected for the "I" and which will be overcome by the "I"...In no philosophy is there a substructure for what is distinctively Christian. It makes no difference whether one constructs a philosophical anthropology after the manner of Plotinus, Thomas Aquinas, Nicholas of Cusa, or Fichte (as Maréchal and his followers do). All this "the heathens also do".[21]

What is unique in Christianity begins with revelation and ends with revelation: the infinite God loves the individual human being infinitely. Over against his understanding of Fichte, Balthasar argues that only in Christ does my "I" become God's "thou" and that in fact I can only be an "I" because God wishes to make himself my "thou". The doctrine of the Trinity expresses the inevitable conclusion:

> God must in himself eternally be "I" and "thou" and the unity of both in love. The mystery of the Trinity is the irreducible prerequisite for the existence of a world. The mystery of the Trinity is required for the possibility of a drama of love between God and the world; it is required if this drama, as an encounter between "I" and "thou", is to fulfil the world's inner need.[22]

Christianity cannot dialogue with the world employing philosophy as its common language, because philosophy can only bring together two instances of a common nature. If we attempt to use philosophy as a bridge, we inevitably reduce theology to its common denominator with philosophy, and then it ceases to be theology. We can summarise Balthasar's position as follows: philosophy, viewed not in itself, but in terms of its usefulness to the theological enterprise, necessarily lacks the required substructure which would enable it to deal with what is distinctively Christian, i.e. the infinite God's infinite love for the individual human being.

What is the alternative? Not I but God's eternal love for me, which I could never have anticipated, must be put at the very centre of things. This is the alternative to

---

[20] art. cit., 31.

[21] art. cit., 33-34 (emphasis mine).

[22] art. cit., 34. In the final chapter it will be noted that Balthasar himself requires a theological account of how the world actually experiences what he calls here its "inner need", how this experience is articulated, and how the world's articulation of its experience is related to the revelation of the mystery of the Trinity.

a transcendentally oriented theology, and Balthasar finds that the two are not
accidentally in direct confrontation with one another:

> What Christianity puts at the very centre of things is so tiny when compared with
> the lordly systems of transcendental and evolutionary anthropology that it remains
> invisible...That the theological factor remains beyond the reach of philosophical
> discovery shows that God has chosen the "lower" way, the "last place", in
> revealing himself. Revelation and the Cross are identical...The more unmistakably
> the whole of Christianity orients itself towards the Cross, the more it appropriates
> the wise foolishness of the Cross and lets its presence shine forth - in deeds and
> not merely in words - the more theophanous will it make the world again.[23]

Though "we must recognise the free working of the grace of Christ even where there
is no explicit Christian belief", which is to our humiliation when non-Christians give
a better example of self-giving than Christians, the task of radiating the glory of the
Lord, the glory which shone most clearly through on the cross, belongs to the
Christian.[24] In Cordula oder der Ernstfall Balthasar reminds Christians of the
urgency of this task.

The Moment of Christian Witness

Of Balthasar's post-conciliar writings, Cordula oder der Ernstfall is probably the best
known for its polemics against Rahner's theology.[25] Quite specifically and
unambiguously the doctrine of the anonymous Christian is ridiculed, especially in a
dialogue between a concerned Christian and a well-meaning Kommisar. On more than
one occasion Balthasar found it necessary to clarify and qualify the position which he
adopted in this book.[26]

---

[23]art. cit., 37.

[24]art. cit., 36. Cf. further: Dare we hope "that all men be saved?". We will later examine
Balthasar's difficulty, which is linked to his rather negative assessment of modern philosophy, in
providing a theological basis for this claim.

[25]This book was first published in 1966, and was translated into English as The moment of
Christian witness, published in 1968. The second (1967) German edition, to which we refer here,
contains an appendix written by Balthasar as a response to widespread criticism of his treatment of
Karl Rahner in the first edition.

[26]Cf. especially the appendix to the third German edition, pp. 121-132; H. U. von Balthasar,
Apologia pro Cordula sua, Civitas 22, 1966/67, 441-442, and an interview with Balthasar: Geist und
Feuer, Herder Korrespondenz 30, 1976, 76. Cf. further P. Henrici, op. cit., 55: "Cordula became
known through its conversation between a Christian and a well-meaning Kommisar - a biting post-
conciliar satire. In its entirety it was seen as a polemic against Karl Rahner, but are not indeed
Rahner's 'anonymous Christians' (not invented by him) the peg for a much broader critique of a
much more widespread attitude?" For explicit references by Rahner to Cordula oder der Ernstfall,
cf. Im Gespräch 1, 242; Gnade als Mitte menschlicher Existenz, Herder Korrespondenz 28, 1974,
85. On theology of ecumenical discussion cf. Theological investigations 11, 59; Observations on the

Why the increased sharpness of Balthasar's critique?[27] As already noted, in the aftermath of the Second Vatican Council with the Church's newly discovered confidence in its openness to dialogue with the world, Rahner's ideas were becoming increasingly influential within theological circles.[28] The notion of God as the "absolute future" was winning widespread acceptance, not only from fellow theologians e.g. E. Schillebeeckx and J.B. Metz, but also among many communists e.g. Roger Geraudy[29], and meetings were held often at this time, especially under the auspices of the Paulusgesellschaft, to further Christian-Marxist dialogue and mutual understanding.[30]   Rahner's basic thesis was that "absolute future is just another name for what is really meant by 'God'"[31]. We understand the human being to be an historical being and therefore someone who is in a state of becoming (werden).[32] The human being finds himself or herself limited by the present but looks to the future, experiences himself or herself as drawn towards the future, and from this concept of the future draws strength for the present.   Can we really hold that the future towards which we continually strain is ultimately nothing? This would imply that our present existence was also nothing, for the future defines the present. But this is not the case.   The future towards which we strain and which we will one day reach is the Future - God.   Now we could not reach this Absolute Future alone, argues Rahner, and at this point he parts company with Marxist philosophy.   No amount of human endeavour - evolutionary or revolutionary - could bring it about.

---

problem of the anonymous Christian, Theological investigations 14, 280.

[27]Commenting on the severity of some of Balthasar's post-conciliar writings de Lubac said: "he has courageously declared war on certain wild abandons that are a betrayal of the Council. Had more allies rushed to his flag, he would have had no need to write certain rather savage pages" (A witness of Christ in the Church: Hans Urs von Balthasar, Communio Winter 1975, 229).

[28]The following articles by Rahner appeared around this time and are reproduced in Theological investigations 6: Marxist Utopia and the Christian future of man, Orientierung XXIX, 9, 1965, 107-110; Reflections on dialogue within a pluralistic society, Stimmen der Zeit, XC, 1965, 321-330; Reflections on the unity of the love of neighbour and the love of God, Geist und Leben XXXVIII, 1965, 168-185. The first article listed above, "Ideology and Christianity" was delivered on the occasion of Rahner's receiving the Reuchlin Prize.

[29]Author of From anathema to dialogue, London: Collins, 1967.

[30]Cf. G. Vass, The faith needed for salvation - 1, The Month New Series 1, 1970, 203-204.

[31]Theological investigations 6, 62.

[32]In the last sections of Hearers of the word, drawing on Heidegger, Rahner developed an understanding of the historical nature of man.

It is something which cannot be foreseen or anticipated by human categories, because it is a transcendental not a categorical reality.[33]

Rahner's intention here was not to develop anything new but merely to accommodate the language of his transcendental theology to that of the Marxists. As this was already rooted in a transcendental philosophical system, the task was not too difficult. Balthasar feared however, that in accommodating his language Rahner had also compromised Christianity.

The purpose of Cordula oder der Ernstfall was twofold: on the one hand, to show the inadequacy of a transcendental theology based upon the Kantian philosophical system to support the fullness of the Christian mystery and provide a basis for the Christian's engagement with the world, and, on the other, to distil the essence of Christian discipleship, which is martyrdom inspired and enabled by Jesus Christ's death on the cross. His critique of Rahner in this book is also double-sided, beginning with an attempt to show that Rahner's system is methodologically erroneous, and ending with an account of the negative consequences of such a method. From the middle sixties onwards Balthasar's critique focuses more on the latter.

In the article reviewed above, Balthasar was at pains to point out that the Church and the world could never enter into dialogue with each other on equal terms. Cordula oder der Ernstfall, drawing heavily on selected biblical texts, begins with a sharp focus on the hostility which must characterise the world's attitude to Christianity.[34] Balthasar finds in Matthew's Gospel the basis for the conclusion that persecution must be the normal condition of the Church in its relation with the world: "...those who confess his name cannot avoid drawing upon themselves the hate of all other men".[35] To confess "the Name" means to be drawn into Jesus' life and death. In the death of Jesus, both the world's rejection of him and his mission in obedience to the Father were accomplished. In martyrdom both the world's hatred for the disciples and the

---

[33]"God - understood as the absolute future - is basically and necessarily the unspeakable mystery, since the original totality of the absolute future, towards which man projects himself, can never really be expressed in the precise characteristics proper to it by determinations taken from intramundane, classifiable experience; thus he is and remains essentially a mystery, i.e. he is known as the essentially transcendent, of whom it is of course said that, understood precisely as this mystery of infinite fullness, he is the self-communicating absolute future of man" (Theological investigations 6, 62).

[34]Balthasar criticises sharply the process of demythologisation which, he claims, robs scripture of any meaning.

[35]Cordula oder der Ernstfall, 13. Balthasar draws particularly on the interpretation of Matt. 10: 19-22 found in Das Evangelium nach Matthäus übersetzt und erklärt von J. Schmid, Regensburg, 1956.

disciples' mission also achieve completion. Both openness to the world and detachment from the world - in short, the Christian's whole attitude to the world - must be based on this call to martyrdom.

The Christian's main enemy is identified as "the philosophical system" which lures the Christian away from the very core of his faith. Sketching the development of German idealism from Kant through Fichte to Hegel, Balthasar outlines this system in terms of four theses.[36] The first thesis (as evident in Kant's Critique of Pure Reason) is that infinity (freedom) is the means of measuring human finite nature.[37] The second thesis holds that freedom exists purely as an intrasubjective phenomenon which is established in dialogue between the "I" and the "non-I" (as shown earlier). Third, the cosmos can only be considered to be the self-mediation of freedom.

> The natural realm becomes the mine which yields the material for a process of hominisation. With Fichte it was only speculative, but with Marx it has become practical and increasingly technical. And since man is seen as the centre and aim of this process, nature itself loses its aura (Nimbus) as mediator of the divine and becomes a "worldly world".[38]

Meanwhile, as the gap between the real and the ideal narrows, the human spirit itself becomes absolute (the fourth thesis):

> ...if the cosmos does indeed represent a process of hominisation, and if the aim of this process (human freedom) is by definition an absolute one (i.e. autonomous), then it must necessarily follow that the causa finalis of evolution is at the same time its causa efficiens and also its primum movens. The existence of the cosmos is explained by its aim - man. But the freedom of man...is self-creating and requires no aid outside itself.

[39]The human being can express awe and wonder only at the ideal of his or her own fulfilment. Thus the path which began by giving God an essential function in relation to humanity (Descartes) inevitably ends in this function turning out not to be essential after all. God is not only dispensable, but in fact must be dispensed with, if human freedom is to be absolute. From the point of view of systematic philosophy, Christianity is unavoidably something which belongs to the world's history and which

---

[36]Cordula oder der Ernstfall, 48-52.

[37]"...Unendlichkeit (Freiheit) ist die Ermessung der eigenen Endlichkeit: der Mensch mißt seinen Durchmesser" (op. cit., 50).

[38]op. cit., 51.

[39]op. cit., 52. Balthasar goes on to say: "Der Triumph des Systems liegt darin, daß es im voraus spekulativ entworfen und im nachhinein empirisch erhärtet worden ist, somit jetzt gefahrlos experimentell manupiliert werden kann" (loc. cit.).

played an important role in the world's development, a role which is now concluded.[40]

It follows that modern philosophical thought cannot be of service to theology for it brings God closer to man by only reducing the difference between them, and at the same time places God at such a distance from man that the unknowable part of God is no longer man's concern.[41]

Christianity has therefore a difficult decision to make. How can it be "modern" and genuinely Christian? In a direct reference to the Second Vatican Council, Balthasar warns that the Christian cannot bracket the serious challenge facing him for the sake of his aggiornamento.[42] The serious challenge facing the Christian can only be met through genuine Christian witness. But why, Balthasar asks, should the Christian wish to give witness any more?

> Karl Rahner frees us from a nightmare with his theory of the anonymous Christian who is dispensed, in any case, from the criterion of martyrdom and nevertheless even in his hiddenness (Verborgenheit) may still claim the mark (Bezeichnung) of being Christian if he, consciously or unconsciously, gives God the honour.[43]

Balthasar continues, in a sardonic tone, to outline Rahner's basis for this doctrine. He focuses particularly on Rahner's apparent identification of love of God with love of neighbour and of the implications of this for our understanding of Christology as anthropology.

Balthasar's first criticism is of the way in which all the mysteries of soteriology are reduced to the mystery of the incarnation.[44] In this way Rahner's system is similar to the evolutionistic Christology which Soloviev, basing his thinking on Schelling, Hegel and Darwin, developed over a century ago. In such a system something fundamental in the Trinitarian drama is lost:

> There is lacking clearly a Theologia Crucis which Rahner still owes us. Admittedly, of course, the emphasis on the doctrine of an anonymous Christianity (with the evolutionary background we have outlined above), so urgently required in the present situation, involves a proportionate de-emphasis of the theology of the

---

[40]op. cit, 58.

[41]op. cit., 65-66.

[42]"Die ganze Alternative...geht bloß darum, ob der Christ um seines aggiornamento willen den Ernstfall einklammern kann" (op. cit., 61).

[43]Cordula oder der Ernstfall, 85. Balthasar is referring to Rahner, K., Theological investigations 6, 390-398.

[44]Balthasar is commenting in particular on Rahner's article "Christology within an evolutionary view of the world", Theological investigations 5, 157-192.

cross and, correspondingly, of the theology of Christian living in terms of the
Ernstfall. For, according to what we have said, the saved person does not owe (his
redemption) to Christ, but to the eternal saving will of God, which becomes
recognisable in the life of Christ (im Existenzvollzug Christi).[45]

What is wrong here, according to Balthasar, is that it is not Christ's deed (his death
on the cross) which moves the will of God to forgive, but rather because of God's
will to forgive it is that the deed takes place.[46] Rahner fails to explain, possibly
because of his misunderstanding of Anselm's doctrine of satisfaction, how we can
claim that Christ bore our sins on the cross.

This relegation of the role of Christ in the saving mystery takes on another form in
Rahner's theology. So that the anonymous Christian can make the act of faith which
is necessary for salvation, an over-simplistic identification between love of God and
love of neighbour takes place.[47] This is only possible, argues Balthasar, if one
"leaves out Christ" and concentrates on selected biblical texts (especially in John).[48]

According to Balthasar, Rahner's position is two-fold: in my love of neighbour, my
love of God is implied, and in expressing my love of God, my love of neighbour is
also implied. This is possible because love is first and foremost a moral act, which
in the present order of human existence may become the supernatural virtue of charity
which is necessary for salvation. This clearly follows from Rahner's transcendental
method. When I genuinely love, I am expressing my openness to the whole of
reality. This includes my openness and acceptance (my love) of the concrete
otherness (the "thou") of my neighbour.[49] In fact, the basic act (Grundakt) in which
one transcends oneself is this love of the "thou" of the neighbour. It is the essential

---

[45]Cordula oder der Ernstfall, 91-92.

[46]"...properly speaking, it is not Christ's action which causes God's will to forgiveness, but vice
versa, and this redemption in Christ (one might also say: in view of Christ) was already effective
from the beginning of humanity" (Theological investigations 5, 187).

[47]Cf. The commandment of love in relation to the other commandments, Theological
investigations 5, 439-459; Reflections on the unity of the love of neighbour and the love of God,
Theological investigations 6, 231-249; Foundations of Christian faith, 456-457.

[48]Cordula oder der Ernstfall, 94.

[49]"Wherever man posits a positively moral act in the full exercise of his free self-disposal, this
act is a positive supernatural salvific act in the actual economy of salvation even when its a posteriori
object and the explicitly given a posteriori motive do not spring tangibly from the positive revelation
of God's Word but are in this sense 'natural'. This is so because God in virtue of his universal
salvific will offers everyone his supernaturally divinising grace and thus elevates the positively moral
act of man" (Theological investigations 6, 239).

moment in self-transcendence. It is a moment made possibly only by grace, whether one is aware of it or not. The virtues of faith, hope and charity are implicit in this act. It follows that the love of one's neighbour is the path to human fulfilment, for this act of love implies love for God as its inexpressible horizon.

When Balthasar uses the word "love" one can assume that he is referring to God's love for us, not our love of God or of neighbour. This is the primary reality of love for Balthasar which cannot be compromised or distracted from. Human love can, at best, be a response to the love which the Christ crucified has for me:

> The Christ who lives within me lives so within my innermost self (and nearer to me than I am to myself) because he died for me, because he took me to himself on the cross and constantly takes me to him again in the eucharist. How could my relationship with a fellow human being be comparable to that - and therefore encourage the same answering love from me? The bridge to brotherly love in the sense of Christ is that what he has done for everyone, he has done for me.[50]

For Balthasar, "the religious act" must be primary. For him, in one's love of neighbour, one's love of God overflows. For Rahner, one's love of neighbour is the expression of one's love of God in which the person making this act of love makes the essential act of acceptance of God's love for him, and is consequently saved.

We have arrived at perhaps the clearest viewing-point for the differences between Rahner's and Balthasar's theology. And, as we will see in the next section, we have here a microcosm of Balthasar's whole critique of Rahner. It will be necessary for us to establish as clearly as possible just how Rahner understands one's neighbour to be a mediator of revelation.

In a footnote, Balthasar remarks that he does not intend to "deny Karl Rahner's legitimate notion that there is a fides implicita and a corresponding supernatural love outside the sphere of Christianity, of the bible, as well as with those who are theoretically atheists".[51] We have already noted a similar remark of Balthasar's in his article (reviewed above) on the relationship between the Church and the world.[52]

---

[50]Cordula oder der Ernstfall, 95.

[51]loc. cit.

[52]Meeting God in today's world, Concilium 6, 1, 1965, 37: "...we must recognise the free working of the grace of Christ even where there is no explicit Christian belief". Once again, the failure to address the question of how this might be accounted for theologically, given especially the intensity of Balthasar's critique of Rahner's proposal, is astonishing. Were the aim of his book only to outline the essence of Christian discipleship, this would be understandable, but his secondary aim, i.e. to show the inadequacies of a theology based on a Kantian transcendental system, is considerably weakened by his failure to provide an alternative theological account of the salvation of non-Christians which he himself describes as being "so urgently required in the present situation" (Cordula oder der Ernstfall, 91).

The unacceptable consequence of the doctrine of the "anonymous" Christian is that

> He who speaks of "anonymous Christian", cannot (and will not wish to) avoid an
> ultimate unequivocality (Univozität) between Christians with the name and
> Christians without - consequently, despite all subsequent protests, it cannot be of
> importance whether or not one confesses the Name. And he who presents Love
> of Neighbour and Love of God as identical, and the Love of Neighbour as the
> primary act of the love of God, may not be (and probably is not) surprised if it
> becomes a matter of indifference whether people confess belief in God or not. The
> main thing is that he has love.[53]

But, he argues, how are we to know what love is? God establishes love's criteria.[54]
All of this, comments Balthasar, has consequences for the basis upon which we
Christians can enter into dialogue with non-Christians. In a satirical dialogue entitled
"If the salt becomes savourless" (Wenn das Salz dumm wird),[55] Balthasar portrays
an enthusiastic Christian, armed with the jewels of Rahnerian theology, attempting
to evangelise an open-minded and well-meaning communist Kommisar. The result,
according to Balthasar is that the Christian has become an anonymous atheist, even
if he or she does not realise it.

But the true Christian is not duped. Like all the saints, he knows that genuine
Christianity involves martyrdom in some form or other. Genuine martyrdom must
spring from the cross of Christ in order to accomplish "all that has still to be
undergone by Christ for the sake of his body, the Church" (Col. 1:24). It involves
a dying to the world. It involves an immersion in God's love for me which is so
radical that I am prepared to lay down my life for my neighbour.[56] If it even came
down to the horrible choice of my salvation or that of my neighbour, like Paul (Rom.
9:3) I would gladly give him my place.[57]

Apologia pro Cordula sua

In general, Balthasar's Cordula oder der Ernstfall got a hostile reception and he was

---

[53]Cordula oder der Ernstfall, 103.

[54]Balthasar quotes 1 Jn. 4:10 and Rom. 5:8: "In this is love, not that we loved God...but that
God shows his love for us in that while we were yet sinners Christ died for us" (Cordula oder der
Ernstfall, 103.

[55]Cordula oder der Ernstfall, 110-112.

[56]"A Christian should be one who offers up his life in the service of his fellow man because he
owes his life to Christ crucified" (Cordula oder der Ernstfall, 114).

[57]"Ich muß...für jeden Bruder so sehr hoffen dürfen, daß ich in einem fiktiven Ernstfall, wenn
es darum ginge, ob er oder ich in Gottes Reich eingehen soll, ihm mit Paulus (Rom. 9:3) den
Vortritt ließe" (Cordula oder der Ernstfall, 108).

particularly annoyed by a review, published anonymously, in Orientierung in 1966. He found it necessary to clarify his position on two further occasions.[58] Balthasar is anxious that the reader appreciates the purpose of his book, which, rather than an attack on the theology of Karl Rahner, was

> to ask Christians, and theologians among them, if they were prepared to shed their blood, in the sense of the Gospel and as the old Church understood it, for the God-made-man who bore the sins of the world and also yours and mine.[59]

This is the criterion of Christian genuineness (Echtheitskriterium). But how can it be seen as such if we really doubt, as some theologians do, that Jesus whom the apostles proclaimed after Easter historically existed, that he shed his blood on the cross, and that he reconciled humanity with God, transforming believers into children of the Father? And is this understanding of our faith furthered if without confessing the name of Christ, i.e. as "anonymous" Christians, people can become blessed in their own way? Nothing less is at risk here than the existence or non-existence of Christianity.[60] If we profess that all those outside the Church must somehow also be Christians we are going to suffer a substantial decline in Church-membership. Only saints and living witnesses can save us now from "the neutral gear (Leerlauf) and endless, shallow chatter of worldliness and evolution".

In the Appendix to the third edition of Cordula oder der Ernstfall, Balthasar expands on his shorter reply in Civitas, and explicitly tackles criticism relating to his treatment of Rahner's theology. He points out that he has never made a secret of his admiration for Rahner's speculative ability and courage, and, in difficult moments, actually defended Rahner against criticism.[61] At the same time, he points out, he was always critical of Rahner's method, which he always considered to be not without its dangers, at times uncoordinated and inconsistent, and to have led to a "stretching" (Ausweitung) of dogma.[62] By this latter comment Balthasar seems to be mean the

---

[58]These clarifications can be found in Apologia pro Cordula sua, Civitas 22, 1966-1967, 441 - 442 and in the appendix to the 3rd (1967) edition of Cordula oder der Ernstfall, 121-132, which reiterates and develops the points made in the Civitas article.

[59]Apologia pro Cordula sua, Civitas 22, 441.

[60]Apologia pro Cordula sua, Civitas 22, 442.

[61]Here Balthasar is referring to the essay he wrote on the occasion of Rahner's sixtieth birthday (Christliche Kultur, Beilage zu Neue Zürcher Nachrichten 1964, 9.), and his review of the first two volumes of Schriften zur Theologie, (Wort und Wahrheit, 1955, 531-533), which we have already examined above.

[62]Cordula oder der Ernstfall, 124-126.

apparent transformation of the content of dogmatic propositions while continuing to use the same terms.

Were this all Balthasar had to say in the Appendix to the third edition of Cordula then perhaps Fiorenza's comment that this appendix is "nothing but a further polemic" would be justified.[63] However, Balthasar goes on to make an important distinction, or more accurately take over an important distinction from de Lubac.

> No Christian would deny that, within the different cultures and life situations there are "anonymous Christians" who have received insights which stem from the Gospel. However, it would be false to conclude from this that there exists overall among humanity an "anonymous Christianity", so to say an "implicit Christianity".[64]

Balthasar still objects to an "implicit" or "anonymous" Christianity which, as de Lubac points out, reduces the task of the Saviour to that of making explicit what was already implicit and overall. This would approximate merely to giving a new label to an old or at least already existing product. The advantage of de Lubac's distinction as Balthasar sees it, is that the proclaimer of the Gospel can understand his mission as indispensable and at the same time accept that Christ, who died for all, is not unknown to the non-Christian in the depths of his heart. Balthasar refers to this distinction again and again in the future and uses it to clarify his opposition to Rahner's doctrine of the "anonymous Christian", on the one hand, and his optimism regarding the possibility of salvation for all, including non-Christians.

Balthasar concludes his Appendix by referring once again to the urgency of the situation facing the Church at the time. It is in the context of Balthasar's perception of this crisis that judgement upon Cordula oder der Ernstfall should be passed.

Truth is Symphonic

In the aftermath of the Second Vatican Council Balthasar felt it necessary to attack some of what he perceived as terrible simplifications inevitably leading to a reduction of Christianity and conversion of the Church to the world, and this led to the publication of books and articles in the same vein as Cordula oder der Ernstfall. At the same time, however, he realised that Christian faith was becoming a very complex matter for many people who were not students of theology and were not likely to be attracted by his more systematic theological writings e.g. The Glory of

---

[63]K. Rahner, Spirit in the world, xxxii,

[64]H. De Lubac, Geheimnis, aus dem wir leben, Einsiedeln: Johannes Verlag 1967, 149 (German translation of Paradoxe et Mystère de l'Eglise, Aubier, 1967 prepared by Balthasar).

<u>the Lord</u>.   Therefore he set about addressing concrete faith questions in simple terms.[65]

One issue which Balthasar felt in particular need of clarifying was the controversial question of pluralism.   The issue first surfaced for him at meetings of the International Theological Commission, of which both he and Rahner were members and it became a source of disagreement between them.[66]   Around this time Balthasar published <u>Einfaltungen. Auf Wegen Aspekte christlicher Einigung</u> (1969) and <u>Die Wahrheit ist symphonisch. Aspekte des christlichen Pluralismus</u> (1972).   In the latter publication Balthasar provides us with a clear understanding of what he considers to be the contribution of philosophy to Christianity and it is clear that, in writing, Rahner's interlocking between philosophy and theology is on his mind.[67]   All "architects of the spirit without exception", he writes, from Plato and Parmenides to Kant and Hegel, enquired into the riddle of being and thus expressed the deepest desire of "philosophising humanity" to discover its ground and purpose.[68]   The purpose of philosophical debate is to prevent the "glowing fire of the question" from being extinguished.   Balthasar points out that this can happen in two ways, both leading to total impoverishment of the human being. The first way in which this can happen is through what Balthasar calls "resignation". The human being becomes disillusioned with life.   He lacks motivation to discover anything or to change anything.[69]   Life only retains a semblance of meaning if, with the aid of modern technology, he limits himself to a small comfortable world.   However within this world he has "deliberately cut the umbilical cord binding himself to the world's

---

[65]Cf. <u>Klarstellungen. Zur Prüfung der Geister</u>. Freiburg: Herderbucherei, 1971 (English translation: <u>Elucidations</u>, London: SPCK, 1975), <u>In Gottes Einsatz leben</u>, Einsiedeln: Johannes Verlag, 1971 (English translation: <u>Engagement with God</u>, London: SPCK, 1975), <u>Neue Klarstellungen</u>, Einsiedeln, 1979 (English translation: <u>New elucidations</u>, San Francisco: Ignatius Press, 1986), <u>Kleine Fibel für verunsicherte Laien</u>, Einsiedeln: Johannes Verlag, 1980.

[66]Cf. P. Henrici, <u>op. cit.</u>, 56.

[67]<u>Die Wahrheit ist symphonisch</u>, Aspekte des christlichen Pluralismus has been translated and published as <u>Truth is symphonic</u>, Aspects of Christian pluralism, San Francisco: Ignatius Press, 1987. References are to this English translation.

[68]<u>op. cit.</u>, 47-50.

[69]Balthasar's description is close to that of Nietzsche's "last man" who exists though he has little desire to live, who knows neither love nor longing and who is bored by the great questions of human existence: "Wherefore live? All is vanity! To live - that means to thrash straw; to live - that means to burn oneself and yet not become warm" (<u>Thus spoke Zarathustra</u>, London: Penguin Classics, 1961, p.221).

ground" and therefore lacks all orientation to the absolute, and goes around in circles "within relative values which mutually threaten and destroy each other".[70]

It must be admitted that more and more people are "deliberately cutting the umbilical cord" with the ground of their existence, as Balthasar suggests. The unwillingness to think deeply about life and the tendency to avoid all depth experiences, cushioned by modern technology insofar as this is possible, characterises the approach to life for far too many as we come to the close of the twentieth century.[71] Karl Rahner expresses the same fear that the human race might in fact be, as he puts it, "evolving backwards".[72] In such a world God would cease to be an issue, as indeed Karl Marx predicted, and both the affirmation and negation of God would disappear without residue, thus heralding not only the real "death of God", but also, as Balthasar and Rahner both claim, the end of humanity, at least as we know it, as well.

The "glowing fire of the question" can be extinguished in yet another way, according to Balthasar. We human beings can also believe that we have in fact arrived at an answer. In this way the question also disappears. But to claim that the question has in fact been answered is to claim that there is no substantial question beyond what is generally knowable. This implies that we are, in fact, identifying ourselves with the principle of life or the ultimate ground of our existence. The concrete has been made absolute and so both have been totally devalued, signifying once again the end both of God and humanity. This is precisely why Balthasar cannot see a happy marriage between modern philosophy as it has developed from Descartes through to Hegel and as it has found political expression in Marx, Feuerbach and Engels, and Christian revelation. There is an unavoidable tendency within this system, which climaxed with German idealism, to seize the absolute and take possession of it, rather than be possessed by it. But in attempting to seize the absolute we totally devalue it and thus ourselves.[73]

---

[70]H. U. von Balthasar, Die Wahrheit ist symphonisch, 50 - 51.

[71]This is the context, I believe, within which contemprary attempts to develop an appropriate approach to the proclamation of the Christian faith in Ireland must be rooted, and which is similar to the context within which both Balthasar and Rahner developed their approaches to theology.

[72]K. Rahner, Theological investigations 20, 6.

[73]Both Kasper and O'Donnell, following Balthasar and Jüngel agree that modern philosophy leads inevitably to atheism and the devaluing of humanity. Cf. p. 136, n. 7 of this chapter. Cf. further E. Jüngel, op. cit., 125 - 126; W. Kasper, Jesus the Christ, 50, 51; The God of Jesus Christ, 19-20 and J. O'Donnell, op. cit., 7 - 11.

But what about non-Christian religions? If I believe in God in some way or another, then at least I am not identifying myself with the ultimate ground of existence. However, some of the more extreme forms of Eastern religions (e.g. Buddhism), Balthasar suggests, are but subtler forms of the human being identifying himself with the ultimate ground of existence.[74]

It would seem that for Balthasar, Hegelian-Marxist ideologies and non-Christian religions which are only philosophies in another form, are at best human attempts to reach the absolute.[75] At best, they express the humanity's yearning for wisdom and truth (philo-sophia). At worst they frustrate or hinder God's reaching out to the human being either by obstructing the human being's attempt to address ultimate questions, i.e. by distracting him, or making him feel resigned to the apparent sheer meaningless of existence, or by deluding him into thinking that he has in fact found an answer to the question. Philosophies or aspects of philosophies which do so are then very clear manifestations of the effects of original sin.

Christian revelation "uncovers the inchoate and essentially incomplete character of philosophies and world views".[76] It dismantles these philosophies and identifies the genuine search - the restless heart - which is common to them all. These philosophical systems and world views must be humbled until all that is left is the realisation that they search without any guarantee of finding, but in the hope that they might, for "it is up to God and his freedom (to decide) if and when he will be found". Their act of humility is expressed in the realisation and acceptance that they of themselves cannot come to any decisive conclusion, leaving the way open for the argument of "greater dissimilarity" of negative theology.[77]

> And since it is only God's free self-disclosure that can produce the key to the riddle
> of why there is a world at all; why sin, suffering and death are allowed in it; and
> what, in his futile existence, the creature may hope for, all philosophies whatsoever

---

[74]H. U. von Balthasar, op. cit., 51. We will discuss Balthasar's attitude to non-Christian religions towards the end of this section.

[75]Daniélou considered religions to belong to the world of creation, to be "man's search for God" and entirely due to "human effort" (J. Daniélou, Le mystère de salut des nations, 17-18). Cf. further R. E. Verestegegui, Christianisme et religions non-chrétiennes: Analyse de la 'tendance Daniélou', Euntes Docete 25, 1970, 227-229. Both articles are referred to in C. Saldanha, Divine Pedagogy A Patristic view of non-Christian religions, thesis submitted to the Faculty of Theology, Pontifical University of Maynooth in 1978.

[76]Die Wahrheit ist symphonisch, 53.

[77]Cf. op. cit., 52, 54.

will need a transvaluation of their fundamental position.[78]

In the concrete, the Christian should proclaim the Gospel according to the example given by St. Paul in his Areopagus address to the men of Athens (Acts 17), which Balthasar considers to be normative for evangelisation. The gods of the philosophers - known and unknown - must be confronted with the God of Jesus Christ.

Balthasar is not very optimistic that these philosophies will in fact be able to transform sufficiently, but admits that "the truth of revelation, which was originally cast in Hellenistic concepts by the great Councils, could equally be recast in Indian or Chinese concepts". However, it must be remembered at all times that "the divine Word... is much richer than can be plumbed by all of mankind's languages and thought forms together".

While Balthasar does not refer to Rahner's theology, his comments on the relationship which he feels must exist between philosophy and revelation are a direct criticism of Rahner's theology. They also bring into sharper focus why he always held, with Karl Barth, that Christian revelation cannot be subsumed within any philosophical system. However, they also raise the question of the status of non-Christian religions and philosophies. Balthasar admits that non-Christian religious search for truth and wisdom

> is guided by the knowledge of a presence, and not only some vague, general presence, but a presence that is personal to each individual.[79]

This search is only in the hope that it might find God and is totally devoid of any guarantee. But is it a graced search? Is this search entirely the human being's own response to his restless heart, or is it aided by God? Is this search inspired by God and even God's first step in reaching out to humankind and therefore a pre-grasp of God's totally free self-disclosure? And if the search is indeed aided by grace, and all grace comes through Christ, how do we give an account of this theologically? Balthasar does not, at least at this point, provide us with answers to these questions.

Sparks from the central fire

The first edition of Communio appeared in 1973 as a result of meetings between some members of the International Theological Commission.[80]

---

[78]op. cit., 55.

[79]op. cit., 54.

[80]"In 1945 a request was made several times through Adrienne that "I should start a review."...I did not think of it seriously again. Then, one evening in a restaurant in the Via Aurelia in Rome, a few of us from the International Theological Commission decided to start the the international

In the beginning Balthasar was not only this journal's coordinator, but he also determined its style and content from the outset and in clear opposition to Concilium. In 1975 Balthasar wrote a very important article in which he summarised his thought and work to date and outlined his main hopes, fears and concerns. His main concern emerges clearly once again as the Church's mission to the world. His main fear in this regard is that the Church would lose its identity, sell itself and the Gospel short. The "christening" of the Enlightenment and liberal theology, according to Balthasar, claims that the religious element in humankind stands as a whole in the light of grace and redemption and that down every religious road one can encounter the God of grace.[81] This is explained on the grounds that

> man as spirit in the world is finalised to the absolute spirit-being, and this transcendental dynamism is again supernaturally finalised through the self-opening of the inner love of God himself, so that whoever strives constantly can be called an "anonymous Christian." This is the christening of German idealism.[82]

This is less a cautious and perhaps also somewhat less precise restatement of both Balthasar's original critique of Rahner's Spirit in the world and what he had to say about German idealism in Cordula oder der Ernstfall. In the original review, of course, Balthasar was not in a position to make a direct link between what he understood as Rahner's "christening of German idealism" and the "anonymous Christian" as he is now:

> Is it not precisely here that the absolute and the divine light up and become understandable to him (man), as (after Fichte's profound speculation) Feuerbach and the modern personalists, Scheler, Ebner, Buber, and Jaspers also propound it? Isn't this almost transparent to the Sermon on the Mount? Doesn't the Parable of the Good Samaritan (where it is the "heretic" who does the right thing and is put forward as the example) 'express precisely this "one thing necessary?" Doesn't the Parable of Judgement Day (Matt. 25) say precisely that even the just are astounded at the judgement ("Lord, when did we see you hungry, thirsty, naked, in exile, sick, and in prison?") and hence that the just too are "anonymous Christians" wherever they make their Christianity really count as genuine fellowmen? Here, at last, the true humanism is begotten. And finally: isn't Heidegger correct when he defines man as openness to being, whose ethical nature does not reside in his being

---

review Communio. It was supposed to be launched first of all in Paris, but fell through, and so it made its first appearance in Germany in 1973. It would never have occurred to me to link this journal, which today comes out in eleven languages, with what had been asked of me almost forty years earlier. When the founding group began to break up, I was left on my own, having been pushed into the coordinating role. Only then did it dawn on me that there might be a connection with that request in the past from heaven. The blessing that rests on this fragile network linking different countries and continents confirms me in this presumption, which gradually became a sure conviction" (H. U. von Balthasar, Unser Auftrag, 68f. In: P. Henrici, op. cit., 46).

[81]Cf. H. U. von Balthasar, In retrospect, Communio Winter, 1975, 200.

[82]H. U. von Balthasar, loc. cit.

> a servant of laws and commandments, but in his ability to heed the call of being
> as a whole in the momentary situation? And since the Holy Spirit of God and of
> Christ holds sway in All, why shouldn't this essentially mysterious call blowing
> hither out of the absolute be inspired in its depths by the command of the personal
> God of love - anonymously, of course - so that even over Heidegger's thought the
> waters of Baptism can be poured?[83]

At first the Christian might feel liberated by such a theology. But

> it has a snag. When everything goes so well with anonymity, it is hard to see why
> a person should still be a name-bearing Christian. And it certainly seems that on
> the basis of this new theological vogue, many are already prepared - perhaps out
> of solidarity with the Russians and the Chinese and in order to become an
> unacknowledged leaven from within -to renounce the troublesome formality of the
> name.[84]

Balthasar goes on to say that the Christian is one who lets himself or herself be killed
for Christ and

> there is no such thing as an anonymous Christian, however so many other men -
> hopefully all! - attain salvation through the grace of Christ. But the grace for all
> depends on the form of life of Him who through the shame of his poverty, his
> obedience, and his bodily "castratedness" (Matt. 19.12) embodied God's grace and
> desired at every stage... that others partake of this form.[85]

Balthasar makes no reference to the distinction made by de Lubac between the
"anonymous Christian" and "anonymous Christianity" and it would seem that
Balthasar has taken back ground which he conceded in the Appendix to Cordula oder
der Ernstfall. However, in the latter, he accepted the phrase "anonymous Christian"
to make it quite clear that he was not limiting the possibility of salvation to baptised
members of the Church. Insofar as this expression described non-baptised individuals
who attain salvation through the grace of Christ, he seemed happy to accept it. He
simply wanted to eliminate any possible misconception that Christianity could in any
way be anonymous. Balthasar contradicts himself here, but only at the level of terms
and not of content.

We can only speculate as to why he was no longer content to accept the term
"anonymous Christian". Perhaps he felt, in retrospect, that the distinction between
"anonymous Christian" and "anonymous Christianity" was too subtle to be
appreciated by many people. What we can be certain of, is that, in Balthasar's eyes,
the teaching of the "anonymous" Christian/Christianity was detrimental to the Church
and undermined it in its relation to the world. While in no way denying the
possibility of salvation to all, Balthasar believes that

---

[83]art. cit., 202.

[84]art.cit., 202-203.

[85]art. cit., 203.

> if everything in the Church is not to be rendered superficial, there remains the true,
> undiminished program for the Church today: namely, the greatest possible radiance
> in the world by virtue of the closest possible following of Christ.[86]

But why bother if, instead, one can be an anonymous Christian? His reason for
rejecting the concept of the anonymous Christian at this point is no longer based on
an argument that the anonymous Christian is the result of a flawed methodology. It
also has clearly nothing to do with the salvation or damnation of non-Christians. The
doctrine of the anonymous Christian is objectionable on the grounds that it relativises
and undermines the work of the Christian and the Church in the world. But if we
think for a moment of what the Church primarily is for Balthasar - the clearest and
most profound radiance of Christ in the world -then Balthasar's main fear emerges.
If the Church is relativised, it follows that Christ will be relativised. Balthasar's main
objection to the doctrine of the anonymous Christian is that it gives the impression
that the salvation of all (including Christians) is not achieved in and through the
historical life, death and resurrection of Jesus the Christ. Therefore the doctrine of
the "anonymous Christian" is objectionable not just because of what it has to say
about Christians and their mission in the world, but more fundamentally, about the
historical Jesus Christ and his mission in the world. Did Christ's life, death and
resurrection, and especially (for Balthasar) Christ's death on the cross, achieve our
salvation, or did the Christ-event simply make our salvation known? This question
lies at the very heart of Balthasar's criticism of the anonymous Christian.

The Call for a theology of the cross

In an interview in 1976 Balthasar relates his critique of Rahner's lack of a theology
of the cross to his critique of the anonymous Christian and points out that both
criticisms must be understood within the context of Rahner's transcendental
Christology. That Balthasar's main objection to Rahner's doctrine of the anonymous
Christian is that it seemingly leads to the relativisation of the historical life, death and
resurrection of Christ, clearly emerges from the following

> Rahner sees the redemptive, the expiative in Christ's death in Jesus' act of
> complete self-giving (Selbstübergabe) to the Father as he died. I ask, is that
> enough? What is terrible about Jesus' death is that he suffered the death of sinners
> and of all sinners. For me the word "representation" (Stellvertretung), totally
> understood, cannot be renounced (unverzichtbar).[87]

Balthasar refers back to what he said in the appendix to Cordula oder der Ernstfall

---

[86]loc. cit.

[87]Geist und Feuer, Herder Korrespondenz 30, 1976, 76.

about the distinction between "anonymous Christianity" and "anonymous Christians" which he borrowed from de Lubac. He seems once again prepared to accept de Lubac's distinction:

> "Anonymous Christians": certainly. There are great human paradigms outside the Church. "Anonymous Christianity": no, because that implies a relativisation of the objective revelation of God in the biblical event, and would sanction the religious paths of other religions as either ordinary or extraordinary means of salvation. That is biblically not on. But also the expression "the anonymous Christian" in my opinion remains unfortunate, because being a Christian simply includes confession of a name, the name of Jesus Christ.[88]

Even if Rahner's transcendental Christology were methodically legitimate, and as we have seen, Balthasar is not prepared to admit this, it would still be unacceptable because it would arrive at Christ independently of biblically-mediated revelation, thus relativising God's objective revelation which culminated in the historical life, death and resurrection of Jesus Christ. It seems to be the case that while it would give us an account (to Balthasar, a dubious account) of how all may "anonymously" experience God's grace and respond to God's grace, at the same time it would render any other mediation of grace superfluous. It robs the objective biblical historical event of any significant meaning.

As Balthasar perceives the Church's present situation vis-à-vis the world, this kind of theology is not only counter-productive but suicidal, and not only theologians but also the magisterium are admonished to examine their consciences.[89]

Current trends in Catholic theology

Balthasar gave two lectures in the United States in October 1977. His lecture notes, and the response papers of certain theologians, were subsequently published in Communio. Balthasar's most interesting comments during these lectures relate to his attitude to non-Christian religions, and as we shall see in the next section, they further help us to bring his criticism of the doctrine of the "anonymous Christian" in focus.

One of the two lectures dealt with "Current trends in Catholic theology". While all contemporary theology is at pains to stress the unity of theory and practice, Balthasar could identify three different approaches: Rahner's transcendental approach,

---

[88] loc. cit.

[89] We have already referred to Balthasar's comments in this interview on the Second Vatican Council.

Balthasar's own theological aesthetics, and Liberation Theology.[90]

Balthasar introduces Rahner as a disciple of Joseph Maréchal whose work attempted to reconcile Thomas Aquinas with German idealism. He summarises Rahner's approach as follows:

> Because it was God's intention from the beginning to surrender himself totally to his creatures, man is from the outset projected beyond himself toward union of God and man, a union that came into existence in the person of Christ. Anthropology thus becomes inchoate or deficient Christology. And because all the truths of revelation have their centre and their foundation in Christ, there is in man a potential that corresponds to every dogma, if not in his objective categorical, finite world of objects, at any rate in the transcending impulsions of his knowledge and his freedom which must be kept expectantly open to God's gratuitous coming into finiteness.[91]

Balthasar admits that Rahner's motive is good - to show how closely Christian truth conforms to the deepest human expectations - but points out that Rahner's greatest difficulty is to prove the necessity of an explicit, historical Christianity. The incarnation is apparently reduced to being the transcending fulfilment in time of all that is human.

> If a man follows the guidance of his own conscience and does what he believes is right, he is caught up in the grace of God and may be called an "anonymous Christian", no matter what religion or atheistic worldview he may adhere to. Here Rahner comes close to Karl Barth who said that the only difference between Christians and non-Christians is that Christians are aware of God's grace to all mankind, and that, therefore, it is their duty to announce it to the world.[92]

It seems to Balthasar that "the relativisation of everything ecclesiastical in the name of an all-pervading grace" inevitably follows.

Balthasar criticises the transcendental approach further in highlighting the clear divergence between Rahner's approach and his own:

> My main argument...is this: It might be true that from the very beginning man was created to be disposed toward's God's revelation, so that with God's grace even the sinner can accept all revelation. Gratia supponit naturam. But when God sends his own living Word to his creatures, he does so, not to instruct them about the mysteries of the world, nor primarily to fulfil their deepest needs and yearnings. Rather he communicates and actively demonstrates such unheard-of things that man feels not satisfied but awestruck by a love which he never could have hoped to experience. For who would dare to have described God as love, without having first received the revelation of the Trinity in the acceptance of the cross by the

---

[90]Current trends in Catholic theology and the responsibility of the Christian, Communio 5, Spring 1978, 77 - 85.

[91]art. cit., 79.

[92]art. cit., 80.

Son.[93]

God's love for us is unique and has no need of, nor can it tolerate, any other proof but itself. Therefore Christianity has no place for a special apologetics, according to Balthasar. Like any work of art, it is its own proof.

> For the Christian it would be a downright betrayal of God's love in Christ were he to look for a "ground of being" while ignoring the cross that Christ suffered for us and his resurrection that includes us. We do not need to search for God; he sought us and found us.[94]

Balthasar's argument against the transcendental approach finds new expression here. All attempts to give an account of the faith which do not originate within the historical Christ event are judged not only anti-Christological but anti-Christian. But does Rahner invite the Christian and non-Christian to look for a "ground of being" while ignoring or bracketing the historical Christ event? As we shall see later, this accusation presupposes a certain understanding of the way in which Rahner interlocks philosophy and theology.

Catholicism and the religions

In one of his two lectures during this American visit, Balthasar set out to show the uniqueness of Christianity and in particular of Catholicism, which he describes as Christianity's "oldest version and the stem from which all other, later branches have sprung".[95] Christianity's claim to absoluteness is grounded in its uniqueness.

Christianity is unique in origin. Whereas all other religions originate in the natural, human search for God, Catholicism originates in "God's condescension to man". This condescension climaxes in the incarnation which is God's final and ultimate Word to humanity. The finality of the incarnation depends on a distinction in the Godhead between a Speaker and a Word. Because both Speaker and Word are God, their otherness from one another must be bridged by the Holy Spirit. Therefore God's ultimate revelation to humanity is also uniquely a trinitarian revelation.

The incarnation is unique in another way. It discloses not only God's unique and final utterance to humanity, but also achieves the most perfect human response to God. Thus in Christ we find a way of responding to God which does not flow from human initiative but is a response to God's pursuit of humanity. Therefore Christianity is unique because "it is the way - shown by God himself - that leads man

---

[93]loc. cit.

[94]art. cit., 83.

[95]Catholicism and the religions, Communio 5, 1978, 6.

to God".[96]   Christian prayer is also unique because it can contemplate the absolute
transcendent God in the concrete Jesus of Nazareth:

> The Christian in meditation does not have to close his eyes to the "categorical" in
> order to experience the "transcendental".[97]

And it follows, that just as Jesus is incomparable as the only eternal Son of the Father
and "the perfect archetype of his lesser brothers", the Church "as the extension of
Christ's reality into time is essentially incomparable with other religious
communities".   It follows that the Church has a unique mission in the world and
must concern itself both with human well-being on earth and more importantly with
humanity's eternal salvation.   And Balthasar warns that

> the idea that grace may also be received outside the Church, that there could be
> something like anonymous Christianity, in no way relieves the Church of her
> missionary obligation.[98]

Balthasar's opposition to the doctrine of the "anonymous" Christian is once again
clearly set in the context of weakening the Church's identity and sense of purpose in
the world.

Can we interpret from the above quotation, an admission by Balthasar that grace is
indeed received outside the Church? Earlier in the same article, when discussing
religion as an anthropological phenomenon he asks:

> ...does mere negation of time and space bring us to that absolute which is God?
> And though the human mind might experience a kind of revelation when it
> transcends the barriers of the finite, including those of the individual ego, and
> penetrates into a sphere where light, freedom, and peace appear to shine forth, the
> same urgent question still remains unanswered: Is this the revelation of the true and
> living God? We do not say a priori "no" - we simply leave the question open.[99]

It seems that some members of Balthasar's audience were not prepared to allow him
to leave this very important question open, and in a response paper D. J. O'Hanlon
challenges what he sees as the theological presuppositions which make it "inevitable
for him to downgrade what happens outside the Christian Church."[100] Unfortunately
O'Hanlon is not very clear on precisely what he considers these theological

---

[96]art. cit., 9.

[97]art. cit., 11.

[98]art. cit., 13

[99]art. cit., 7. Cf. Glory of the Lord 1, 144ff.

[100]D. J. O'Hanlon, Hans Urs von Balthasar on non-Christian religions and meditation,
Communio 5, Spring 1978, 60-68. The same issue of Communio contains both a critical essay on
Balthasar's entire method and approach (D. J. O'Keefe, A methodological critique of von Balthasar's
theological aesthetics) and Balthasar's article "Response to my critics".

presuppositions to be which lead Balthasar to claim that for all non-Christian religions, religion is a movement coming only from the world to the Absolute. This has implications for all forms of prayer which are non-Christian (O'Hanlon notices that Balthasar is even reluctant to use the words "prayer" or "contemplation" to describe non-Christian worship), and

> when (Balthasar) implies that only Christianity reaches a God who is both absolute and personal, it seems to me that he goes too far.[101]

While Balthasar claims that he wishes to leave open the question of non-Christians experiencing Christian revelation, O'Hanlon says that the whole tenor of both of Balthasar's papers answers this question in the negative and challenges Balthasar directly to prove him wrong.

In Balthasar's subsequent response to O'Hanlon's criticisms perhaps what is most significant is the context within which he justifies his position on non-Christian religions. Balthasar says that he is writing from the perspective of a Europe whose "Christian substance is being hollowed out".[102]   It would seem that Balthasar's (arguably theological) presupposition is the decline of Christianity in Europe, and in this context he specifically mentions "anonymous Christianity". But by so doing he does not mean to deny that

> God's free grace in Christ embraces all mankind. If men humbly seek their God, this grace can be well received and lived by non-Christians.[103]

Can we take this as an affirmative answer to Balthasar's own question as to whether the human mind, when it transcended the barriers of the finite could arrive at a revelation of the one living and true God? It seems hard to interpret it as otherwise, yet at no point has Balthasar offered us an account of how this grace might be present, and in fact, not only is Balthasar's overall stance as portrayed in his two lectures dubious or at least dismissive of this, as O'Hanlon points out, but in fact Balthasar seems to close off the most significant avenues for the mediation of grace outside the Christian Church. It will be important to our assessment of the validity of Balthasar's critique of the "anonymous Christian" to come to a clearer understanding of Balthasar's position on grace outside the Church.

New Elucidations

In 1979 Balthasar wrote on the relationship which should exist between the Church

---

[101]O'Hanlon, art. cit., 62.

[102]Response to my critics, Communio 5, Spring 1978, 69-76.

[103]H.U: von Balthasar, art. cit., 70.

and non-Christians, with the purpose of arriving at "some practical conclusions for our inner-ecclesial situation".[104] It is interesting that this should prove once again to be his context for examining non-Christian religions.

Balthasar considers that the New Testament lays down the norm for relations between the Church and the world in the way in which the relationship between Jew and Gentile developed.[105] In this context the Christian is the contemporary "Jew", enjoying a Christian upbringing and inheriting a rich ecclesial tradition.

The latter day Gentile is untouched by this tradition but "has direct access by sheer grace, without any tradition".[106] At some time or other they may come across the phenomenon of a God-man called Jesus, but it comes to them as if out of nowhere and as something that they could not have foreseen or expected. While the Church must be open to the human values in these non-Christian cultures

> Within global world history, biblical salvation history is imbedded as a permanent leaven and continues in the history of the Church; of course it can be effective as leaven only if it is mixed into the dough of humanity as a whole...Who belongs to her? The Christian who expressly confesses to be such, or likewise anyone who comes within the Church's influence and does not join her? Both may be correct, each at his own level, but we have no right to equate levels: that is God's affair.[107]

Balthasar makes it quite clear that grace is available outside the Church, he even admits that the Church is in some way in need of non-Christian cultures and is here at his most affirmative regarding them (he even says that it would be best for latter day "Jew" and "Gentile" to admit their mutual neediness and poverty, p.71). However he remains uncompromising regarding the doctrine of the anonymous Christian which is the context in which the remarks about "equating levels" is made. This is clear from Balthasar's footnote to the sentence quoted above

> Here we need not address the question of the "anonymous Christian". The best and clearest answer to this question that I have found is at the end of the foreword

---

[104]New Elucidations, San Francisco: Ignatius Press, 1986, 61. (English translation of Neue Klarstellungen, Einsiedeln: Johannes Verlag, 1979).

[105]op. cit., 60 - 74.

[106]op. cit., 71. This is not to imply that the Gentile is totally without tradition. On p.72 we read: "the "Gentile" does not come to the Church without a tradition of his own. Inevitably he brings his culture along with him. The Fathers of the Church took this very seriously as did the Jesuit missionaries. Augustine expresses the opinion that even the Gentiles had their prophets. And Henri de Lubac does not hesitate to assert that when a nation is converted, its forefathers are also included in the conversion process, since they have made the current process possible."

[107]op. cit., 72 - 73.

to <u>Mere Christianity</u> by C.S. Lewis.[108]

By now an answer to the question as to why Balthasar does not provide us with an account of how non-Christians can experience grace is beginning to emerge. Following de Lubac, he believes that this is best left as "God's affair". Why? It would seem that his principal fear is that for the Church and for theologians to occupy themselves with this question at this time will have a detrimental effect upon the Church's own sense of identity and uniqueness of mission.

C.S. Lewis defines a Christian as one who accepts the common doctrines of Christianity.[109] In response to objections that some one who cannot hold these doctrines actually could be far more a Christian and far closer to the spirit of Christ, Lewis says:

> ...this objection is in one sense very right, very charitable, very spiritual, very sensitive. It has every available quality except that of being useful. We simply cannot, without disaster, use language as these objectors want us to use it.[110]

Lewis goes on to say that his point is not a moral or theological one but only, though presumably no less importantly, a question of clarity of language. He also makes the interesting comment that to use "Christian" to describe someone who is close to the spirit of Christ rather than simply to describe someone who accepts the doctrines of Christianity involves the Christian in passing judgement upon his neighbour. But we cannot look into our neighbour's hearts and are in fact, as Christians, forbidden to judge. Further, the use by non-Christians of the word "Christian" to describe someone who is close to the spirit of Christ will lead eventually to the word simply becoming another term of praise. It must be admitted that the word "Christian" is already in use to some extent in this sense. When someone who accepts the doctrines of Christianity lives unworthily of them, suggests Lewis, it is much better to say he is a bad Christian than to say that he is not a Christian.

It is strange that Balthasar considers that Lewis's comments represent "the best and clearest answer" to the question of the "anonymous" Christian.[111] Balthasar's own critique, as we have already seen, runs much deeper. His endorsement of Lewis clarifies further why he is uncomfortable even to accept de Lubac's distinction between the terms "anonymous Christian" and "anonymous Christianity".

---

[108]<u>op. cit.</u>, 73.

[109]Cf. <u>Mere Christianity</u>, 9 (first printed in 1955).

[110]<u>op. cit.</u>, 10.

[111]<u>New Elucidations</u>, 73.

Lewis's objection is not, as he himself admits, theological. Balthasar's endorsement of Lewis's comments make it clear that his objections are not just theological. The Theodramatik, though conceived before Herrlichkeit, represents the final part of Balthasar's trilogy.[112] In it Balthasar seeks to give an account of how God's love is made manifest in the world. In the course of outlining the mechanics of God's self-giving to the world, Rahner's doctrine of the anonymous Christian is attacked specifically on two occasions. The first of these is in the context of a discussion of the salvation of non-Christians. Balthasar is particularly critical of Rahner's account of how non-Christians experience grace. We have already given an account of Balthasar's objections to the supernatural existential which questioned the usefulness of Rahner's use of natura pura as a Restbegriff which underpins the supernatural existential. His objections then were in the context of attempting to establish the correct relationship which must exist between nature and grace. He now returns to attack the supernatural existential. This time however, his purpose is to show that there is a danger that the supernatural existential does away with the need for a categorical-historical revelation. Balthasar relates his comments to an address on the relationship between the Church and non--Christians which Rahner gave in 1961.[113]

Rahner believes that it is an increasingly urgent task for the Church to outline its relationship to non-Christian religions in the light of an ever increasing pluralism. How can Christians continue to defend their claim that Christianity is the absolute religion intended for all? How can it claim that its interpretation of God's activity is instituted by God himself? If we take seriously God's will regarding salvation for all, this implies that the individual must be capable of partaking in a genuine saving relationship with God at all times and in all historical situations. At the same time we hold that all salvation comes only through Christ and is effected in this life. It must follow that

> every human being is really and truly exposed to the influence of the divine
> supernatural grace which offers an interior union with God.[114]

---

[112]Theodramatik consists of the following volumes: Band 1: Prologomena, Band 2: Die Personen des Spiels (Teil 1: Der Mensch in Gott, Teil 2: Die Personen in Christus), Band 3: Die Handlung and Band 4: Das Endspiel.

[113]Cf. K. Rahner, Christianity and the non-Christian religions, Theological investigations 5, 115-135. Balthasar is also targeting J. Heislbetz, (Theologische Gründe der nichtchristlichen Religionen, Quaestiones Disputatae 33, Herder: Freiburg, 1967) and A. Darlap, (Fundamental Theologie der Heilsgeschichte, Mysterium Salutis 1, 1965.

[114]op. cit., 123.

We must conclude that supernatural grace is offered to all and is accepted by at least some. The non-Christian religions clearly have a role in the mediation of this grace outside the Church.[115] They can have this role even though they contain erroneous elements, for even the Old Testament though "lawful" was not free from error. In fact they must have this role if we take into account the social nature of the human being. The human religious sense cannot exist or develop apart from a social expression of it. Religion has an inalienable social dimension.

It follows that Christianity should view non-Christian religions as already at least to some extent touched by God's grace and truth, and to this extent to have among their members "anonymous Christians". This is not in any way to wish to weaken the mission of the Church which must be considered to be "the incarnational and social structure of grace".[116] But rather than the Church viewing itself as the body of those who have some claim on salvation, the Church should understand itself to be

> the historically tangible vanguard and the historically and socially constituted explicit expression of what the Christian hopes is present as a hidden reality even outside the visible Church.[117]

Balthasar cannot accept this definition of Church. There must be more to the Church than being the explicit expression of what is already a hidden reality outside of it. He does not deny that human nature is in some way supernaturally modified -this follows if we accept God's universal salvific will for all. But is it correct to consider the human spirit's supernatural openness to transcendence to be an experience of grace, by which Balthasar means an experience of being addressed by a personal word from God? Balthasar claims that if the human being's openness to a supernatural horizon is in fact an experience of grace the need for an a posteriori categorical revelation of

---

[115]Rahner also tackles here the question as to whether such religions can be considered to be "lawful". He accepts that once other religions come into contact with the religion (Christianity), they are invalidated, but argues that this "coming into contact" is difficult to judge, must be understood historically and cannot be taken to be chronologically simultaneous for all. Therefore even after the period of the apostolic age other religions may continue to have a period of validity and of being willed by God.

[116]Rahner also says that "the individual who grasps Christianity in a clearer, purer and more reflective way has, other things being equal, a still greater chance of salvation than someone who is merely an anonymous Christian" (op. cit., 132). At first this may seem surprising but Weger's interpretation of what Rahner means here would seem to be the correct one: "The explicit knowledge of God's revelation...which the explicitly believing Christian, unlike the anonymous Christian, possesses is not simply a knowledge which may or may not be present and which has no influence on the life of the one who has it. On the contrary, this knowledge of faith is an existential knowledge which has a direct influence on life" (K.- H. Weger, op. cit., 121).

[117]K. Rahner, Christianity and non-Christian religions, Theological investigations 5, 133.

God disappears.[118] De Lubac, it seems to Balthasar, without in any way impinging on the universality of grace, has correctly established the limit of the supernatural existential as a desire for the living God which must itself be elevated.[119]

In the third volume of the Theodramatik Balthasar tackles Rahner's soteriology and in particular Rahner's lack of a theology of the cross. While he relates his comments in particular to selected passages in Foundations of Christian faith, his criticism is largely as already presented in Cordula oder der Ernstfall.

Balthasar is critical of Rahner's attempt to get behind what Rahner calls the "late" New Testament Christologies to the disciples' first experience of the crucified and risen Jesus. Arguing that Jesus did not interpret himself as a "sin-offering", Rahner rejects the understanding of Jesus' death as expiatory or as atonement which we find in the scriptures, the Fathers and Anselm, and which he feels compromises our understanding of the immutability of God.   But according to Balthasar it also undermines the whole centrality of the cross in the saving event.   Together with Rahner's warnings against a "mere biblicism" (einem bloßen Biblizismus) and in Rahner's system the bible must be relegated, since biblical revelation is only a part of revelation history, historical revelation as a whole becomes merely the explicit expression (Ausdrücklichkeit) of what has always been already at least implicitly present through grace.[120]

Thus Christ's death, characterised as it is by self-surrender into the hands of a loving Father becomes merely an example for us of how we too should face death. Balthasar asks, could Mary's death not be of equal significance for us?[121]

---

[118]"Wenn die Eröffnung des übernatürlichen Horizonts für den Menschen wirklich schon eine "Gnadenerfahrung" und darin der Zuspruch eines personalen Wortes von Gott her besagt, muß dann nicht überall dort, wo die Objektivierung dieses apriorisch-tranzendentalen Wortes zwar notwendig versucht, aber durch keine eigene aposteriorisch-kategoriale Offenbarung Gottes als entsprechend verbürgt wird, die Gestalt der objektiven Religion notwendig mißlingen"? (Theodramatik 2, 2, 380).

[119]"Il ne nous est pas seulement permis, il nous est imposé de croire que la lumière du Verbe éclaire tout homme venant en ce monde, et que, sous mille formes anonymes, la grace du Christ peut etre partout à l'oeuvre" (H. De Lubac, Le fondement théologique des missions. In: Theodramatik 2, 2, 382). Balthasar first made many of the points he makes here in his book on Karl Barth which we have already dealt with. There we also saw that Rahner felt that while de Lubac successfully avoided extrinsicism, there was a danger of nature and grace collapsing into each other in his position.

[120]Theodramatik 3, 253.

[121]Cf. further Herrlichkeit 3, 2, 147. Cf. also W. Kasper, Jesus the Christ, 51-52.

Chapter 4
The Anonymous Christian: a Reduction ?

Introduction
The previous chapters have demonstrated clearly that Hans Urs von Balthasar's main objection to Karl Rahner's concept of the anonymous Christian is that it derives from a theological method which ultimately presents the historical Christ-event merely as the manifestation of God's salvific will in history rather than as the actual event (Ereignis) of salvation. According to Balthasar, this theological method errs in the same way as German idealism errs i.e. it attempts to deduce the reality of the absolute from the human spirit's openness to the absolute. More fundamentally it is erroneous to allow theology to be subsumed within an alienating philosophical system. Further, the consequences of Rahner's concept of the anonymous Christian are undesirable for the individual Christian's self-understanding, for the Church's self-understanding and for the Church's relationship to the world.

The aim of this chapter is to evaluate Balthasar's criticism of the anonymous Christian from the perspective that in its method it represents a reduction of the Christian mystery. The next chapter will examine the question of a possible relativisation of biblical revelation and the Church.

A proper evaluation of Balthasar's criticisms demands that we confront them with key elements of Rahner's theological method. We must also pay attention to what Rahner has said about his own method in an effort to discern precisely how he interlocks philosophy with theology and attend, in the course of this examination, to the few isolated specific responses Rahner makes to Balthasar.[1]

Karl Rahner's method
Often God is encountered as distant and vague, at best as a mysterious flickering light in an almost overwhelming darkness. At the same time existentialism for the most part appears to offer an alternative and coherent world-view which excludes God. Europe is experiencing widespread atheism for the first time. The European Christian has no other choice but to dialogue with people who hold world-views which conflict with Christianity. This is only possible if a common language can be found. A theology which begins exclusively "from above" is unable both to account for the

---

[1] Prof. H. Vorgrimler, a former assistant of Rahner's, has provided me with the following references made by Rahner to Balthasar: Theological investigations 7, 12; Theological investigations 11, 39; Gnade als Mitte menschlicher Existenz, Herder Korrespondenz 28, 1974, 77-92, esp. 85; Im Gespräch 1, 242, 245ff. Rahner did not defend himself systematically against Balthasar or any other of his critics.

Christian's own faith and to enable him to enter into dialogue with others.[2] The contemporary pastoral situation, as Rahner perceives it, determines how theology is done.[3] The Church's contemporary situation within the world convinces Rahner that it is only through an interlocking (Verschränkung) between philosophy and theology that he can

> give people confidence from the very content of Christian dogma itself that they can believe with intellectual honesty.[4]

To evaluate Balthasar's criticisms of this approach we must examine two grounds upon which Rahner seeks to justify his method. First, Rahner acknowledges the influence of Ignatius of Loyola, admitting it as

> a historical fact ...that his own theological thinking sprang from the practice of the Ignatian Exercises and so in fact was fashioned in the light of reflection on the effective operation of the Spirit.[5]

The influence of Ignatius of Loyola on Rahner should not be underestimated: it convinced Rahner from the very beginning that theology must help one not just to talk about God but also to experience God.[6] It must help one to become a mystic. Rahner was convinced that the Christian of the future would be a mystic or he would not be a Christian at all.[7] In his later writings, responding to the Christian's

---

[2] While attending the Second Vatican Council, Rahner wrote to Vorgrimler (5 Nov. 1962): "I also notice there that I'm not yet all that old, even when I sit at a table with Daniélou, Congar, Ratzinger, Schillebeeckx and so on. I find that these still do not realise clearly enough how little e.g. a christology "from above", which simply begins with the declaration that God has become man, can be understood today" (H. Vorgrimler, Understanding Karl Rahner, 158).

[3] Cf. Reflections on methodology in theology, Theological investigations 11, 68-114, especially p. 70.

[4] Foundations of Christian faith, 12. Rahner summarises precisely what he means by an interlocking of philosophy and theology on pp. 24-25.

[5] Theological investigations 16, x - xi. In a Festschrift to commemorate his eightieth birthday Rahner writes: "Ich hoffe, daß mein großer Ordensvater Ignatius von Loyola mir zubilligt, daß in meiner Theologie so ein kleinwenig von seinem Geist und seiner ihm eigenen Spiritualität merkbar ist. Ich hoffe es wenigstens! Ich bin sogar der etwas unbescheidenen Meinung, daß in diesem oder jenem Punkt ich näher bei Ignatius stehe als die große Jesuitentheologie der Barockzeit..." (K. Lehmann, ed. Vor dem Geheimnis Gottes den Menschen verstehen, 114).

[6] "A task for any genuine fundamental theology is to develop a theology of the Ignatian choice as a precondition of the availability of an absolute decision of faith. Such an openness must at least theoretically contain the process of reflection proper to fundamental theology, a process which never reaches a definitive conclusion" (Theological investigations 16, 165).

[7] Cf. Im Gespräch II, 34-41. Concerning the importance of Ignatius of Loyola for Rahner see K. Fischer, Der Mensch als Geheimnis, 7, 28, 149. Fischer describes the Ignatian spirituality as Rahner's Sitz-im-Leben. Cf. H. D. Egan's support for Fischer's position in H. Vorgrimler, ed.,

contemporary difficulty in experiencing God's presence, Rahner began to speak more and more about God being fundamentally experienced as "absolute Mystery".[8] We have already noted Martin Heidegger's influence on Rahner. If metaphysics is defined as the enquiry about being as such and in its totality, insofar as it enquires into the universal basis of being it must also embrace theology, taking <u>theos</u> to be (for Heidegger) no more than the name given to the universal ground of being. Metaphysics must therefore be, according to Rahner's interpretation of Heidegger, an <u>ontotheology</u>, an unlimited enquiry into being as such and the ground of being through which the traditional limits of enquiry in philosophy and theology can be transcended.[9]

It must be noted that Rahner, unlike Balthasar, was required first of all to prepare to teach philosophy and later actually to teach theology within the Jesuit scholastic tradition. Thus Rahner was less free than Balthasar to reflect creatively on the ideal method in theology. Rahner had to find a compromise between his own wish to provide theology which was orthodox, credible, coherent and articulate, and the discipline which had been imposed upon him in his own Jesuit seminary training and which still guided his teaching in Catholic theological faculties.

Rahner commented upon his own method in theology on a number of occasions, especially in the latter years. These writings do not refer specifically to criticisms of his method. Nevertheless, they are defensive in tone, and they constitute an implicit response to all his critics, including Hans Urs von Balthasar.

In 1970 Peter Eicher published his dissertation, a philosophical work on Rahner's anthropological starting-point.[10] In his foreword to Eicher's book Rahner dismisses

---

"Wagnis"-Theologie: Erfahrungen mit der Theologie K. Rahners, Mystik und die Theologie Karl Rahners, 99-112. A. Grün, also treats of the influence of Ignatius on Rahner's theology of the cross in Erlösung durch das Kreuz. Karl Rahners Beitrag zu einem heutigen Erlösungsverständnis, Münsterschwarzach: Vier-Türme Verlag, 1975.

[8]Cf. for example: Foundations of Christian faith, 44-89; Theological investigations 21, 60, 196-207.

[9]Cf. K. Rahner, The concept of existential philosophy in Heidegger, Philosophy today 13, 1969, 126-137. Cf. further J. Macquarrie, Twentieth century religious thought, 353-358; ibid., Existentialism, 190-202.

[10]P. Eicher, Die anthropologische Wende. Karl Rahners philosophischer Weg vom Wesen des Menschen zur personalen Existenz. An abridged version of Rahner's introduction to this work is reproduced in Theological investigations 17, 243-248. C. Fabro, in an appendix to his La svolta antropologica di Karl Rahner (237-247), has sharply criticised Eicher's work.

any claims to being, or to having been, a philosopher.[11] He is even cautious about claiming to be a theologian, admitting that

> apart from a few essays on the history of penance nothing I have written can be called theological scholarship, let alone (professional) philosophy. It is all far too amateurish for that - but rightly so, in the modern situation we have described; I am not ashamed of the fact. I do not believe that a judgement of this kind involves a depreciation of what I have written. I even believe that when one talks to people today who want to know something "existential", it is the only way one can talk and write.[12]

It is the only way one can write, according to Rahner, because everywhere today knowledge is characterised by the existence of pluralities of disciplines. In an age of "gnoseological concupiscence", no one individual can hope to express his convictions on the basis of a process of reflection which has investigated each and every detail.[13] What has to be said today can no longer be said with scholarly exactitude and complete reflection.[14] But it still must be said. Therefore Rahner maintains that

> a new literary genre (Genus litterarium) is developing because it simply has to develop. This genre is neither theological nor philosophical scholarship; nor is it literature; nor is it the popularisation of theology and philosophy; it is - yes, what is it? At all events, it is the case today that if one works on philosophy in a specialised and scholarly way...one ceases to get anywhere at all.[15]

What Rahner precisely means by this new literary genre is difficult to discern. He comes closest to a definition when he describes his own writings as at once much more and much less than scholarship: less than scholarship in that the dimensions of the reflections which are collectively possible today are beyond the reach of any one individual; more than scholarship because an attempt is made to say something which "may minister salvation". Rahner ends his introduction to Eicher's book by asking the reader to pay more attention to what he wanted to say than to what he actually said, pleading that in matters of theology and philosophy today "the difference

---

[11]"Denn Sie sind ein Philosoph und haben was ich schrieb, als solcher Philosoph der Aufmerksamkeit wert gehalten. Und ich bin halt Theologe, vorsichtiger: ich möchte Theologe sein und eigentlich sonst nichts. Einfach, weil ich kein Philosoph bin und mir nicht einbilde, einer sein zu können. Nicht weil ich die Philosophie verachte oder unwichtig halte, sondern gerade, weil ich einen Heidenrespekt vor ihr habe" (K. Rahner. In: P. Eicher, op. cit., ix).

[12]Theological investigations 17, 247.

[13]Concerning "gnoseological concupiscence" see Theological investigations 11, 74-75; Sacramentum Mundi 5, 21.

[14]Theological investigations 17, 246-247.

[15]Theological investigations 17, 246.

between what is said and what is meant is greater than ever before".[16] In a Festschrift to commemorate his eightieth birthday, Rahner comments on his own method in more detailed terms which are of ultimate significance in our evaluation of Balthasar's criticisms, and indeed of all criticism of Karl Rahner. Acknowledging the influence which Ignatius of Loyola had upon him, Rahner goes on to admit that

> as a Jesuit, I do not feel myself bound to a particular school of theology and even less to a particular school of philosophy. On the whole I have valued Maréchal's interpretation of thomistic philosophy more than that of Suarez in which I was first educated. Naturally one can make the reproach against such a contemporary philosophy and theology which I have pursued that it results in eclecticism (Eklektizismus). But where in the world is there a systematic philosophy and theology which avoids the reproach of eclecticism? And how else can one pursue theology today than in the widest possible confrontation and widest possible dialogue with all the enormous diversity in the anthropological sciences? How can such a theology, which tries above all to listen, and wants above all to learn, avoid the reproach of eclecticism? Naturally I know that in my theology perhaps much that is said is unclear and does not fit together clearly (nicht klar zusammenpaßt). Because of the pluralism in the sources of one's knowledge, one is not at all in the position to conduct an adequate and comprehensive reflection on the coherence of one's sentences.[17]

These admissions by Rahner regarding his own method might seem at first sight to remove the need for any further discussion of Balthasar's criticisms. However, that is not the case. If we re-examine Balthasar's critcisms in the light of the above comment by Rahner on his own method it becomes clear that Rahner avoids the kind of reduction Balthasar accuses him of, precisely because he is eclectic. In fact Rahner must be methodologically eclectic to avoid deducing the reality of the absolute from the human spirit's openness to the absolute. To show that this is the case we must re-examine that part of Rahner's method which most concerns us, i.e. the functioning of the "agent intellect" as presented in Spirit in the world and Hearers of the word.

The agent intellect is the power which makes all rational knowledge possible by enabling us to know something in particular precisely as something in particular.

---

[16]op. cit., 248

[17]K. Rahner. In: K. Lehmann, ed. Vor dem Geheimnis Gottes den Menschen verstehen, 114-115. Cornelio Fabro (op. cit.) sharply rejects Rahner's eclecticism, queries his interpretation of Aquinas, stresses his reliance on the early Heidegger and argues that Rahner's methodological difficulties result from his excessive preoccupation with addressing contemporary questions: "Un mistificare ascendente allora: da Heidegger, attraverso Kant, fino a san Tommaso? Se non Rahner, troppo occupato nello scrivere sui nuovi problemi del giorno almeno qualche rahneriano potrebbe, anzi dovrebbe, rispondere a simili interrogativi (p.96) ....Se Rahner non avesse avuto, come sembra, l'appoggio di una parte notevole dell'episcopato tedesco, tutto sarebbe finito in una bolla di sapone" (p.97, n.122). Cf. further especially pp. 87, 95, 203. Rahner never replied to Fabro's criticisms.

When we examine the agent intellect we realise that a process of <u>abstraction</u> is at work, itself based on two logical principles: the principles of identity and of non-contradiction.   My ability to distinguish between two beings depends upon my realisation that they have something in common. My grasp that they have something in common is logically prior to my grasp that they are different. But I only become aware of this prior grasp simultaneously with my awareness of the distinction between the objects under discussion.

It is in and through my grasping of particular objects <u>as</u> distinct and particular objects that I realise that I have a grasp of their common element. In other words, I know beings because I know being, but it is only in coming to know beings as beings that I realise that I also know being. Because the structures of human knowledge are not a finite system, the process of abstraction can disclose a notion of absolute being.[18] This is so because whenever I come up against a limit if I am able to recognise it as a limit, then in some way I have already gone beyond it. Take the human eye. It is a finite system in that it can only recognise colours. Is it aware that it can only recognise colours? Obviously not, for if it were aware that it sees only colours then it would have some implicit grasp of what belongs to the world of non-colour. It would have at least a negative understanding of what is not colour. A truly finite system cannot reach beyond itself, which it must do if it is even to be aware of its finiteness. Putting this more technically, the knowing power specified by a finite formal object cannot recognise its own finiteness as such.

Now returning to the system which is the human intellect, what do we consider to represent its ultimate limitations? Space and time? How do we know that these represent the limitations of human knowledge? It would seem to follow from the above that the fact that we realise that we are restricted (limited) by space and time implies that we possess at least a negative notion of what lies beyond space and time. Another way of putting this is that the fact that we can recognise things as <u>contingent</u> implies that we have an implicit grasp of the <u>absolute</u>. To be aware that there are realities beyond one's grasp is already to have some implicit grasp of them, some pre-understanding. This <u>Vorgriff</u> (literally, pre-grasp) functions throughout the whole system of being.

The agent intellect discloses a <u>Vorgriff</u> which is of unlimited possibility. We become aware of it in and through the process of abstraction, i.e. in which we think away particular limits until we arrive at limitlessness. We have a <u>Vorgriff</u> of the infinite;

---

[18]This understanding of the structures of human knowledge Rahner has borrowed from Heidegger.

we have a <u>Vorgriff</u> of God.

An anthropological reduction?

The core of Balthasar's argument in his review of <u>Spirit in the world</u>, in <u>Love alone the way of revelation</u>, <u>Cordula oder der Ernstfall</u> and in <u>Theodramatik</u>, is that Rahner grounds his theology upon the framework of idealistic philosophy and inevitably must argue directly from the human spirit's openness to the infinite to the reality of the infinite. Were Rahner to ground his theology consistently in idealistic philosophy, Balthasar's criticisms would be entirely valid, and Rahner's chosen starting-point would lead him where he would rather not go. However, Rahner, by his own admission, does not ground his argument consistently in any one system. His own method presents a totally new system and not only has he borrowed concepts but he has given them a meaning of his own. Rahner's concept of the <u>Vorgriff</u> comes closest to that of Heidegger, as Balthasar recognises.[19] But Rahner's concept of the <u>Vorgriff</u> differs critically and fundamentally from Heidegger's as we shall now show.

For Heidegger the <u>Vorgriff</u> reveals a pre-grasp of the universal ground of being (<u>Sein</u>). First, if one's search for the ultimate ground of being is to be truly philosophical one must admit the possibility that the universal ground of being is nothingness. Second, Heidegger does not identify being with the Christian notion of God, i.e. he does not identify absolute being with Being, and is in fact dismissive of crypto-theologians passing themselves off as philosophers who make a gigantic leap with the aid of a capital letter.[20] For Heidegger, the agent intellect reveals either being or nothingness, and the possibility of the human being in his or her ontological situation (<u>Dasein</u>) becoming nothing must be taken seriously. For Heidegger <u>Dasein</u> can only live authentically by reckoning with the possibility of ceasing to exist, i.e. the possibility of becoming non-being. <u>Dasein</u> must accept "the possibility of his pure and simple impossibility".[21] This is a precondition of authentic existence. <u>Dasein</u> must learn how to die in order to live. Death is the veil which reveals being. To detract from, or transform in any way, the radical nature of "nothingness" in

---

[19] review of <u>Geist in Welt</u>, 372.

[20] Cf. J. P. Mackey, <u>Modern theology</u>, 20; H. U. von Balthasar, Meeting God in today's world, <u>Concilium</u> 6, 1, 28.

[21] K. Rahner, The concept of existential philosophy in Heidegger, <u>Philosophy today</u>, 13, 1969, 134.

Heidegger is to depart radically from him.[22] This is precisely what Rahner does. He argues that the Vorgriff must be the ground of that towards which it reaches.[23] If the Vorgriff exists then it cannot be reaching toward nothing. Were the Vorgriff to reach towards absolute nothingness then we would not be able to draw a distinction between what is contingent and what is necessary. All we would know is what is contingent and not only would the need for this distinction or for two categories not arise, but the distinction itself would be impossible. The very fact that we can distinguish between what is absolute and what is contingent implies that the Vorgriff is not empty but possesses some content. It cannot therefore be nothing. Even if our knowledge of the absolute is a negative knowledge, it is nevertheless real. The agent intellect necessarily reveals the absolute as real, but unknown. It provokes the question, which one must ask oneself, whether God has revealed himself in the world. This is a radical departure from Heidegger and represents the kind of argumentation which Heidegger not only deliberately avoided but severely criticised.[24] It is an argument which is theological rather than ontotheological.

In addition to ruling out nothingness as a possibility, Rahner also shifts from Heidegger's notion of being to the Christian notion of God. For Heidegger's notion of being (Sein) cannot be spoken about apart from the individual being (Dasein) who, in his or her existential situation, possesses a Vorgriff of Sein and in whom Sein comes to expression. For Rahner, the first a priori of human transcendence reveals itself as the infinity of the absolute and Dasein's true destiny becomes a choice between eternal death and eternal life before God, and not merely resoluteness toward death. Rahner argues that to jar one loose from the pure idea and cast one into one's own existence and into history, as Heidegger does, is to prepare one in advance for

---

[22]As Rahner himself admits, "This transcendence towards nothingness thus becomes the express condition, first and last, in order that a being appears for Dasein in the light of being" (The concept of existential philosophy in Heidegger, Philosophy today 13, 1969, 135).

[23]"To ground" means to draw and set in motion the reality which one experiences as one's real life (Foundations of Christian faith, 33).

[24]"In Heidegger's view, religious people commonly use what they choose to call religious faith for the sorry purpose of suppressing the most elemental consciousness of reality which human beings can have and which is indeed definitive of the human condition. And this misrepresents the whole of reality. For although reflective consciousness is the inevitable source of the awareness of that insidious nothingness which taints everything, it is not, so far as it is aware, the source of that nothingness. If it were the source of nothingness it could conceivably, by a self-injection of some verbally revealed certainty, rid itself and all reality of the fatal disease. Reflective consciousness does taint all it perceives with the awareness of nothingness - it must consider the non-existence even of God..." (J. P. Mackey, op.cit., 20).

the existential and historical fact of a divine revelation. It is to open one to the God of Abraham, Isaac, and Jacob, "to the Word of Life, seen, heard, touched by human hands, Jesus of Nazareth".[25]

It is at this point that the interlocking between philosophy and theology takes place. Rahner, while still arguing "philosophically" (insofar as he argues purely philosophically at all), assumes God, and thereby avoids deducing the reality of God from the reality of the desire for God.

In addition, when Rahner claims that "what grounds man's openness and his reaching out in the unlimited expanse of his transcendence cannot be nothingness",[26] he is making a theological claim, for another reason: were this a purely philosophical claim, Rahner would be providing us with a philosophical-logical argument for the existence of God - which he never claimed to do. In fact he specifically claimed the opposite in Spirit in the world:

> This is in no sense an a priori proof of God's existence. For the pre-apprehension and its "whither" can be proven and affirmed as present and necessary for all knowledge only in the a posteriori apprehension of a real existent and as the necessary condition of the latter.

[27]Rahner avoids attempting to provide a philosophical proof for the existence of God because he is not arguing purely philosophically. As Ratzinger comments,

> the transcendental method does not pretend to deduce Christianity purely from itself; it is a presupposition of understanding (Verstehensvorgang) which becomes possible because the faith had already opened up the field of thought...[28]

And according to Lehmann, one can only postulate a reduction in Rahner's theology

---

[25]K. Rahner, The concept of existential philosophy in Heidegger, 137.

[26]Foundations of Christian faith, 34.

[27]K. Rahner, Spirit in the world, 181.

[28]J. Ratzinger, Vom Verstehen des Glaubens. Anmerkungen zu Rahners Grundkurs des Glaubens, Theologische Revue, 74, 1978, 184. Ratzinger describes the critical moment in Rahner's theology as providing the necessary Verschmelzung, i.e. a merging or a blending: "Im Begriff der Aszendenzchristologie scheinen mir gemeinhin zwei unterschiedliche Moment miteinander verknüpt. Einmal meint er, daß der Weg vom Menschen Jesus her zum Logos und zum Sohn genommen, also Theologie aus Anthropologie entwickelt wird und nicht umgekehrt, wie es in der Deszendenzchristologie geschieht. Zum anderen verbindet sich damit die Vorstellung, daß der Ausgangspunkt bei dem in der Bibel begegnenden Menschen Jesus genommen und von diesem aposteriorischen Befund her die Christologie als Ganze aufgebaut wird. Was den ersten Gesichtspunkt anlangt, so zeigt Rahners ganze philosophisch-theologische Konstruktion m. E. recht gut die notwendige Verschmelzung der beiden Wege. Einerseits wird der Gottesbegriff vermittelt, aber andererseits kann gerade hypostatische Union nicht allein vom Ausgriff des Menschen her entfaltet werden, sondern bedarf der geschehenen Antwort Gottes, die im Ausgriff irgendwie erwartbar, aber nicht aus ihm deduzierbar ist" (art. cit., 182, emphasis mine).

if one presumes

> that he first developed a philosophical system which he then applied to theological questions. Basically one cannot in fact distil a philosophically pure structure (kein reines philosophisches Gefüge) out of this theology.[29]

While acknowledging, significantly, that the reader of Spirit in the world could be forgiven for having this impression, he says that for Rahner (and this includes the Rahner of Hearers of the word)

> within the framework of catholic theology there is no pure philosophy which is capable of being delimited or separated.[30]

At the end of this chapter we will examine in more general terms Rahner's understanding of the relationship between philosophy and theology. As a result of our examination it will be clear that for Rahner there is no such thing as a pure philosophy and that such is the interlocking (Verschränkung) which exists between human experience and divine revelation that it is impossible in theology to argue solely "from above" or "from below".

Knowledge and the senses

Balthasar is also concerned about the way in which, as he sees it, for both Maréchal

---

[29]K. Lehmann, Karl Rahner. Ein Porträt. In: K. Lehmann, and A. Raffelt, Rechenschafts des Glaubens, 33.

[30]loc. cit. Schwerdtfeger, a student of Lehmann's, fully endorses Lehmann's assessment of Rahner and consequently dismisses Balthasar's criticisms of Rahner as presented in Cordula oder der Ernstfall (N. Schwerdtfeger, Gnade und Welt, Freiburg: Herder, 1982, 56). Schwerdtfeger has provided a very detailed and precise evaluation of Balthasar's critisms of Rahner and I am indebted to his work here. Winterholler in his dissertation on the concept of freedom in Rahner's theology is also convinced that Rahner avoids an anthropological reduction:"The human being in his spiritual existence is referred to the absolute mystery. With this concept Rahner prevents an anthropological reduction from the outset and clearly refuses an absolute anthropocentricism" (H. Winterholler, Schöpferische Freiheit in christlicher Anthropozentrik. Zur Freiheitslehre Karl Rahners, Diss. theol. Pont. Univ. Gregoriana, Rome, 1973). Fiorenza, in his introduction to Spirit in the world (p. xli) also claims that Rahner, through his use of Heidegger, avoids a reduction. C. Geffré agrees that, "Rahner can only avoid the danger of a necessary deduction by using an anthropology which already owes much to the light of revelation" (Recent developments in fundamental theology, Concilium 5, 1969, 9). In his analysis of transcendental Thomism, MacKinnon points out that transcendental Thomists, Rahner included, while taking the linguistic turn, have no great difficulty in establishing a metaphysics, whereas non-Thomists, e.g. Heidegger, do not seem to have this facility at all. This is because, he argues, the non-Thomists are sincerely questioning the possibility of a metaphysics while the Thomists are merely using an analysis of questioning as a methodological device for justifying a metaphysics whose validity has not really been questioned. Such questioning is readily satisfied by answers that lead from the chosen starting-point to the pre-determined conclusion. Cf. E. MacKinnon, The transcendental turn: necessary but not sufficient, Continuum 6, 1968, 225.

and Rahner knowledge is made dependent upon the senses for its content.[31] But Rahner's position, once again through the influence of Heidegger, differs significantly from Maréchal's.

Whereas for Kant, the act of knowing is passive and what we perceive is brought automatically into accordance with pre-determined categories of the human mind, Maréchal argues by contrast that the act of knowing is already a kind of reality. When I know something I am actively doing something. Therefore knowledge is not something passively received or undergone but an active dynamic process. Being is already an a priori condition of knowing. This means that the innate ideas of the world, the soul and God, which Kant excluded as invalid or illusory sources of objective knowledge, are a priori conditions of possibility for the objective categorical judgements of human reason. In arriving at this conclusion Maréchal was influenced by Fichte. Fichte had argued that the human subject has an intellectual intuition of its own spiritual activity of knowing and willing. This makes one aware that one's activity of knowing and willing is fundamentally a striving toward the absolute. He claimed that the dynamism of the mind is a constitutive element of both speculative and practical reason. A real dynamism must have a real goal as its term. Therefore if the mind's striving toward the absolute is one of the a priori conditions of the speculative reason's objective judgements, God's real existence is an a priori condition of possibility of every categorical judgement of the speculative reason. Further, God's real existence is an a priori condition of possibility for any judgement whatsoever. Therefore a judgement which denies God's existence is a contradiction.

Maréchal relied upon on a neo-Kantian interpretation of Kant's theory of knowledge, in which the importance of judgement was played down, all judgements being taken to be purely logical, i.e. a synthesis of subject and predicate, and in which it was considered that intuitions have a greater role to play. Heidegger's understanding of Kant restored proper importance to the role played by the judgement.

Now Maréchal, as Balthasar correctly observes, attempts to establish the metaphysical significance of the judgement primarily as a result of a transcendental reduction. Rahner however, asserts the primary unity and convertibility of being and knowledge, within which the dependence of knowledge upon the senses must be understood. As Heidegger's understanding of the circular structure of all knowledge illustrates, being

---

[31]"Der Ansatz der Problematik ist (wie bei Maréchal) die absolute Bindung der Erkenntnis an die Sinnlichkeit; nicht nur als Ausgangspunkt, sondern als einzige Quelle inhaltlichen Wissens" (H. U. von Balthasar, Zeitschrift für Katholische Theologie 63, 1939, 375).

is at once known and unknown.[32] <u>Dasein</u> knows <u>a priori</u> about being, since the intellect cannot inquire about that which is totally unknown. But the fact that <u>Dasein</u> can and indeed must ask about being, means that <u>Dasein</u> is not already present to the goal of enquiry. Rahner holds that the human being is able to continue questioning because, in contrast to the position adopted by German idealism, the human being's possession of being is not absolute but finite. Rahner can only make this claim to an absolute/finite distinction, i.e. he can only argue that the human being's possession of being is finite, because, parting company with Heidegger, he cannot but assume God into his system from the very outset.[33]

Philosophy and theology

In order to allay fully Balthasar's fear that Rahner's theological system has been subsumed within a philosophical system which alienates theology from its purpose and goal, it is necessary at this point to dwell a little on Rahner's overall position concerning the relationship between philosophy and theology.[34] But before doing this, perhaps a clarification regarding Balthasar's attitude to philosophy is necessary. Perhaps I have painted a bleak picture of how Balthasar views philosophy. It would be wrong to form a judgement on Balthasar's attitude to philosophy as a whole based entirely on his criticism of Rahner's reliance upon philosophy. Balthasar has respect for philosophy.[35] He recognises that philosophy has a role to play, but this role is much minor and very different from that envisaged by Karl Rahner. It has been possible to examine here only Balthasar's criticism of what he considers to be the improper employment of modern philosophy. It is philosophy's role with respect to theology which is on trial.

Tor return to a consideration of the relationship between philosophy and theology according to Rahner, the first point is that according to Rahner this relationshp is a

---

[32]Heidegger tries to develop a corresponding understanding of truth as a process of unconcealment, rather than as <u>adaequatio rei et intellectus</u>.

[33]For a more detailed account of the influence of Maréchal on Rahner see Fiorenza, <u>op. cit.</u>, xxxv-xlv; G. McCool, <u>A Rahner Reader</u>, xiii-xvi.

[34]The following articles provide us with this overview: Philosophy and theology, <u>Theological investigations</u> 6, 71-81; Philosophy and philosophising in theology, <u>Theological investigations</u> 9, 46-63, and On the current relationship between philosophy and theology, <u>Theological investigations</u> 13, 61-79.

[35]See, for example, the third part of Balthasar's trilogy, <u>Theologik</u>.

particular case of the relationship which exists between nature and grace.[36] We have
already examined Rahner's understanding of the relationship which exists between
nature and grace in describing the supernatural existential and in the next chapter we
will examine Rahner's overall presentation of the structure of revelation more closely.
At this stage, however, one of Rahner's most important presuppositions must be
stressed: God's universal will to save implies that there is a general revelation of God
which is co-extensive with the history of the world.[37] It follows from this, according
to Rahner, that there cannot be any such thing as a pure philosophy:

> In his thinking, man as philosopher is in fact constantly subject to a theological a
> priori, namely that transcendental determination which orientates him towards the
> immediate presence of God.[38]

What Rahner is saying here is that the human being's theologising does not begin
when he or she encounters pronouncements of the Church, or scripture. On account
of God's universal desire for the salvation of all humankind it has already begun in
a gracious self-communication which has previously taken place at the transcendental
level. For this reason, there can be no such thing as pure philosophy. In fact,
because the person philosophising is theologically determined from the outset, it is
more accurate to describe philosophy - and this is an important point - as an inner
moment within theology, just as nature is understood as an inner moment within
grace.[39] Rahner, I believe, understands theology as liberating the believer to do
philosophy with confidence.

To further demonstrate the unity which must exist between philosophy and theology
we need only to recall that the human being seeks unity in knowledge. When I learn
something new, I immediately confront it with the knowledge I already possess.
Philosophising happens in theology whenever I radically confront the message of faith

---

[36]Cf. Theological investigations 6, 72-73; Theological investigations 9, 46.

[37]Theological investigations 13, 62. This point is more fully explained in the next chapter.

[38]Theological investigations 13, 63.

[39]Theological investigations 6, 72. It is interesting in this context to note that in the mid-19th
century John Henry Newman articulated a similar view in his classic, The idea of a university, which
began as his foundation discourse for the ill-fated Catholic university for Ireland. Defending the right
of theology to a place in the university programme he insisted that "university teaching without
theology is simply unphilosophical" (Discourse II, p. 80). In the subsequent discourse, "The bearing
of theology on other knowledge", he concluded thus: "In a word, religious truth is not only a portion
but a condition of general knowledge. To blot it out is nothing short, if I may so speak, of
unravelling the web of university teaching. It is, according to the Greek proverb, to take the Spring
from out of the year; it is to imitate the preposterous proceeding of those tragedians who represented
a drama with the omission of its principal part" (Discourse III, p.103).

with my understanding of existence and the world. My knowledge of the Christian faith and of the world continues to expand and interlock as I grow in understanding. Insofar as philosophy is genuine philosophy - an unrestricted search for the truth - there can be no irreconcilable contradiction between philosophy and theology. Both have as their ultimate source God, the one Truth. Contradictions arise only when philosophy restricts its field of operations, when it excludes something from the outset as a subject which is a priori alien to it.

Rahner is arguing, therefore, that if philosophy, in an attempt to remain "pure", a priori brackets the possibility of the human spirit's ultimate orientation to the immediate presence of God out of its field of study, then it ceases to be philosophy.

Why then, maintain a distinction between philosophy and theology at all? From the theologian's point of view there would not seem to be any point. Balthasar argues, for example, that

> Christianity places man in a relationship which leaves far behind the services of a metaphysical knowledge of God and makes this practically superfluous. Therefore, theological metaphysics actually died the day Christ was born...Heidegger asserts that a Christian metaphysics is a contradiction, since one who already knows God can no longer honestly ask about the mystery of being.[40]

And on this point Rahner would seem to be in agreement with both Balthasar and Heidegger. He says that

> philosophy is properly speaking a theology that has not yet arrived at the fullness of its own nature.[41]

Insofar as philosophy arrives at a full recognition of the human being's transcendental determination by virtue of God's self-communication which is present always and everywhere, it should no longer be called philosophy, but theology. Rahner recognises first that, to adapt Balthasar's words, purely philosophical knowledge of God is not possible (in the light of our understanding of salvation history as co-extensive with the history of the world), and second that even "impurely" philosophical knowledge of God died the day Christ was born.

However, Rahner recognises that "the day Christ is born" dawns at different times and in different places for each individual, and, perhaps we could add, within each individual as well. Philosophy is still necessary if we wish to enter into dialogue with those who have not yet come to an explicit knowledge of the revelation which takes place in Jesus Christ, or with systems which do not recognise divine revelation. It is

---

[40]Meeting God in today's world, Concilium 6, 1, 1965, 28. For a further account of how Balthasar understands philosophy to be superseded by theology see The Glory of the Lord 1, 144ff.

[41]Theological investigations 13, 65.

even necessary - I think Rahner would argue - to do philosophy if we are to enter into dialogue with the unbeliever within ourselves. It is therefore both possible and necessary to maintain a distinction between philosophy and theology within that study which is seen by the theologian as an ever greater and more obvious unity.

Whereas Balthasar sees the relationship between philosophy and theology only from the theologian's point of view, Rahner is prepared to see the situation from the philosopher's point of view, intending the word "philosopher" here to describe the person who philosophises, the person who has not as yet arrived at a satisfactorily explicit recognition that he or she is living in the immediate presence of God's gracious self-communication personally addressed to him or her. Philosophy, which the theologian might recognise as a defective theology, is indispensable to theology if as theologians we are

> not taking the easy way out, not trying to talk merely to the person who believes in any case, but to the doubter, to the person who is earnestly questioning and to him who does not believe; not by quoting the formal authority of scripture and the magisterium in particular questions of dogma, but by trying to render the matter intrinsically worthy of belief.[42]

This understanding of the unity and distinction which must exist between theology and philosophy, and of the indispensability of philosophy to theology if theology is to mediate the Christian faith credibly, is totally endorsed by Kasper when he writes:

> Theology can preserve its identity only if it has the courage to immerse itself in the alien realm of philosophy - not to commit suicide there or to degenerate into a philosophy of religion, but to truly find itself. In losing itself, theology will be able to show how its faith overcomes the world (1 Jn. 5: 4). In other words, theology cannot be reflected in the common heritage of human thought unless it moves this heritage beyond itself as well.[43]

What happens when theology finds itself confronted with a philosophy which is not only suspicious of theology's most precious claims, but actually rejects these claims and proposes a contradictory claim to the truth about the ultimate determination of humankind? In this situation, as we saw already, Balthasar believed that theology could have nothing to do with such a modern philosophy. Rahner has no hesitation in admitting that philosophy is subject to the judgement of theology. However, he cautions the theologian in exercising such judgement, to avoid thinking that he or she is the sole representative of the Spirit of God.[44] When theology exercises critical judgement on philosophy, however:

---

[42]Theological investigations 9, 52.

[43]W. Kasper, The methods of theology, 60.

[44]Theological investigations 13, 65.

it is attempting first and foremost to lay bare the hidden sinfulness or the hidden
state of grace bestowed upon it by the Spirit, inherent in all philosophy, even
though philosophy itself does not recognise either of these states at the level of
conscious reflection.[45]

To conclude this section we return to consider the particular case of the nature of the
relationship which must exist between contemporary philosophy and theology.
According to Rahner, the contemporary situation is significantly different from that
of previous ages in that no one, ready-made, uniform and coherent philosophical
system is at theology's disposal. Our age is, to use Rahner's description again, one
of "gnoseological concupiscence": there is a pluralism of understandings of the world
and existence which no one individual is capable of integrating adequately. Indeed,
not only have we an irreducible pluralism in philosophies, we also have a pluralism
in theologies.[46] In such a situation the theologian must either avoid all philosophy,
which is arguably impossible and which in any case would compromise theology in
its attempt to mediate the Christian faith credibly and in a language which can be
understood by all, or the theologian must take the risk of engaging in dialogue with
philosophy, but on theology's terms and therefore eclectically.

From the above examination of Rahner's understanding of the relationship between
philosophy and theology it is clear that for him theology cannot be subsumed within
an alien philosophical system. Rather, genuine philosophy is always a moment within
theology, and one which enables theology to find itself. Viewing philosophy as
theologians, Balthasar and Rahner are substantially in agreement. However, Rahner
recognises that many of those whom theology seeks to address do not share the
theologian's perspective on reality at least at the explicit level and for him philosophy
- even contemporary philosophy, carefully discerned - provides a bridge between
these people and the theologian. The theologian cannot ignore these people: the
theologian has a responsibility to mediate the Christian faith credibly to them.

---

[45]Theological investigations 13, 66.

[46]Theological investigations 9, 54-56.

Chapter 5
The Anonymous Christian: a relativisation?

Introduction

The aim of this chapter is to examine Rahner's presentation of how grace is present to, and active in, the lives of non-Christians in the light of Balthasar's conviction that this constitutes an unacceptable relativisation of Jesus Christ and the Church.

In his biography of Rahner, Vorgrimler points out Rahner's personal loyalty and devotion to the Church. In every sense of the word, he claims, Rahner was essentially a "Churchman" and was critical of those who voiced non-constructive criticism of the Church.[1] Vorgrimler recalls that one of the few times Rahner became angry over matters theological was when a journal, of whose advisory body he was a member, published a letter supporting Küng's criticism of infallibility. For Rahner, who strove to be a faithful disciple of Ignatius as did Balthasar, the latter's criticism must have given him cause for serious reflection. Yet Rahner did not respond specifically to the objection that his theology undermined explicit Christianity. Nevertheless, references in certain articles in Theological investigations would seem to take this criticism into account. For example, in discussing the possibility of faith in contemporary society, Rahner stresses that Christianity is the "recognition and homecoming of everything in the way of truth and love which exists or could exist anywhere else."[2] And in an effort to underline Christianity's uniqueness he urges:

Try to understand what Christianity means! Make comparisons! Listen carefully to what Christianity has to say! Hear its message most exactly but also listen with all the breadth of the spirit and the heart. If you do this you will never hear anything elsewhere which is good, true and redemptive, which illuminates man's existence and opens up his reality into the infinity of the divine mystery - anything which is not to be found also in Christianity.[3]

On one occasion Rahner even suggests that Christians have a better chance of salvation than non-Christians.[4] With Heinrich Ott, Weger explains this as follows: the aspect of consciousness in Christian knowledge is not only a "plus" in knowledge

---

[1]H. Vorgrimler, Understanding Karl Rahner, 36.

[2]Theological investigations 5, 9.

[3]loc. cit.

[4]"...the individual who grasps Christianity in a clearer, purer and more reflective way has, other things being equal, a still greater chance of salvation than someone who is merely an anonymous Christian" (K. Rahner, Theological investigations 5, 132). For an account of how the conferring of a sacrament can increase justifying grace see Theological investigations 12, 173.

but also a "plus" in being, and results in a commitment of life in the light of faith.[5] However, as Weger partially admits, this argument is incompatible with Rahner's basic premise. Rahner does not really wish to imply that it is harder for the non-Christian to be saved, for this would introduce a kind of a "lottery" element into the plan of salvation. At the same time the non-Christian lacks something, for

> (he) is not a Christian at the social level (through baptism and membership of the Church) or in the sense of having consciously objectified his Christianity to himself in his own mind (by explicit Christian faith resulting from having harkened to the explicit Christian message).[6]

But whatever the non-Christian lacks, it is not essential to the attaining of salvation, for he or she can be addressed by the God of Jesus Christ through the Holy Spirit, and enabled by God's grace to make a free response which may be an acceptance of God's gracious self-offer. Rahner is keen to point out that this is not the ideal or most desirable situation. But it is the most common one, and insofar as we can be optimistic about the effectiveness of God's universal salvific will, it must be admitted that this would seem to be how the majority of people are saved. Does this doctrine of the Church regarding the universal salvific will not itself relativise the role of the Church? Is there any way of remaining optimistic about the possibility of salvation for those lacking explicit contact with the Church and explicit knowledge of the historical Christ-event, without at the same time assigning only a relative role vis-à-vis their salvation, to the historical Jesus of Nazareth and to the Church?

Whereas non-Christian religions and philosophies provide categorical interpretations of transcendental revelation which are sometimes more or less successful, according to Rahner it is only in Jesus Christ that the absolute, irrevocable and irreversible interpretation of the revelation of God has taken place.[7] All human beings, before and after the time of Jesus Christ, have sought this ultimate interpretation of what they have already transcendentally experienced. In this ultimate interpretation both the relationship between God and humanity, and the relationship among human beings themselves, reach their truest and highest expression. This ultimate interpretation lives on in the Church. But how is this ultimate interpretation essential, related to, and determining of the other partial interpretations? How are these extra-ecclesial

---

[5]K. - H. Weger, op. cit., 121.

[6]Theological investigations, 283.

[7]This answers Williams' question: "Given that the transcendental Vorgriff cannot operate without some categorical occasion, how are we to understand the categorical element in revelation to non-Christians?" (Balthasar and Rahner. In: J. Riches, ed., The analogy of beauty, 18).

interpretations absolutely dependent upon the ecclesial interpretation?

Before examining specific aspects of Balthasar's criticism, e.g. his objections to Rahner's supernatural existential, to the apparent over-simplistic identification of love of God with love of neighbour and to Rahner's seeming lack of a theology of the cross, it is necessary to situate these particular aspects of Rahner's theology within his presentation of the structure of revelation and salvation as a whole.

The structure of revelation according to Rahner

Rahner's most fundamental conviction is that those who do not close themselves to God through an ultimate act of free and personal sin for which they are culpable, find salvation. For Rahner this is a clear consequence of the Church's teaching on God's universal salvific will and the Church's obligation to be optimistic about the effectiveness of this salvific will.[8] Rahner's presentation of revelation and salvation, and arguably his theology as a whole, is an attempt to clarify the implications of the Church's conviction that it is God's will that all people be saved, a conviction which is only possible because of, and can only be rooted in, the saving mystery of Jesus Christ.

As Rahner already made clear in his earliest writings, God cannot reveal himself to historical human beings except in and through history.[9] The history of salvation and revelation must take place wherever individual and collective human history is taking place.[10] This means that human history, and the history of revelation and of salvation, must be co-extensive with each other. They are not, of course, the same. "Profane" history also embraces elements opposed to salvation which are a rejection of God e.g. guilt and sin. And salvation is essentially the result of God's self-offer enabling a free decision for the individual, a decision which cannot be recorded in the annals of history books. Yet the whole purpose of profane human history is human redemption, and despite the distinctions, profane history and salvation history are united towards this goal.

When we examine human history, we discover first of all what we may describe as "natural" revelation. Natural revelation describes the knowledge of God which human

---

[8]"Because of God's universal salvific will, a Christian has no right to limit the actual event of salvation to the explicit history of salvation in the Old and New Testaments, despite the theological axiom which has been current from the time of the Fathers down to our own times, namely, that outside the Church there is no salvation" (Foundations of Christian faith, 148).

[9]Hearers of the word, 133.

[10]Foundations of Christian faith, 145.

beings possess by virtue of the fact that they are finite creatures of God. In and through natural revelation, according to Rahner, God is present at best as a question, not as an answer.[11] God is known only as the unknown one, as mystery, negatively. His relationship with creatures remains ambiguous. By the light of natural revelation only, it is still unclear to us whether or not God wishes to be "a silent and impenetrable mystery keeping us at a distance in our finiteness" or whether he wishes to confront us in radical closeness and to communicate himself to us.[12] The history of natural revelation is recorded in the history of religious and philosophical knowledge of God, though the two histories cannot simply be identified one with the other, because, according to Rahner, in the concrete history of human knowledge of God, grace has also been at work.

When we speak about grace, we are speaking about God's coming to us in absolute freedom, offering himself to us in and through our concrete history. The human being can never begin to have anything to do with God without already having being addressed by God and borne by his grace.[13] Therefore, according to Rahner, every human being at all times in history and everywhere is informed not only by the light of natural revelation, but also by the light of supernatural revelation within the transcendental depths of one's being. Because this being addressed constitutes an existential modification of one's transcendental consciousness produced permanently by God's grace, it calls forth a response which, in freedom, may be either for or against God's self-offer. Though we are not, as yet, talking about thematically reflexive verbal or "propositional" revelation, what we are talking about differs critically from mere natural revelation because the transcendental moment in revelation orientates the human being towards the absolute immediacy and closeness of God. There is not any doubt or ambiguity regarding God's intention to enter into a relationship with humankind. Grace is offered and responded to, either positively or negatively.

For two reasons supernatural transcendental revelation necessarily seeks categorical expression.[14] On God's side, God's transcendental self-communication has its own dynamism which intends to bring about the divinisation of the creature in all its

---

[11]Foundations of Christian faith, 170-171.

[12]Foundations of Christian faith, 170.

[13]Foundations of Christian faith, 146.

[14]Cf. Foundations of Christian faith, 173.

dimensions. On the human side, this offer of grace occurs within human history and if we accept that history is moving the human being along towards an ever more adequate self-interpretation, it follows that there must be some self-interpretation of the supernatural, transcendental revelation at the historical categorical level. In other words, viewed both from human and divine standpoints, the transcendental and supernatural experience of God necessarily interprets itself historically and therefore forms a categorical history of revelation. If we now admit, with Rahner, that history is moving us along not only to an ever more adequate self-interpretation at the categorical level, but also to an ultimate self-interpretation at this level, it follows that there must be an ultimate historical, categorical interpretation of transcendental revelation. In Jesus Christ

> we have an event which, as an eschatological event, fundamentally and absolutely precludes any historical corruption or any distorted interpretation in the further history of categorical revelation and of false religion.[15]

The history of categorical revelation in the Old and New Testaments can and must be understood as the valid self-interpretation of God's transcendental communication to human beings. It is important to point out, however, that Rahner does not simply equate the history of categorical revelation with the Old and New Testament history of revelation.[16] By "categorical revelation" is meant an explicitly religious history of revelation which knows itself to be willed positively by God and to be directed by him. Categorical revelation, being the necessary historical manifestation of the transcendental and supernatural experience of God, is co-extensive with all of human history and therefore may be obscured by human guilt and depravity, but at the same time knows itself to be guided and directed by God, and this guarantees the success of its interpretation.

As Rahner points out, it is not detrimental to Christianity's absolute claims if, in the course of an examination of the history of religion, we see that other religions have managed a partially successful categorical interpretation of God's self-communication to them. It is merely an indication that the God of the Old and New Testament has in fact been at work among them despite their primitiveness or even depravity. We will return at the end of this chapter to examine the implications of the above for Rahner's understanding of non-Christian religions.

During his presentation of revelation Rahner is at pains to point out that it is only

---

[15]Foundations of Christian faith, 157.

[16]"...the categorical history of revelation... does not simply coincide unambiguously and exclusively with the Old and New Testament history of revelation" (Foundations of Christian faith, 155).

possible to structure the whole history of revelation in the light of Jesus Christ.[17]
This is true with regard to the Old Testament, for example. It is also only in the light
of Christ that we Christians can distinguish between the categorical history of
revelation in its pure and ultimate sense, and other less successful interpretations and
interpretations which are merely human substitutes.[18] Jesus Christ is the norm and
the measure.

If we accept that Christ is the fullness of revelation, then we are in a position to
recognise other incomplete elements of revelation, and entirely false interpretations.
Herein lies for Rahner the justification for making the otherwise outrageous claim that
we Christians can interpret non-Christians better than non-Christians can interpret
themselves. While it is entirely understandable that non-Christians may not wish to
be called anonymous Christians, it is a direct consequence of the claim that Christ is
the fullness of revelation and that all salvation comes through him that the Christian
is in a position to propose such an understanding.[19]

The centrality of Christ in Rahner's presentation of the structure of revelation is
already, of course, a partial response to Balthasar's criticism that Rahner relativises
the historical Christ-event. In answer to this objection, Rahner could argue that if the
term "relativisation" implies a dislocation of the Christ-event, this is simply not the
case. Rather, he seeks to re-locate within the history of revelation as a whole what
he holds to be the ultimate and normative revelation which takes place in the
incarnation.

We have already discussed the relationship between the transcendental and
categorical moments in revelation. If we take "categorical", to refer to our conscious
and explicit relationships with others and with the world around us, Rahner has
clearly shown that a categorical dimension is essential to transcendental revelation.
But if Balthasar were to frame his objection in these terms, he would surely ask: how
essential to this categorical dimension is the categorical revelation in the concrete
sense of what took place in the life, death and resurrection of Jesus Christ? When we
come to examine Rahner's soteriology we will see that this is precisely what is at
stake when Rahner attempts to show how for him the historical Christ-event (not just

---

[17]Foundations of Christian faith, 164-166.

[18]Foundations of Christian faith, 157.

[19]It must again be stressed, however, that it was not Rahner's original intention to describe non-
Christians as anonymous Christians. The term was originally intended only to be at the service of
the Christian's understanding of Christianity.

the incarnation but also Jesus' death on the cross), is both the "cause" and the "effect" of the Father's universal salvific will. As we shall see - and here Rahner comes very close to Balthasar's own position - he argues that in Jesus Christ, God's love-creating condescension becomes irreversible and unequivocally accessible in the salvation history of the world because through the cross the Holy Spirit is sent out into the hearts of all men and women. Transcendental revelation is essentially related to and dependent upon categorical revelation and the two can never really be spoken about independently of one another.

Salvation through Christ: symbol and sacrament

The different elements of God's self-communication, which, as the Christian recognises, climax in the ultimate revelation of God in Jesus Christ, all have one common goal and common purpose: redemption. This is the whole purpose of the created world, its history and God's breaking-in to this history. Towards this goal the order of creation and the order of redemption are united.[20]

Rahner's account of how this goal is actually realised in history is profoundly Christocentric. To understand this we must examine how Rahner understands Christ to be the sacrament of God the Father, and the Church to be the sacrament of Christ. But this can be understood only if we first grasp Rahner's understanding of symbol, which fulfils a similar function in his theology to that which the concept of form (Gestalt), developed from Goethe, does in Balthasar's aesthetics.

By "symbol" Rahner means the highest and most primordial manner in which one reality can represent another and still allow the other to be present.[21] The most basic principle of an ontology of symbolism is that all beings are by their nature symbolic: they necessarily express themselves in order to attain their own nature. The reason this is the case is that, according to the classic principle which Rahner inherits from Aristotle through Aquinas, all beings must realise themselves through a plurality in unity. This statement needs to be carefully understood: it is a cornerstone of Rahner's

---

[20]"God has not created two realities needing subsequently to be, so to speak, harmonised. Rather, he has constituted the whole of reality distinct from himself, to which he communicates himself according to one, ultimate, primordial intention, so that it all has a primordial unity and every difference in it springs from the unity as a mode of the unity itself, the unity preceding the differences which arise from it and which must precisely for its sake be respected" (K. Rahner, The Christian commitment, 52).

[21]K. Rahner, Theological investigations 4, 225.

whole theological system.[22]

First of all, to show that all beings are multiple and at the same time one, we can, with Haight, simply take the example of the human person.[23] The human person is a unity of matter and spirit where the human soul is taken as the substantial "form" which gives substance and shape to human "matter". Different and even paradoxical statements can be made about the human person: spirit is not matter; by definition, matter is non-spirit. One's body is not one's spirit, yet one's body is the presence of the spirit. Spirit and matter are different, yet they cause each other to be and are therefore a unity:

> Matter determines spirit by being that which spirit informs; spirit informs this matter making it to be what it is. They are one because they are reciprocally causative of each other.[24]

The plural moments in the unity of a being have an inner agreement among themselves because of the unity of the being. At the same time, the fact that a being can be expressed in plurality is critical with regard to its perfection. Rahner says that a being emerges into a plurality "for its perfection", or "on account of its being perfect".[25] According to its degree of being, therefore, each being forms something distinct from itself and yet one with itself for or on account of its own perfection. What is formed or originated is different from, but always in agreement with its origin, and therefore has the character of a symbol with regard to its origin. This returns us to our original statement that "being is of itself symbolic, because it necessarily expresses itself".

Through expressing itself, i.e. through being symbolic, a being realises itself and comes to itself or takes possession of itself.[26] A symbol is therefore not a randomly established secondary relationship between two beings. Rather, a being is essentially symbolic and comes to itself and possesses itself to the extent that it is symbolic. The

---

[22]The philosophical background to this principle is already dealt with by Rahner in his outline of "conversion to the phantasm" in Spirit in the world, 237-383.

[23]R. Haight, The experience and language of grace, 121.

[24]R. Haight, art. cit., 121. Haight goes on to stress the importance of this concept for Rahner, recognising that "this ontologically grounded principle of simultaneous identity or unity and distinction and diversity (plurality) runs all through Rahner's theology and is particularly operative in his theology of grace" (loc. cit.).

[25]Cf. Theological investigations 4, 228.

[26]We have already seen this statement inverted: the degree of reditio completa in seipsum, i.e. the degree of a being's being-present-to-self, is another way of describing its degree of self-realisation. Cf. Theological investigations 4, 228, and the earlier summary of Spirit in the world.

main implication of the fact that a being is essentially symbolic is that by realising itself in its own intrinsic otherness, which is constitutive of itself, a being makes itself known:

> The being is known in this symbol, without which it cannot be known at all: thus it is symbol in the original (transcendental) sense of the word.[27]

A being comes to possess itself while making itself known to the other. One very important consequence of this particular aspect of Thomistic ontology emerges when we apply it to formal causality. Rahner says that the form gives itself away from itself by imparting itself to the material cause. It does not work upon the cause externally by bringing about something different from itself or alien to itself. In a very real way, the "effect" is the "cause".[28]

We can summarise our investigation so far by saying that the principle with which we began, i.e. that all beings are of their nature symbolic (meaning that beings necessarily express themselves to attain their nature), has led us to a definition of a symbol as "the self-realisation of a being in the other, which is constitutive of its essence". This definition has very obvious implications for our understanding of the Trinity. According to Rahner, the theology of the Logos is the supreme form of the theology of the symbol:

> The Logos is the "word" of the Father, his perfect "image", his "imprint", his radiance, his self-expression. Whatever answer is to be given to the question...whether the Father utters the eternal Word because he knows himself or in order to know himself, two items at any rate must be retained. One, the Word - as reality of the immanent divine life - is "generated" by the Father as the image and expression of the Father. Two, this process is necessarily given with the divine act of self-knowledge, and without it the absolute act of divine self-possession in knowledge cannot exist.[29]

It necessarily follows that the Logos is the symbol of the Father in the fullest sense of the word: "To have seen me is to have seen the Father..."[30] What is symbolised (the Father) expresses himself and possesses himself; the symbol (the Logos) remains distinct from what is symbolised (the Father), but is constituted by what is symbolised. As the appearance of the Logos, the humanity of Christ can be understood as the symbolic reality of the Logos. When God expresses himself in

---

[27]Theological investigations 4, 231.

[28]Theological investigations 4, 233-234. The precise meaning and importance of this will become clearer when we examine Balthasar's criticism of Rahner's soteriology, later in this chapter.

[29]Theological investigations 4, 236.

[30]John 14: 9.

history, what appears is the humanity of the Logos. It follows that

> the Son of the Father is truly, in his humanity as such, the revelatory symbol in
> which the Father annunciates himself, in this Son, to the world - revelatory because
> the symbol renders present what is revealed.[31]

When we reflect upon the full implications of this insight we become aware of what Rahner calls "the natural depth of the symbolic reality" which all things possess through the Logos. We come to realise the full meaning of the Pauline statement that all things are held together in Christ (Col. 1:17), because

> every God-given reality, when it has not been degraded to a purely human tool and
> to merely utilitarian purposes, states much more than itself: each in its own way
> is an echo of all reality.[32]

Each individual reality can speak of God.

The Church, according to Rahner, is the persisting presence of the incarnate Word in history, a social entity which is a free creation of the redemptive act of Christ. As the primary sacrament of the grace of God, it does not merely designate but really possesses what was brought definitively and irreversibly into the world by Christ. Later in this chapter we will return to examine in more detail precisely what Rahner means by the Church as sacrament. We will now examine specific aspects of Rahner's account of revelation and salvation in the light of Balthasar's criticisms, beginning with Rahner's account of the relationship between grace and nature.

The supernatural existential

Rahner's concept of the supernatural existential enables him to account for the presence of grace among Christians and non-Christians alike. It is his attempt to account for the relationship between nature and grace in such a way that God's self-communication is no way due to human achievement, that it is not owed to the human being, and yet that it constitutes at the same time the human being's completion. Balthasar's criticism of the supernatural existential is therefore not just a criticism of the anonymous Christian but of Rahner's whole theology. He criticises in particular the use of natura pura as a remainder concept (Restbegriff), upon which the supernatural existential depends if the gratuitousness of grace is to be safeguarded, i.e. if intrinsicism is to be avoided. He argues that it is senseless for Rahner to claim, on the one hand, that the whole meaning and purpose of creation was God's willingness to give himself to the human being and that grace represents the innermost completion of the human being, and, on the other hand, to try to abstract from this

---

[31]Theological investigations 4, 239.

[32]loc. cit..

ultimate meaning to arrive at "pure nature"?[33] But Rahner does not propose the state of nature as an alternative or even a possible world. He means the concept of pure nature as an abstract but valid presupposition for the human being. It simply describes the state of nature unaffected by grace, a state of which we have no experience, according to Rahner, but which must be theoretically possible to explain the unexactedness of grace.

It represents the human being in an ontic state, a state in accordance with being, in which he is endowed with an obediential potency which has not been supernaturally enhanced. However, we never encounter the human being in this state, though it is still necessary for us to postulate such a state. Rather, we always and everywhere encounter the human being in a state of "thrownness", an ontological state, the state of a being immersed in an historical, existential situation. In this state one is conscious of one's ontic existence and aware that one is subject to a number of a priori dispositions, determinations or existentials which affect one before one acts in freedom and which are pre-conditions upon which one engages in one's historical situation.[34] The supernatural existential is an ontological principle whereas the concept of pure nature is an ontic principle and perfectly admissible as a Restbegriff.[35] In fact, it is indispensable if grace is to be shown to be extrinsic to the human being's ontic existence, but intrinsic to his ontological existence and if both intrinsicism and extrinsicism are to be avoided.

But Balthasar has a more serious objection to the supernatural existential. Does it not involve the equating of the human spirit's openness to transcendence with the experience of being addressed personally by the God of Jesus Christ? Were Rahner entirely faithful to Heidegger, this would be the case.

However, for Rahner the first a priori of human transcendence is supernaturally enhanced and therefore reveals itself as the infinity of the absolute as Absolute, and Dasein's true destiny becomes a choice between eternal death and eternal life before God, and not merely, as Heidegger believes, a resoluteness toward death. As we have

---

[33]H. U. von Balthasar, Karl Barth, 310. In this context see also J.P. Mackey Life and grace, 55-57, who also objects to Rahner's use of natura pura as a remainder concept.

[34]"Ontic means 'in accordance with being', in other words, what is; ontological, in the sense in which Rahner uses the term, means becoming conscious of what is ontic" (K. - H. Weger, Karl Rahner, 198, n.29).

[35]As Vass puts it, "when Balthasar charges (Rahner) with vain speculation about possible worlds, Rahner can simply parry the objection: in the natura pura he envisages only an abstract, but valid, presupposition for man, not however a world in which it could be realised" (G. Vass, The mystery of man and the foundations of a theological system, 73).

already seen, Rahner argues that to cast the human being into history and existence
is to prepare him or her for the existential and historical fact of a divine revelation.
It is to open the person to God, "to the Word of Life, seen, heard, touched by human
hands, Jesus of Nazareth".[36] Dasein's acceptance of the existential situation within
which he or she finds himself or herself (Daseinannahme), as Rahner understands
Dasein, is the acceptance of an existential situation in which God as Christians
understand God, is already a factor. Rahner's Dasein counts among his or her many
existentials a supernatural existential. Dasein's openness to transcendence has already
been permanently and unavoidably enhanced by grace. God has already addressed
Dasein. Since all grace comes through Christ, Dasein has been addressed by Christ
and must respond with a "yes" or a "no". A "yes", a Daseinannahme, can therefore
be equated with an acceptance of Christ (Christusannahme).[37] Should Dasein answer
with a "no", as in all freedom Dasein may, the supernatural existential being a
permanent disposition continues to exercise an influence. Dasein is then living in a
state not only contrary to God but contrary to his own ontological state.[38]

Prevenient Grace
A further related point for Balthasar, is that the unilateral nature of God's reaching
out to humanity is compromised when the human response to grace is not presented
as also dependent upon grace:

> Before the individual can encounter the love of God at a particular moment in
> history, he must have experienced another primary, archetypal meeting, which is
> one of the conditions for the appearance of divine love on earth. This sort of
> meeting is one in which we understand the unilateral gesture of God's love for
> man, and understanding includes appropriate reception and answer. Were the
> answer not in some sort adequate, Love would not have been revealed - for it
> cannot be revealed simply in terms of being - it must at the same time achieve
> spiritual consciousness. But if the answer were not included in God's unilateral
> gesture, which presupposes its own action in giving grace, the relationship would
> be bilateral from the first and we would find ourselves back in the anthropological

---

[36]K. Rahner, The concept of existential philosophy in Heidegger, 137.

[37]This is the only way Rahner can answer Ratzinger when he asks: "Ist die Grundfigur richtig,
die Christentum mit Daseinannahme (natürlich in letzter Tiefe) identifiziert? Gnoseologisch
gewendet: Ist das Verhältnis des allgemein-Menschlichen und des Christlichen richtig bestimmt oder
ist Christentum nicht doch etwas ganz anderes als die Annahme, sozusagen die Reduplikation des
Daseins und seine Reflexion?" (Ratzinger, K., art. cit., 184).

[38]Cf. the sections on The question of personal existence as a question of salvation, 39-41, and
The possibility of a decision against God, 97-106, in Foundations of Christian faith, 39-41.

scheme.[39]

Were the human response to grace independent of grace then the human-divine relationship would be bilateral, as in fact it is in the "anthropological scheme". Williams agrees that the anthropological scheme Balthasar has in mind here is none other than Rahner's.[40] Yet Rahner's supernatural existential, properly understood, accounts for the human response to God's gracious self-offer as itself dependent upon grace. Existentials affect the human being before he or she acts in freedom.[41] They are pre-conditions upon which one engages in one's historical situation.[42] Therefore the freedom with which one answers with a "yes" or a "no" to God is itself a "graced" freedom. This is why should one answer with a "no", it is not just a "no" against God: it is now also a "no" against oneself. Were the human being to respond to God's offer of grace out of his or her ontic state - a state unaffected by grace - then the human-divine relationship would indeed be bilateral. However, as we have just stated, human beings are never found in this state. Human beings always and everywhere exist within an ontological situation in which God has already addressed them and enabled them to respond. Rahner's anthropological scheme is not bilateral:

> God's self-communication is given not only as gift, but also as the necessary condition which makes possible an acceptance of the gift which can allow the gift really to be God, and can prevent the gift in its acceptance from being changed from God into a finite and created gift which only represents God, but is not God himself. In order to be able to accept God without reducing him, as it were, in this acceptance to our finiteness, this acceptance must be borne by God himself. God's self-communication as offer is also the necessary condition which makes its acceptance possible...God's self-communication must always be present in man as the prior condition of possibility for its acceptance.[43]

Here Rahner is echoing the teaching of scholastic theology that the salvific love for Jesus occurs by the power of and as the consummation of the infused supernatural virtue of divine faith, in which God, through his prevenient grace, is himself

---

[39]Love alone: the way of revelation, 62.

[40]Cf. the article by R. Williams in: J. Riches, ed., The analogy of beauty, 12. Williams refers to p.62 of Love alone: the way of revelation as a specific criticism of Rahner.

[41]Rahner understands God's self-communication to be "...an offer...given prior to man's freedom as a task and as the condition of freedom's highest possibility..." (Foundations of Christian faith, 129).

[42]Whereas an existential characterises an individual before his free action takes place, Rahner refers to a quality which accrues to a personal existent on account of free activity as an existentiell.

[43]Foundations of Christian faith, 128.

principle, guarantor, and vessel of this love of a human being for God.

The non-Christian's faith expressed as love of neighbour

Accepting with both Rahner and Balthasar that God himself enables the human being to respond to him, how does this response manifest itself concretely in the non-Christian? For Christian and non-Christian alike an act of faith is necessary for salvation. Rahner argues that the supernatural virtue of charity which is necessary for salvation can manifest itself in one's love of neighbour. If one has faith (even implicitly), hope and love, these are inevitably expressed in the categorical and material spatio-temporality of one's existence: they "cannot simply remain closed within man's transcendental subjectivity".[44] Here we find an expression of the unity which necessarily exists between transcendental and categorical revelation. The path to salvation, for Christian and non-Christian alike, involves endorsing one's transcendental encounter with God in categorical word and action. Putting this more concretely, one's love of neighbour is an expression of one's love of God.

Balthasar was repulsed by the simplistic identification between love of God and love of neighbour which he understood to be implied here. Whereas, according to Rahner, for both Christian and non-Christian alike, love of neighbour constitutes an explicit expression of one's implicit love of God, for Balthasar love of neighbour is distinctive for the Christian because it is a consequence of his or her awareness of God's explicit love for him. The Christian loves others because Christ loved others. For Balthasar, Christ is the essential bridge between oneself and one's neighbour.

Balthasar cannot accept that an implicit act of love of God can substitute for the kind of love of God to which a Christian is called. As he argues forcibly in Cordula oder der Ernstfall, the Christian's conscious awareness of God's love in Christ calls him to martyrdom. The Christian must be prepared to offer his or her life for God, and for his or her neighbour for God's sake.

Contrary to what Balthasar's criticism suggests, Rahner never intended to imply that the non-Christian's implicit act of love of God could be a substitute for a conscious and explicit loving response to God in Jesus Christ. The implicit act of love merely constitutes the minimum essential act of confession of faith, so to speak, which should evolve into the kind of explicit act upon which Balthasar insists. As we have already seen

> ...the faith as it exists in the pagan is properly speaking designed to follow its own inherent dynamism in such a way as to develop into that faith which we simply call

---

[44]Cf. K. - H. Weger, op. cit., 134.

> the Christian faith. The seed has no right to seek not to grow into a plant...the fact
> that it is not yet developed into a plant is no reason for refusing to give the name
> which we give to the plant destined to grow from it to the seed as well.[45]

Just as the seed possesses all that is essential to its future life as a plant, so the anonymous Christian possesses what is essential in being a Christian: the anonymous Christian has made an act of faith.[46] In response to Balthasar, Rahner can answer that the non-Christian is not dispensed from what is essential in martyrdom, i.e. the confession of faith, concretely expressed in love of neighbour.[47] The anonymous Christian can even be considered to be a witness to Christ, though in an anonymous sense.[48] Balthasar's real concern must be acknowledged, that Christ would not be left out of Christianity and that altruism, however well-grounded, would not become a substitute for Christian faith. However, even though Rahner expressed himself in terms accessible to the modern questioning and agnostic mind, in an attempt to develop a common language for dialogue, the unity and distinction between love of God and love of neighbour which he proposes, properly understood, does not relegate God to second place.

---

[45]Theological investigations 14, 291.

[46]It would take us too far afield to examine precisely here the kind of faith which the anonymous Christian is held to possess. Albert Nolan's reflections on the nature of faith (Jesus before Christianity, 30-34) provide Rahner's approach with a biblical basis. He points out that Jesus relied upon the power of faith, not prayer, to save. He repeatedly said "your faith has healed you" (Mk. 5:34, 10:52; Mt. 9:28-29, Lk. 17:19). Clearly this saving faith was not the same as subscribing to a creed or dogmas. It was a very strong conviction, but as Nolan points out, not any kind of conviction but the most powerful conviction that truth and goodness will triumph over darkness and evil; the conviction that faith will conquer fatalism. It can be argued that there is an anonymous element in this act of faith: clearly many of those whom Jesus healed did not know who he was. Their faith was expressed in their belief in the power of goodness and truth and this faith saved them.

[47]Balthasar calls into question the ability of love of neighbour to mediate love of God. But another problem arises here. Is the love of one's neighbour merely a means to an end? Is one's neighbour merely a channel through which one's love of God flows, or is one's neighbour loved for his or her own sake? The fact that one's transcendental relationship is realised in one's love of neighbour does not in itself mean that the position of one's neighbour is non-essential or secondary. The mediation of oneself through another "self" does not necessarily imply a degradation of the other. However it must be admitted that Rahner is not entirely unambiguous here and Balthasar's accusation that a theology associated with an idealistic philosophy is unable to give the totally other, the "thou", its proper place and worth, is unable to conceive of the "thou" as more than a "non-I" and to avoid reducing it to a function of the "I" - this accusation is difficult to refute. Given that for Balthasar love of neighbour is essentially an overflow of one's love of God, is Balthasar himself entirely free from the same criticism?

[48]Cf. Theological investigations 13, 157-158. In a passage which we have already quoted (Geist und Feuer, Herder Korrespondenz 30, 1976, 76), Balthasar himself admits that non-Christians can be witnesses: "Wir haben große Vorbilder von Menschen außerhalb des Christentums."

Perhaps the difficulty here lies in evaluating Rahner's account of the relationship between love of God and love of neighbour within the context of his attempt to establish the minimum faith-response necessary for the non-Christian if he or she is to accept salvation. Rahner's actual position on the relationship between love of God and love of neighbour differs only from Balthasar's in that he is more insistent that love of God and love of neighbour do not become separated:

> ...ordinary love for neighbour is a prerequisite of our love for Jesus. Here we may safely paraphrase what we read in John: How can we love Jesus, whom we cannot see, if we do not love our neighbour, whom we do see? And the other way about: This love for neighbour can and should actually grow through a love for Jesus, for it is only in a loving relationship with Jesus that we conceive the possibilities of love for neighbour that otherwise we should hold simply not to be feasible, but which present themselves nonetheless wherever we subsume our neighbour in our love for Jesus because he or she is Jesus' brother or sister.[49]

Like Balthasar, Rahner sees love of God in Jesus as the bridge between oneself and one's neighbour. He even goes further, as will become clearer in the next section, in claiming that God in Jesus Christ is the ground of all love of neighbour, and, one could add, of self-acceptance or self-love too. This is true because it is God's love and acceptance of us, irreversibly confirmed in Jesus Christ, which constitutes the sole basis upon which we can take the risk of abandoning ourselves unreservedly and of loving unconditionally. This is the case even for one who does not consciously know Jesus Christ:

> Where love can really abandon all reservations, definitively and with absolute assurance, where love can really live out to the last its most proper, most original nature as unconditional self-giving and surrender to the other, there Jesus as such is "co-loved" as the Ground of this love - even where that blessed Name is as yet altogether unknown to the one who loves. But we Christians can name this primordially and radically loved person. We call him Jesus of Nazareth. And when one really knows what takes place in a love like this - if that love is not to be the most enormous perversion or ultimate absurdity of existence - one sees that the prerequisites and conditions for such a love in the beloved include everything basically posited in what the Christian faith confesses of Jesus of Nazareth, as the one who exists in a union with God that is absolute and of a substantial order.[50]

The fact that God condescended to love us and continues to love us, is the sole basis of our love of ourselves, of others and of God.

A relativisation of the cross of Christ?

In the course of his argument that Karl Rahner's concept of the anonymous Christian relativises the role of the historical Christ-event in the saving mystery, Balthasar

---

[49] The love of Jesus and love of neighbour, 23-24.

[50] K. Rahner, op. cit., 44.

focuses his criticism repeatedly on Rahner's theology of the cross. He does this firstly because the cross is the Leit-motiv of his own theology. Secondly, Balthasar believes that Rahner's transcendental emphasis, which enables Rahner to develop the concept of the anonymous Christian, at the same time precludes a proper redemptive role being assigned to the historical Christ in his theology, and especially to the death of Christ. According to Balthasar, Rahner's inadequate theology of the cross is one of the casualties of the anonymous Christian.[51]

In order to assess the validity of Balthasar's criticism, it is necessary both to examine more closely Rahner's actual position and to place Balthasar's criticism more fully in the context of his own theology as a whole.

The first point which must be made is that Rahner has a theology of the cross, worked out and expressed in a number of different articles, both spiritual and theological.[52] On the surface however, the cross does not occupy the central role for Rahner which Balthasar gives it in his theology. Anselm Grün, in his work on Rahner's soteriology, claims that the cross is central to what Rahner means by the categorical-historical, which never exists separately from the transcendental, and he shows that, for Rahner, the incarnated spirit can only reach God and be reached by God in and through the historical-categorical.[53]

Is it true that Rahner presents the cross merely as the event which reveals the salvific will of the Father? Although this is not an accurate summary of Rahner's position,

---

[51]As we have already noted Balthasar sees a direct connection between the doctrine of the anonymous Christian and Rahner's (as he views it) flawed theology of the cross: "Hier fehlt deutlich eine Theologia Crucis, die uns Rahner bisher schuldig geblieben ist. Freilich, die für die heutige Lage so dringend gefordete Aufwertung der Lehre vom anonymen Christentum (...) bedingt eine proportionale Abwertung der Kreuzetheologie und entsprechend der Theologie des christlichen Lebens vom Ernstfall her" (Cordula oder der Ernstfall, 91).Balthasar is also critical of Rahner's Theologie des Todes as not reaching sufficient Christological depth: see The Glory of the Lord 7, 218. Cf. also H. Vorgrimler, Understanding Karl Rahner, 124.

[52]Working in collaboration with Balthasar in 1939 on a proposed schema for dogmatic theology, Rahner agreed that a theology of the cross should include reflection on the cross as Jesus' reality in his own eyes, the cross as vicarious sacrifice and expiation for humanity and the descent into hell. This schema, the original of which is in the Rahner archives in Innsbruck, is reproduced in Theological investigations 1, 1-37. Among Rahner's more important writings on the cross are: Current problems in Christology, Theological investigations 1, 192-197; Dogmatic questions on Easter, Theological investigations 4, 121-133; The scandal of death, Theological investigations 7, 140-144; Self-realisation and taking up one's cross, Theological investigations 9, 253-257; Following the Crucified, Theological investigations 18, 157-170; Foundations of Christian faith, 228-284; Our Christian faith, 195-123.

[53]A. Grün, Erlösung durch das Kreuz. Karl Rahners Beitrag zu einem heutigen Erlösungsverständnis.

as we shall now show, it nevertheless points out the clear emphasis in Rahner's soteriology. Rahner differs very significantly from Balthasar in how he understands the cross as the "cause" of our salvation. In addition, as we shall see, "how" Jesus died is not as important for Rahner as "that" he died.[54]

While Rahner believes that sense must be made of the statement that "the expiatory death of Jesus on the cross made satisfaction to God for our sins and thus won for us our redemption", this must be achieved without in any way compromising or obscuring the Christian's understanding of God as a God of Love, or as a God with a universal salvific will already operative at all times and in all places in human history. Our image of God can be compromised in two ways. First, God understood as a loving and caring Father may become blurred by an image of a bloodthirsty, vengeful God demanding retribution. Second, our understanding of the immutability of God may be weakened by too simplistic an explanation of how a change in God's attitude to humankind can be brought about by the obedience of the God-man. Because of the way in which the theory of satisfaction can contribute to a crisis in the credibility of Christian faith, Rahner prefers to choose as the focal point for his soteriology the salvific will of God:

> ...this whole work of redemption, which is supposed to placate God and make him merciful, is the result all along of God's spontaneous desire to save, so that we must also clearly say, the saving work of Jesus Christ exists because even before it God was the God who forgives and triumphs over the sins of the world, and not (only) that God is merciful because of the saving work of Christ.[55]

It is equally difficult to account for Jesus' obedience unto death on the cross as the cause of the Father's salvific will without in any way overshadowing or denigrating God's supernatural salvific will, really operative in the world, which implies the possibility of supernatural revelation everywhere and at every time in history. In other words, Jesus' death on the cross must be accounted for simultaneously as cause and effect of the Father's universal salvific will.

The problem with the way this was handled in the teaching of the dogmatic theology of the schools (that the Spirit who makes faith possible is given at all times and places intuitu meritorum Christi) was that it failed to make sufficiently clear how the grace of the Spirit universally given and the historical event of the cross at a particular time and place were connected one to the other. While the Second Vatican Council is

---

[54]For example, one one occasion Rahner wrote: "The way Jesus died is not the important thing - though it is interesting to consider whether it would have been different if Jesus had died at an appropriate age and not in his youth, say from a heart attack" (Our Christian faith, 105).

[55]Our Christian faith, 115.

reserved about how such a salvific faith in a real revelation can come about outside
the Old and New Testaments, it nevertheless explicitly teaches about the universal
possibility of faith.[56] This leaves the theologian with the task of showing how this
faith can and must be related to the historic Christ-event. While it may be
presupposed - with the theology of the schools - that Christ is present and operative
in non-Christian believers through his Spirit which proceeds from the Father and the
Son, the task remains to show how this Spirit - the Spirit of the eternal Logos - is
properly speaking the Spirit of Jesus Christ.[57]

To do this we must show how the cross can be understood both as the "effect" and
"cause" of the Father's universal salvific will.

Rahner applies his understanding of symbol as follows. There are events which can
be regarded both as the effects of a will and also as its cause:

> ...insofar as a will has to implement itself by bringing about something other than
> itself in which it expresses itself and becomes definitive, then this objectifying
> expression of this will is not only an effect, but also a cause of this will insofar as
> that will would not really have existed in ultimate seriousness and irreversibility if
> this expression had not existed.[58]

While from the beginning Christ's life and death is initiated by God's salvific will to
forgive and sanctify sinful humanity, i.e. while it is the effect of God's salvific will,
it is also the cause of the same will, in that through Christ's death this will becomes
expressed in ultimate seriousness and irreversibility.

It is in this sense that Rahner's claim that the cross derives totally from God's
merciful will to communicate himself and has no other cause than God himself, must
be understood. Rahner interprets Jesus' death not only as the appearance of the
Father's salvific will in history, but also as the fulfilment of this will. In a real sense,
the cross is the cause of the Holy Spirit's appearance in history.[59] Insofar as the
Spirit is always oriented toward the highest point of its historical mediation, it can be
said that the Spirit is always and everywhere the Spirit of Jesus Christ, the Logos of

---

[56]I am following Rahner's concise handling of this question in Foundations of Christian faith,
311-321.

[57]op. cit., 316.

[58]K. Rahner, Our Christian Faith, 116.

[59]"...we see the incarnation and the cross as what scholastic terminology calls the 'final cause'
of God's universal self-communication to the world, given with God's saving will, which knows no
reason outside itself and which we call the Holy Spirit; and...we view the incarnation and cross in
this sense as the cause of the imparting of the Holy Spirit at all times and in all places in the world"
(Theological investigations 17, 46).

God who became man.[60]

According to Rahner, the Second Vatican Council could only define the Church as "the sign and instrument of the innermost union with God and of the unity of the whole of mankind"[61], because the cross of Jesus Christ is the primary sacrament (Ursakrament) which causes the Church to be this sign and instrument of salvation:

> the cross can and should be understood in this sense as the cause of the salvation signified and not merely regarded as the cause of our awareness of salvation in faith. Of course the cross possesses this latter function for us and for our faith as well, but the cross of Jesus as the universal primary sacrament of the salvation of the whole world expresses more than this, and indeed says everything, always assuming that 'sacrament' is correctly interpreted and is seen to possess the specific type of causality which is proper to the cross as the instrument of salvation for all men.[62]

For Rahner, the importance of how Jesus died lies in his full commitment, abandonment and complete trust in his heavenly Father. That Jesus faced death with confidence in his Father's love for him, enables us to have confidence too.[63] As we saw earlier, it is God's love for us which gives us the courage to love, to take the risk of venturing outside of ourselves and even of abandoning ourselves to one another and to God. The life, death and resurrection of Jesus of Nazareth testify to this love in a manner which renders this love irrevocable and irreversible. Jesus of Nazareth makes the loving of oneself, others and God not only possible, but he makes the risk, inevitably a part of loving, seem reasonable, and the taking of this risk unavoidable, for those wishing to live fully human lives.[64]

Balthasar would agree that Jesus Christ, through his life, death and resurrection, testifies uniquely and irrevocably to God's eternal love for us. However, he chooses

---

[60]Foundations of Christian faith, 318.

[61]Lumen Gentium, n.1.

[62]Theological investigations 16, 215.

[63]Heidegger's influence on Rahner's attitude toward death in general, and Jesus' death in particular, is substantial: "...essentially Dasein is a being-toward-death (Dasein ist wesentlich Sein zum Tode); only there in fact does he reach his fullness, only there is his disposition of his existence effective, total, definitive, and unforfeitable. To be resolved to his being-toward-death, such is the fundamental attitude demanded of Dasein; to bear the anxiety of nothingness, such is the courage to live, a courage drawn from heroic acceptance of an intrinsic finitude, a finitude to which every other perspective but nothingness is closed" (K. Rahner, The concept of existential philosophy in Heidegger, 133-134, 136); "There-being, becomes conscious through the veil of not-being, of being, as the most fundamental aspect of all, the term with the richest and most comprehensive reference" (J. P. Mackey, Modern theology, 19). Cf. further K. Rahner, On the theology of death, Freiburg: Herder, 1961.

[64]Cf. K. Rahner, The love of Jesus and love of neighbour, 17, 33, 42.

to emphasise a different aspect of this love from that which Karl Rahner emphasises. According to Balthasar, we must not forget that God reveals himself in Jesus Christ to sinners, sinners who deserve death on account of their sins. Therefore the manner of Jesus' death is more than an example for us, more than a gesture of solidarity to give us courage and confidence. Both the fact and the manner of Jesus' death, the death on behalf of all sinners on the cross, in total abandonment, and especially abandoned by his Father, is the unique eschatological judgement death deserved by all men and women because of their sins. It is a carrying of the world's guilt.

Whereas Rahner is afraid that an overemphasis on the doctrine of satisfaction will contribute to a credibility crisis for faith in the God who loves, Balthasar is reacting to the contemporary trend to run away from the reality of sin and the failure to recognise human sin as the cause of suffering, pain and offence to God. Balthasar is aware of the double danger of an overemphasis on the doctrine of satisfaction, i.e. a flawed image of God as demanding revenge or at least placation, as well as the immutability of God being compromised, but he is even more anxious that the full meaning of the pro nobis in Christ's death not be jeopardized.

In his own theology, Balthasar presents the cross as a Trinitarian event. Through the power of the Holy Spirit, the Son can remain one with the Father and at the same time, in obedience to the Father, enter into the total Godforsakenness of sin.[65] This is necessary because if Jesus' death is to be redemptive for all of humankind, it must be an identification with and an assumption (Übernahme) of all human sin and disobedience.[66] Jesus must experience total godforsakenness on the cross, because sin, in essence, is separation from God: it is hell.[67] The Son takes this terrible step in obedience to the Father, an obedience made possible by the bond of love between Father and Son, maintained by the Holy Spirit.

The ultimate moment of Jesus' suffering - Jesus' abandonment by the Father - is expressed in the prayer "My God, my God, why have you deserted me?" (Mk. 15, 34). Balthasar rejects any attempt to explain away the stark reality which this prayer reveals: out of love for sinful humankind God the Father allowed his Son to suffer in our place, really abandoning his Son on the cross, and out of love for his Father

---

[65]H. U. von Balthasar, Theodramatik 3, 324.

[66]"For our sake God made the sinless one into sin, so that in him we might become the goodness of God" (2 Cor. 5:21).

[67]Cf. J. O'Donnell, The mystery of the triune God, 63. O'Donnell highlights the difference between Balthasar and Anselm on this point: "in the soteriology of Anselm, Jesus suffers the punishment of sin, but is not touched by the reality of sin as such in his own being".

and for us, and in complete obedience to his will, Jesus willingly underwent this suffering.[68] The other prayer is taken from Psalm 31, which we find in Luke's account of the passion: "Father, into your hands I commit my spirit" (Luke 23, 46). This prayer is understood by Balthasar not to be expressing confidence which Jesus himself had that he might be glorified, but rather a hope that the will of the God who abandoned him has been accomplished.

Balthasar's Trinitarian understanding, as outlined above, allows God to take seriously the depth of human rejection of God through the abuse of human freedom. It allows God to judge sin, to hold it to be despicable, and at the same time to forgive sin by absorbing the suffering and evil caused by sin into his own person, and all without loss of either human or divine dignity.

In one of his few specific responses to Balthasar's criticism of him, Rahner expressed his fear that Balthasar's theology of the cross as outlined above had not overcome one of the difficulties of the satisfaction theory:

> ...if I wanted to enter into a counter-attack then I would have to say that there is a modern tendency (I do not want to say theory but nevertheless a tendency) as much with Balthasar as with Adrienne von Speyr (naturally more with the latter), but also independently from them with Moltmann - which conceives of a theology of the death of God, which seems to me to be basically gnostic. Said rather primitively, to become extracted from my dirt and mess and my doubt, it is of no use if God - to put it crudely - is just as dirty.[69]

Behind this criticism of Balthasar is Rahner's concern, which as we saw dominates his own "pure Chalcedonian" theology of the cross, to safeguard the immutability of God. God's immutability is protected by careful attention to the Council of Chalcedon's teaching of the communicatio idiomatum. The exchange of concrete attributes must not be misinterpreted as a simple identity of concrete attributes in both

---

[68] Some scholars prefer to place this line from Psalm 22 in the context of the psalm as a whole e.g. D. Lane, Christ at the centre, 57-58: "...the apparent abandonment of Jesus by God the Father in suffering and death on the cross is overcome by the prayerful recitation of Psalm 22 by Jesus on the cross. The words 'My God, My God, why have you forsaken me' (Mt 27:46) are merely the opening lines of this psalm. The rest of the psalm, which we can presume was well-known to Jesus, moves from absence to presence, from loss to gain, from complaint to praise in regard to the mystery of God. To be sure, according to all outward appearances God seems to have forsaken Jesus. At the same time, however, the prayerful recitation of Psalm 22 for help uttered by Jesus goes beyond his apparent aloneness in death."

[69] Im Gespräch 1, 245-246. N. D. O'Donoghue (Mystics for our time, 25, n.12) criticises what he sees as Balthasar's over-dependence on von Speyr: "Curiously, von Balthasar's writing on hell is based on the experienced 'descent into hell' of the twentieth-century mystic, Adrienne von Speyr (1902-67), whose visionary world is the context of all von Balthasar's theology. This is the first time in the history of theology that a major theologian has based his system on private revelation. It is a powerful system based, however, on a dangerous precedent; for easy or cheap knowledge is harmful to men and women."

natures. For Rahner, the divine identification with suffering humanity lies in the Son's victorious death in solidarity with sinful humankind.[70] The immutability of God is protected because God only changes in "the other" and not "in himself".[71] According to Rahner,

> the pure Chalcedonian will always hold that it is God's impassible, holy blessedness that has "formally" redeemed us, not something earthly and finite that has been speculatively introduced into the interiority of God qua God.[72]

In suspecting Balthasar of gnostic tendencies, Rahner seems to be implying that Balthasar is less than careful regarding the communicatio idiomatum. In the context of his Trinitarian theology as a whole, which is the only context in which judgement may be passed on Balthasar's theology of the cross, Balthasar seeks to avoid just such tendencies.

According to Balthasar, the Father's abandonment of the Son has been embraced from all eternity, for from all eternity the Father has risked himself by giving himself away to the Son, and from all eternity the Son has been a "yes" in loving obedience to the Father.[73]

It is the eternal separation and union within the divine life itself which makes possible the separation and the union on the cross. It would seem that for Balthasar, "the dramatic action of the economic Trinity is made possible and embraced within the primordial drama of the eternal Trinity".[74] This would seem to imply that the dramatic action of the economic Trinity is an effect of the primordial drama of the eternal Trinity, which is similar to saying as Balthasar's does, though admittedly within a much more strongly Trinitarian and a more dramatic perspective than Rahner's, that it was God's will from all eternity to forgive and save.

Balthasar's development of the doctrine of satisfaction within a theology of the Trinity makes it possible for him to reconcile the central theological insights of this doctrine with a more authentically Christian image of God. The purpose of Balthasar's whole theological system is to reveal the God of Love and to show that only love is the way of revelation. Nevertheless, in attempting, through a renovation of the doctrine of satisfaction, to disclose fully the depth of God's love for us - God loved us enough

---

[70]The love of Jesus and the love of neighbour, 56-57.

[71]Cf. especially Theological investigations 4, 123-129.

[72]The love of Jesus and the love of neighbour, 57.

[73]Cf. J. O'Donnell, op. cit, 65

[74]loc. cit.

even to abandon his only Son for our sake - and to highlight the price of this love, it would seem to be impossible to exorcise from the doctrine of satisfaction a lurking image of a vengeful God who punishes. While protecting the dignity both of God and of humankind, an authentic soteriology must at the same time avoid presenting the cross as a magic wand which transforms an angry God into a gracious one.

Regarding the salvation of non-Christians, we know from Balthasar's writings elsewhere that he considers it a Christian's responsibility to hope for the salvation of all.[75] However, he fails to provide us with an account of how this optimism can be grounded in and related to his theology of the cross. His theology of the cross does not, of course, contradict such an optimism and one can see how such an optimism could be quite easily accommodated within his Trinitarian portrayal of the cross-event. Balthasar understands the incarnation as the moment marking the sending forth of the Son by the Father and the Holy Spirit. By maintaining a loving bond between Father and Son, the Holy Spirit makes possible the Father's abandonment of the Son on the cross which is necessary if the Son is to complete his task of taking upon himself the whole burden of the world's sin. When this has been accomplished, the Son surrenders his Spirit on the cross into the Father's hands.

At the moment of Jesus' death, a reversal in mission occurs in which the Son and the Father now send the Spirit forth into the hearts of all men and women.[76] Though, as Sachs points out, Balthasar does not discuss the problem of the relationship between the Holy Spirit and the human spirit of Jesus in a sufficiently detailed way,[77] one can see how Balthasar's understanding of the emission of the Holy Spirit on the cross may be linked to Rahner's explanation of how "Christ is present and operative in non-Christian believers and hence in non-Christian religions in and through his Spirit".[78]

Since Balthasar was so critical of Rahner's account of how non-Christians can attain salvation yet at the same time defensive of the Church's optimism regarding the salvation of all, why did he not develop the theological implications of his

[75]Cf., for example, Dare we hope "that all men be saved"?

[76]Spiritus Creator, 111.

[77]Cf. J. R. Sachs, Spirit and life: the pneumatology and Christian spirituality of Hans Urs von Balthasar, Univ. of Tübingen dissertation, 1984, 554, n.128.

[78]Foundations of Christian faith,316. Rahner goes on to say: "...the Incarnation and the cross are, in scholastic terminology, the "final cause" of the universal self-communication of God to the world which we call the Holy Spirit, a self-communication given with God's salvific will which has no cause outside God" (op. cit., 316-317).

understanding of the emission of the Holy Spirit on the cross? Such an omission is arguably a consequence of Balthasar's choosing as his chief theological concern the defence of the unique role of Christ and the Church in the salvation of the world. Rahner has shown, however, that the claim that the salvation of the whole of humanity at all times and everywhere comes through the historical Jesus of Nazareth, the claim which both Balthasar and Rahner would agree is the most threatened in a pluralistic age, is credible only when we can account theologically for the salvation of those both before and after the time of Christ who have had no explicit contact with Christ and the Church. And perhaps we need to remind ourselves here that we are in fact talking about providing a theological account of the means of salvation of the vast majority of humanity.

This comparison of Rahner's and Balthasar's theologies of the cross though necessarily brief has been nonetheless adequate to show that both theologians seek to strike a balance between two extremes. On the one hand a soteriology must clearly show that God reconciled the world to himself in Christ (2 Cor. 5:19). This means that the historical Christ event is more than merely a manifestation of God's salvific will from all eternity. On the other hand, full weight must also be given to the statement that "God loved the world so much that he gave his only Son" (Jn 3:16). It was God's love for us which brought about the saving event. These are the two pincer-jaws of an authentic soteriology. While Balthasar and Rahner seek to accommodate both, Balthasar emphasises the former and Rahner the latter. Both theologians alert us to the difficulties and the dangers in each other's approach.

Perhaps both presentations could benefit from closer attention to scriptural exegesis and the proper use of scripture within dogmatic theology.[79] For example, if more attention were paid to the Old Testament understanding of sacrifice as a means of purification, and of how this understanding is the context for reading both St. John's Gospel and St. Paul's letters, it would be easier to reconcile a doctrine of satisfaction with an understanding of God as love. Whereas sin disrupts the human-divine relationship, initiated by God who wishes to share himself totally with Israel, sacrifice first and foremost expresses a commitment to re-direct one's life wholly towards God

---

[79]G. O'Hanlon, ("Does God change? - H. U. von Balthasar on the immutability of God", 179) points to the need for better scriptural underpinning in the case of Balthasar. W. Kasper (The methods of dogmatic theology, 27-28) comments that "the initiative and the whole questioning process must start from Scripture; we should not go back to Scripture to find arguments for theses and concepts that have been laid down beforehand...Scripture is not to be utilised within the framework of the Church's teaching; on the contrary, the teaching of the Church must be presented within the framework of Scripture's testimony".

in loving submission and acceptance.[80]

It is also important to stress the link between the death of Jesus Christ and his life and resurrection.[81] The unifying principle in Balthasar's Christology is Jesus' eternal and loving obedience to the Father, but this is stressed predominantly with regard to the Paschal Mystery. For Rahner, the whole historical Christ-event is a unity in itself with one unique and ultimate meaning for humanity. That the Word became flesh (and this is why Rahner speaks mainly about the incarnation, which is completed by the Paschal Mystery), means that "God's love-creating condescension has become unequivocally accessible and irreversible in the salvation history of the world".[82]

Perhaps both Balthasar's and Rahner's soteriologies could be complemented by placing the Paschal Mystery more fully in the context of the bringing about of the Reign of God. In this way the full significance of Jesus' death on the cross is articulated in terms more accessible to the contemporary believer and, in addition, the events of Jesus' life, death and resurrection are given greater unity. Jesus placed the events and circumstances of his life and death totally at the service of a reign of peace, justice and love, in obedience to God whose stance towards humanity has always been compassion and love, and out of love for this God and for all humankind. Jesus' death on the cross is best understood within the context of the coming of the reign of God, through which all the effects of human sin, suffering,

---

[80]Cf., for example, S. Freyne, "Theology 23: Sacrifice for Sin", The Furrow 25, 4, April 1974, 193-212. Freyne shows that the understanding of sacrifice in the Old Testament as a means of placating an angry God is the result of a process of syncretism. The authentic Old Testament understanding of sacrament is one of purification.

[81]Balthasar would insist on including here the event of Holy Saturday which is of particular significance for him in bringing out the full depths of God's love for us and of Christ's suffering on our behalf. Rahner also discusses the descent into Hell, but sees its significance as emphasising that Jesus was not simply a human being who died,
but one who also shared in the state of being dead. This state was also experienced by the God-man with the result that "there is no longer any abyss in human experience in which man is abandoned and alone. There is one who has gone before him and endured all such abysses, so that we might conquer" (He descended into hell, Theological investigations 7, 150). Even though Balthasar's more dramatic portrayal of hell, based on the visions of Adrienne von Speyr, emphasises hell much more as the place of absolute Godforsakenness, it ultimately leads to the same theological conclusion, i.e. however far a creature may remove himself or herself from God through the abuse of the gift of freedom, through the Trinity, which is absolute unity in diversity, the creature is never beyond the loving arms of the Father. This is because the Son, in obedience to the Father is present in co-solitude (Miteinsamkeit).

[82]K. Rahner, Love of Jesus and love of neighbour, 43.

pain, injustice and evil are conquered.[83] Jesus expressed total solidarity and total compassion (i.e. "suffering with") in his death on the cross through which, in dying for all humankind, he embraced the suffering of all.[84]

Both Rahner and Balthasar have been criticised for failing to bring out the full significance of their Christologies in socio-political terms. J.B. Metz, a student and later colleague of Rahner's, saw the need for this particular development within Rahner's theology.[85] Balthasar, whose account of God as one totally caught up even in the darker side of human existence, also stops short of developing the full implications of such an understanding of God in terms of social justice.[86]

Balthasar is undoubtedly correct in claiming that Rahner's transcendental emphasis, which enables him to account for the salvation of non-Christians, also forces him to develop his theology of the cross in a certain direction. However, Rahner is more anxious to account for the cross as both the "cause" and the "effect" of God's eternal salvific will than Balthasar's criticism acknowledges him to be. Even though it is arguable how successfully Rahner does this, it is beyond dispute that Rahner's goal is to account for the salvation of non-Christians through the historical Jesus of Nazareth, and he is dismissive of the possibility of an act of faith which would lack a Christological character.

Regarding the specific accusation of a relativisation: while Rahner does not contradict Balthasar's position, and is in fact closer to it than Balthasar's criticisms seem to allow in that he at least acknowledges the need to account for the historical Christ-event as the "cause" of salvation, Rahner's emphasis clearly lies elsewhere. In comparison with Balthasar, Rahner certainly relativises the historical Christ-event to the extent that his emphasis is on the Father's salvific-will from all eternity rather than on the Son's loving obedience. Rahner locates the Son's loving obedience at the heart of the Father's salvific will and purpose. Indeed, had Rahner wished to enter

---

[83]Cf. D. Lane, op. cit., 57.

[84]"Compassion and love compel a man to do everything for others. But the man who says he lives for others but is not willing to suffer and die for them is a liar and he is dead. Jesus was fully alive because he was willing to suffer and die not for a cause but for people. The willingness to die for others...is not a willingness to die for someone or for some people; it is a willingness to die for all men. The willingness to die for some people would be an expression of group solidarity. The willingness to die for mankind is an expression of universal solidarity" (A. Nolan, Jesus before Christianity, 114).

[85]Rahner recognised the need for and the value of Metz's development of his thought. Cf. Im Gespräch 2, 115-116.

[86]Cf. G. O'Hanlon, art. cit., 179.

into debate with Balthasar, he could have asked him if, in response to his perception of "the signs of the times", he does not over-emphasise the historical Christ-event with detrimental consequences for his ability to account for the availability of grace outside of explicit Christianity. When we take into account the Church's optimism regarding the success of God's universal salvific will, should it not be one of the theologian's main concerns to provide a theological basis for understanding how the majority achieve salvation? In addition, given the increasing disillusionment among many Church members, particularly in Europe, regarding their perception of Christ, the Church and the Christian life, is it not vital for the theologian to address honestly and credibly the question: "What good deed must I do to possess eternal life?[87]"

A relativisation of the Church?

For Balthasar, the Church should represent the greatest possible radiance of Christ in the world because the members of the Church in their day-to-day lives struggle to follow the Lord as closely as possible.[88] But if one can be an anonymous Christian, why be a name-bearing one?[89] In its mission to the world is the Church not losing its identity? Is the salt losing its savour? Is the Church like a watering-can with a hole in it?[90]

The aim of this section is show that Rahner also believes that the Church should represent the greatest radiance of Christ in the world. If Balthasar chooses to present the Church as the form of Christ, for Rahner the Church is Christ's sacrament, in the fullest sense and meaning of this term.[91] The anonymous Christian cannot be conceived of, or understood, apart from the Church.

According to Rahner, the Church has a two-fold function. It is "the proclaiming bearer of the revealing word of God as his utterance of salvation to the world" and at the same time it is the body of those who listen to and believe in the word of

---

[87]Mt. 19:16

[88]In retrospect, Communio, Winter 1975, 203.

[89]Rechenschaft 1965, 12.

[90]Cordula oder der Ernstfall, 110; Geist und Feuer, Herder Korrespondenz 30, 1976, 78.

[91]Rahner has presented the Church in these terms throughout his works. The main references include: Foundations of Christian faith, 342ff.; Theological investigations 4, 240-245; Theological investigations 14, 142-148; Theological investigations 21, 142-150.

salvation which is addressed not just to the Church, but to the world.[92]

The Second Vatican Council clearly implies that the grace made present in the world through the Church can be active and effective in ways, some of which may remain known only to God, because through no fault of their own many will not become baptised. For these people, no less than for the baptised, the Church points to and renders present the grace which has irrevocably come into the world. The Council's optimism regarding the possibility of salvation for non-culpable atheists is beyond doubt. In addition to the best known section in Lumen Gentium[93] we also find:

> All this holds good not for Christians only but also for all men of good will in whose hearts grace is active invisibly. For since Christ died for all, and since all men are in fact called to one and the same destiny, which is divine, we must hold that the Holy Spirit offers to all the possibility of being made partners, in a way known to God, in the paschal mystery.[94]

> ...in ways known to himself God can lead those who, through no fault of their own, are ignorant of the Gospel to that faith without which it is impossible to please him (Heb. 11:6)...[95]

Though the Second Vatican Council spoke of the Church as "in the nature of sacrament - sign and instrument, that is, of communion with God and of unity among all men", according to Rahner it did not develop this concept fully, which means that it is more difficult to discern precisely what the Council meant.[96] At the least, however, a distinction and a unity is being claimed simultaneously between the Church and the salvation of the world, such that the Church is understood as the sign in history which manifests the will of God, thereby effecting this will which is salvific. The terms "sign" and "effect" must be understood here in the full sense which was outlined when we discussed Rahner's understanding of symbol.

In one of his later lectures, Rahner expands on how he understands this as being possible.[97] When the Council speaks of the Church as the sacrament of the world, it is relying on its faith in the salvific will of God. In optimism which is rooted in hope, it is convinced that God's grace successfully brings about the salvation of many

---

[92]Theological investigations 14, 143.

[93]Lumen Gentium, n. 16, cited towards the end of this chapter.

[94]Gaudium et Spes, n. 22.

[95]Ad Gentes, n. 7.

[96]Lumen Gentium n. 1. Cf. K. Rahner, Theological investigations 14, 142.

[97]The Church and atheism, at the Urban University, Rome, 1980, text reproduced in Theological investigations 21, 137-150

who never become baptised in the Church. When we claim that the Church is sacrament of the world, we are claiming that the Church is somehow instrumental in their salvation. The Church is instrumental in that it makes God's historical promise of himself to all humankind present, and bears witness to this promise irrevocably. The Church functions in this way for the vast majority of people who never become baptised, for non-Christians and even for atheists, whether they lived before or after Christ.

However and wherever it manifests itself, the grace of Christ has as its goal the salvation of human beings in all their historical dimensions and is of its nature oriented towards a full historical tangibility in the Church. Grace is one, and the grace present implicitly in the atheist is the same grace which is incarnated in the Church.

It is clearly not Rahner's intention to account for the salvation of non-Christians in such a way that the Church can be simply by-passed. Non-Christians and atheists are not dispensed from faith or from dependence for their salvation on the Church:

> ... we must call to mind that at all times and in all places the inner, metahistorical
> dimension of grace and faith and the dimension of a historical, social, ultimately
> sacramental tangibility of this grace in the explicit word, in the social character of
> the Church, in the sacrament, have both a necessary interdependence as well as a
> variability in their relationship to one another.

[98]We now have the beginning of an answer to Balthasar's specific question as to why one should bother being a name-bearing Christian, if all goes so well for the non-Christian: the non-Christian's faith is incomplete. It lacks the most proper historical expression which can be found only in the Church, towards which this faith is oriented and on which it is dependent for its full identity and self-understanding.[99] The grace of God intends to bring human beings in all their historical dimensions into God's salvation. The proper historical categorical expression of faith in Christ is

---

[98]Rahner recognises how tempting it is to relativise the role of the Church in accounting for the salvation of the non-believer: "One could of course be first tempted to dismiss the theory of the Church as sacrament of universal grace for the whole world as something that amounts to idle speculation. One could say that one can understand that the grace of Christ even outside of the visible bond of the Church is everywhere at work producing salvation and that the positively upright conscience that we can, in principle, concede to an atheist is already in an unreflexive way an anonymous actualization of faith through the grace of Christ. But then one could object that the relationship of the Church to this non-explicit salvific process of faith and salvation is not brought out clearly in this way and hence is superfluous" (Theological investigations 21, 144).

[99]"Anonymous Christianity serves precisely to express the fact that in the case of a Christianity asserted to be present in this way something is missing from the fullness of its due nature, something which it should have and towards which the nature already present is tending" (Theological investigations 12, 164).

membership of the Church. Grace works towards the Church and intends to bring all into the Church. The fact that this is not as yet achieved, and in concrete cases - in fact in most cases - will not be achieved, does not mean that we must deny that grace is active. On the contrary, our faith calls us to believe not only that grace is active among the non-baptised, but active with success. Were we to believe otherwise, we would in fact be defining the Church as the faithful remnant who are saved and the claim that the Church was the sacrament of Christ for the world would make no sense at all.

Rahner argued repeatedly that anonymous Christianity properly comes to itself (reflex zu sich selber kommt) in the Church. When an anonymous Christian becomes a Christian,

> it is not thereby denied, but on the contrary implied, that this explicit self-realisation of his previous anonymous Christianity is itself part of the development of this Christianity itself - a higher stage of this Christianity demanded by his being - and that it is therefore intended by God in the same way as everything else about his salvation.[100]

Between explicit and implicit Christianity, a kind of analogy exists.[101] Implicit Christianity is referred up towards (hinauf-bezogen), makes towards (hinstrebt) or is ordered towards (hinordnet) explicit Christianity.[102] To understand fully the nature of this ordering, we must return again to our understanding of grace and sacrament. The key theological point to be grasped is that justifying grace can actually be present before the reception of a particular sacrament.[103] That this can be the case has been long recognised in tradition. In Acts 10:47 we find an account of how the Spirit could be present before baptism. Ambrose taught that the catechumen who died before baptism, could be saved. The medievals taught the doctrine of the votum baptismi which was later confirmed by Trent. For Thomas Aquinas it was clear that the sinner, for example, was already justified through penitence before celebrating the sacrament of penance. At the same time it was taught that the sacrament of penance was necessary for salvation. As Rahner says,

---

[100]Theological investigations 5, 132.

[101]The term "implicit Christianity" is not, as Rahner clarified in his debate with de Lubac, meant to represent a particular independent branch of Christianity.

[102]"In der Rede von der impliziten Christlichkeit liegt aber zugleich, daß wie alle Vollzüge des Menschen auch dieser Grundvollzug nicht in seiner Implizität stehenbleiben kann und will, sondern daß er auf seine Ausdrücklichkeit, seinen Namen hinstrebt" (K. Rahner, Sacramentum mundi III, 549-550). Cf. further Sacramentum mundi II, 1209-1215; N. Schwerdtfeger, Gnade und Welt, 383.

[103]Cf. Theological investigations 12, 166-170.

...the theologians did not in the least feel it to be any objection to ask how in that case the sacrament was still necessary and meaningful, seeing that the res sacramenti, the justification, is already conferred even before the reception of the sacrament. Manifestly in their theology of saving history and grace at the collective and individual levels it was obvious to them that the signs of grace as found in the historical dimension and in the Church were not rendered superfluous and meaningless by the fact that grace is already prior to them, for there is an incarnational order such that this grace itself of its very nature seeks its historical embodiment in the word and above all in the sacrament, so that it itself would be denied if an individual sought in principle to frustrate this incarnational dynamism inherent in grace itself.[104]

What difference does the actual reception of the sacrament really make? Rahner gives a two-fold answer.[105] First, he says that the sacrament increases the justifying grace. It is for this reason that Rahner argues, as we saw, that the explicit Christian has a better chance of salvation. Second (and this is based on Rahner's understanding of a symbol and the reciprocal relationship between cause and effect), as the incarnation and effective symbol of this grace the sacrament can constitute one side of a mutually conditioning relationship, being simultaneously the effect and the cause of this original grace. Just as one being becomes expressed in another which is its symbol and which is constitutive of its essence caused by or bringing about its perfection, the anonymous Christian is expressed in the Church and is dependent upon the Church for his or her true identity. Anonymous Christianity demands explicit Christianity in such a way that if an individual "frustrates this incarnational dynamism inherent in grace itself", he or she may only do so culpably.[106]

The anonymous Christian and non-Christian religions
Rahner did not intend the doctrine of the anonymous Christian to be used as an excuse to abandon evangelisation, or even as an explanation for a lack of the Church's success in the mission field.[107] It clearly did have implications, however, for the Christian's self-understanding and for his or her a priori understanding of

[104]Theological investigations 12, 173-174.

[105]Cf. Theological investigations 12, 172. Compare Theological investigations 5, 132.

[106]Cf. Theological investigations 12, 171-172. This is an expression of the Second Vatican Council's insistence that only atheists and non-Christians who are inculpably so can be justified, and it is in accordance with Rahner's insistence on the supernatural existential determining the individual in such a way that he or she must make a decision to accept or reject God's gracious self-offer.

[107]"What is said about the 'anonymous Christian' would therefore be completely misunderstood if it were thought that it represents merely a last desperate attempt in a world where Christian faith is fast disappearing to 'rescue' in its ultimate significance all that is good and human for the Church - against every freedom of the spirit" (Theological investigations 6, 395-396).

those to whom he or she was sent to bring the Gospel.[108] In the first chapter we made the point that the missionary who accepted Rahner's teaching on the anonymous Christian should see the non-Christian as one to whom salvific grace was already present at least as an offer, and as a person who might already have made an implicit act of faith accepting God's gracious self-offer. Other than Balthasar, most of those who criticised the concept of the anonymous Christian, criticised the manner in which it weakened the missionary zeal of the Church. As Rahner made quite clear on a number of occasions, he never intended this to happen.[109]

In the final section of this chapter I intend to situate Rahner's teaching on the anonymous Christian briefly in the context of his teaching on non-Christian religions as a whole. I will then summarise Balthasar's position again, and situate the standpoints of both theologians in the wider context of the Church's teaching on non-Christian religions as it has developed over the last century.

Rahner's approach to non-Christian religions - and here we are including religions other than Judaism, Islam and Hinduism - follows directly from his understanding of how grace can be present and active in the life of the individual non-Christian.[110] First, Rahner recognises among the greatest threats posed to Christian faith by the dawn of pluralism, the threat to Christianity's claim to uniqueness. Nevertheless he sees it as an unavoidable conclusion from the Church's claim regarding the universality of God's saving will that a positive role in the fulfilment of this will must be permitted to non-Christian religions. Rahner argues that if it is possible for all to have justifying faith through the activity of the Holy Spirit, it is against Christianity's own historic nature to assert that this faith could be achieved ahistorically or non-socially. Further, there is no reason to presume that non-Christian religions play merely a neutral or even a negative role: if Christ is present throughout the whole history of salvation, why should he be absent where the concrete man is religious in his history?[111] Rahner is in no doubt that non-Christian religions play an important part in the coming to being of an act of faith in the life of a non-Christian. Such an

---

[108]Cf. K. Rahner, Theological investigations 5, 134; Theological investigations 12, 161-178; Theological investigations 21, 145.

[109]Cf. for example Theological investigations 12, 177-178.

[110]Cf. where Rahner addresses the subject of non-Christian religions: Theological investigations 5, 115-134; Theological investigations 17, 39-50; Theological investigations 18, 288-295; Foundations of Christian faith, 311-321 (which is similar to the article in Theological investigations 17).

[111]Cf. Foundations of Christian faith, 313.

act of faith must have a categorical dimension, and religions as specific historical and social phenomena participate in this categorical dimension. However, the extent to which they participate, i.e. the extent to which their categorical interpretation is more or less successful, can be measured only against the ultimate interpretation which we find in Christianity.

It is only logical, according to Rahner, to admit that Christ can be present in non-Christian religions in the same way as he is present in the lives of non-Christians: through his Holy Spirit.

One of Rahner's main criticisms of the Second Vatican Council is that it did not follow through fully to this logical conclusion drawn from its teaching on the salvation of individual non-Christians. Despite its caution and reserve in this regard, the Council nevertheless acknowledges the relationship of the Church to non-Christian religions (and not just the Church's relationship to non-Christians as individuals) as important and urges us to take these religions seriously.[112]

When we examine the Church's teaching on non-Christian religions historically we realise that it is really only in the last century that we have taken into account that, within the span of human history as a whole, the Judaeo-Christian tradition occupies a very small space. Pessimistic or negative statements about the possibility of salvation being achieved in and through non-Christian religions were usually made in the context of emphasising the uniqueness of Jesus Christ as the only mediator between God and humanity (1 Tim. 2:5). Confronted with rationalism and indifferentism in the middle of the last century, such statements found a new level of intensity:

> We now come to another important cause of the evils with which we regret to see
> the Church afflicted, namely indifferentism, or that wrong opinion according to
> which...man can attain the eternal salvation of his soul by any profession of faith,
> provided his moral conduct conforms to the norms of right and good...From this
> foulest source of indifferentism there flows the absurd and wrong view, or rather
> insanity, according to which freedom of conscience must be asserted and vindicated
> for everybody.[113]

While Pius IX accepted that it is "far from us to want to penetrate the secret plans and judgements of God which are like the great deep, impenetrable to human thought", he urged bishops to

> keep away from men's minds, by all possible efforts, that opinion which is as
> unholy as it is deadly, namely that the way of eternal salvation can be found in any

---

[112]Theological investigations 18, 289. Rahner is referring specifically to Nostra aetate.

[113]Gregory XVI, encyclical letter Mirari Nos Arbitramur 1832, quoted in J. Neuner, and J. Dupuis, The Christian faith in the doctrinal documents of the Church, 280.

religion whatever. With all the learning and ingenuity that is yours, teach the people entrusted to your care that the dogmas of the Catholic faith are not in the slightest manner opposed to divine mercy and justice.[114]

Perhaps here we see most clearly the dilemma with which the Church was and is confronted: on the one hand to acknowledge the limits of our knowledge and the limitlessness of God's mercy and love, and on the other hand to express clearly and unambiguously the conviction that all salvation comes through Jesus Christ.

Eventually responding to a request from the Council in Spoleto in 1851, Pius IX listed the gravest of errors confronting the Catholic Church in 1864. They included the error that

> we should at least have good hopes for the eternal salvation of those who are in no way in the true Church of Christ.[115]

The above statements contrast sharply with the following paragraph from Lumen Gentium, which represents the Church's teaching exactly one hundred years after the Syllabus of Errors:

> For those also can find eternal salvation who without fault on their part do not know the Gospel of Christ and his Church, but seek God with a sincere heart, and under the influence of grace endeavour to do his will as recognised through the promptings of their conscience. Nor does divine Providence deny the help necessary for salvation to those who, without fault on their part, have not yet reached an explicit knowledge of God, and yet endeavour, not without divine grace, to live a good life, for whatever goodness or truth is found among them is considered by the Church as a preparation for the Gospel, a gift from Him who enlightens every man that he may finally have life.

[116]The general attitude of the Second Vatican Council is that there are elements of truth and grace to be found among non-Christian religions which are like a secret presence of God which needs to be illumined by the light of the Gospel.[117] Above all, non-Christian religions are to be respected as "the living expression of the soul of vast groups of people".[118] This is the position which we find reiterated in the new Catechism for the universal Church, and also in the recent encyclical from Pope

---

[114]Singulari Quadam 1854, J. Neuner and J. Dupuis, op. cit., 281-282.

[115]Taken from A Syllabus containing the most important errors of our time which have been condemned by our Holy Father Pius IX in allocutions, at consistories, in encyclicals and other apostolic letters. In: J. Neuner and J. Dupuis, op. cit., 283.

[116]Lumen Gentium n. 16.

[117]Cf. Ad Gentes, n. 9, n. 11.

[118]Paul VI, Evangelii Nuntiandi, n. 53.

John Paul II on the necessity of mission, Redemptoris Missio.[119] In the latter document the Pope reiterates the Council's teaching and stresses that mission has not been replaced by interreligious dialogue or work for human development. He also reminds missionaries that respect for religious freedom and for conscience does not exclude efforts to bring about conversion.

According to Balthasar, Pius IX's fear of the "deadliness" of the teaching that "eternal salvation can be found in any religion whatever" would seem to be realised in the wake of the Second Vatican Council. He believes that Rahner's theology, in any case, approximates to this, and that the teaching of the Second Vatican Council is in danger of being misinterpreted in this way.[120] While it is clear particularly from his book Dare we hope "that all men may be saved?" that Balthasar, like Pius IX, in no way wishes to compromise the Church's teaching on divine mercy and justice, he seems to agree that this must be imparted with as much learning and ingenuity as is possible. As we have already seen, on a number of occasions he seems to adopt almost contradictory positions on the question of the availability of grace outside the Church. His overall position, however, would seem to be as follows. Clearly, individuals outside of the Church, i.e. who are not baptised, may be justified through God's grace. God may indeed be active in their lives. It is our Christian duty to believe this, and Balthasar admits that there are many examples of non-Christians who have given their lives heroically in defence of Gospel values. However, he does not accept that non-Christian religions and philosophies are, in themselves, graced: non-Christians, yes; non-Christian religions, no. According to Balthasar, these are, at best, human attempts to reach God and he is reluctant to claim that these attempts are aided by grace.[121] While Balthasar freely admits the availabilty of grace active in the lives of individuals outside the Church, he is reluctant to provide a theological explanation of how this grace can be active and, as we have already pointed out, his position as a whole makes such an explanation quite difficult. This is clear, for example, when one examines his position on non-Christian prayer which he seems to think is often no more than an urgent and often desperate desire to flee from the senseless merry-go-round of technical civilisation to a transcendental sphere of peace.

---

[119]Redemptoris Missio, especially chapters 1 - 4.

[120]Cf. Geist und Feuer, Herder Korrespondenz 30, 1976, 76, where Balthasar criticises the theory of the anonymous Christian on the grounds that it approximates to a sanctioning of the religious paths of other religions as either ordinary or extraordinary means to salvation.

[121]Cf. Geist und Feuer, Herder Korrespondenz 30, 1976, 72-82; Catholicism and the religions, Communio 5, 1978, 6-14, Response to my critics, Communio 5, 1978, 68-76.

It does not seem to matter whether the sphere is God's or the seeker's own self (sic), or something neutral in between...[122]

In reacting to Balthasar's criticism of him, Rahner has noted this anomaly in Balthasar's recognition of the availability of grace outside the Church:

> ...such an authority as Balthasar himself puts forward the very same doctrine as that which he disputes in my interpretation.[123]

Karl-Heinz Weger has also recognised this inconsistency. Writing very much in defence of Rahner he says

> Hans urs von Balthasar, for example, has rejected Rahner's theologoumenon of anonymous Christianity because 'it implies a relativisation of God in the biblical event and a sanctioning of the objective religious ways of other religions as ordinary and extraordinary ways of salvation'. It is difficult to see how Balthasar can reconcile this statement with those made at Vatican II, but that is his affair. What I cannot understand is how it is possible to maintain that non-Christians have a possibility of salvation on the one hand and, on the other, not to recognise an 'extraordinary' way of salvation in the other religions.[124]

In reply to criticism of his position Balthasar provides us with what is arguably the context in which we are to interpret all his standpoints and emphases which we have hitherto encountered:

> In this Europe, the unique and indivisible "form" of Catholicism - of which no essential factor can be relinquished - has been waived with the justification of pluralism in theology (applied already to Scripture) and the existence in other religions and cultures of certain analogous elements. ("Anonymous Christianity", "all religions are roads to salvation," etc., etc.) Given this acute situation, my theses might sound abrupt and, to some extent, polemical.[125]

Rahner has shown the impossibility of making the kind of distinction between non-Christians and non-Christian religions along the lines which Balthasar seems to suggest, but at the same time he establishes a clear distinction between Christianity as the religion among other religions. Despite his optimism regarding the role played by non-Christian religions, Rahner also clearly recognises their limitations.

In this age of pluralism the Church faces a great dilemma. On the one hand it must account positively, and not just with pious phrases but with theological substance, for the salvation of non-Christians and of those baptised Christians who at one level or another have opted out of the Church. On the other hand, the Church must not cash

---

[122]H. U. von Balthasar, Christian Prayer, Communio 5, 1978, 16.

[123]K. Rahner (Theological investigations 11, 39, n.15) refers us to Cordula oder der Ernstfall, 95, and Wer ist ein Christ?, 100.

[124]Karl Rahner, 119.

[125]Response to my Critics, Communio 5, 1978, 69. Cf. further J. B. Cobb, A question for Hans Urs von Balthasar, Communio 5, 1978, 53-59.

in Christianity's claim to the universal salvific significance of Jesus Christ, thus forfeiting its own essential identity.[126] Balthasar's great fear is that the latter is already happening. However, if the Church's claim to uniqueness is to be credible in a pluralistic society, such a positive account is absolutely necessary.[127] More fundamentally, the provision of such a credible account is required if we are to be faithful to promulgating the Church's teaching on the universality and efficacy of God's will to save. Balthasar's is rightly concerned with the combat against indifferentism. However, the problem of safeguarding the Church's uniqueness cannot be resolved by devaluing non-Christian religions or by playing down the efficacy of grace outside explicit Christianity.

---

[126]We find this dilemma recognised in Pope John Paul II's enyclical, Redemptoris Missio, n.9.

[127]J. Dupuis agrees with Rahner that this is the most urgent task facing the contemporary Church: "Entretemps, contenons-nous d'observer avec Karl Rahner, que la tache christologique la plus urgente aujourd'hui consiste sans doute à montrer la signification universelle et la dimension cosmique de l'événement Jésus-Christ" (Jésus Christ à la rencontre des religions, 132). Cf. further his sections Le débat actuel de la Théologie des religions (133-141) and Deux Positions contrastantes (163-169).

Chapter 6
The Anonymous Christian: Conclusions

Introduction

In the last two chapters we examined particular criticisms which Balthasar made of
Rahner's anonymous Christian and of Rahner's theological method as a whole. In all
major points we found that Rahner's theology, central to which is the theory of the
anonymous Christian, does not constitute a reduction or a relativisation of the
Christian mystery as revealed in biblical revelation.

The subject of our research has been disagreement regarding one of the main tasks
of fundamental theology: the analysis and organisation of our pre-comprehension of
God.[1] Disagreement regarding method would not be possible were it not for
pluralism in theology. One of the advantages of theological pluralism is that one
methodological approach can complement, enhance or correct another. The aim of
this final chapter is to show how Balthasar's and Rahner's approaches to organising
the human pre-comprehension of God can complement each other, and how the
subject of this research is relevant to the contemporary Church and in particular, to
contemporary efforts at evangelisation.

The first part of the chapter examines the similarities and differences between
Balthasar's and Rahner's analysis of the pre-comprehension of God, and it points out
the value of Balthasar's criticisms. We find that Balthasar cannot do without some
concept of a Vorverständnis which, in fact, is very similar to Rahner's, but that
Balthasar is more aware of a danger in the method characterised by Rahner's
theology, even if it cannot be proven that this danger is realised in Rahner's work.
While I am making explicit here the complementarity in Balthasar's and Rahner's
understandings of the a priori by drawing the reader's attention especially to this
element of Balthasar's theology of revelation, it should be clearly borne in mind that
for Balthasar and Rahner the a priori and the a posteriori form an integral whole and
are only to be considered separately for the purposes of elucidation.

The second part re-enforces the complementary nature of the work of Balthasar and
Rahner by drawing some practical conclusions regarding the contemporary usefulness
and possible implications of the doctrine of the anonymous Christian for the Church's
contemporary missionary task in Europe. We will find that the theory of the
anonymous Christian offers us a theological understanding of how those who do not
identify with explicit Christianity can be saved, an understanding which, though

---

[1]Cf. C. Geffré, Recent developments in fundamental theology: an interpretation, Concilium,
1965, 11.

bearing in mind the cautionary notes sounded by Balthasar, still does not necessarily undermine explicit Christian faith. Such an understanding can offer those who evangelise both a motivation and a sense of direction.

The final part of the chapter reflects on the importance of providing such a theological understanding in the context of the contemporary faith situation in Europe.

On Balthasar's understanding of the pre-comprehension of God and on the importance of his criticisms

In the course of examining Balthasar's criticisms of Rahner we already have had cause to refer to Balthasar's position on the availability of grace outside the Church. However, the articles examined were not written with the intention of providing such an account and it was impossible to get a clear picture of Balthasar's own understanding.[2]

Balthasar deals systematically with theology's task of organising and presenting the human being's pre-comprehension of God in the first volume of his major trilogy, The Glory of the Lord.[3] His main argument here is that the Cartesian-Kantian influence on theology has led to the imposing of the measure of the human spirit on divine revelation with the consequent relegation of aesthetics to the periphery of theology. However, Balthasar's theological aesthetics cannot function without some understanding of an a priori either. Balthasar acknowledges this himself:

> He (the human being) certainly has a pre-understanding (Vorverständnis) of what
> love is; if he did not he could not make out the sign Jesus Christ. It would be
> objectively insoluble and contradictory, because here has appeared the love of God
> in the form of flesh, i.e. in the form of human love. But he cannot proceed beyond
> this pre-understanding to a recognition of the sign without a radical conversion...[4]

Balthasar's understanding of how this a priori manifests itself is, in fact, remarkably similar to Rahner's.

Balthasar speaks of the human being as endowed with both a religious a priori and a theological a priori which never exist apart from each other but whose distinction must be posited to explain the human experience of the gratuitousness of grace.

The religious a priori is the human being's natural pursuit of the transcendent:

---

[2]Cf. Section 2: Chapter 2, pp. 167-171.

[3]The Glory of the Lord 1: Seeing the form. Cf. especially 131-417.

[4]Love alone: the way of revelation, 51. This point is also made by C. Geffré:"...von Balthasar himself cannot do wholly without some kind of pre-understanding. I can only apprehend the beauty of the mystery of Christ if I already have within me some kind of norm of beauty, and it is because I perceive there a certain affinity that I can come to credibility" (loc. cit.).

> There is a natural religious a priori, given with the essence of the creature as such,
> which coincides with its ability to understand all existents in the light of Being,
> which is analogous to and points to God. Provided it does not get caught up in
> detailed analysis of partial aspects of Being, natural ontology is very largely always
> also a form of natural theology.[5]

The theological a priori is the graced transformation of the religious a priori:

> ...the ontological and epistemological elevation and illumination of this a priori by
> the light of the interior fullness of God's life as he reveals himself...this
> manifestation of God does not dawn only on those who expressly call themselves
> Christian, but basically on all men. This is because we are all called to the vision
> of God in eternal life and, therefore, however secretly, all are placed by God's
> grace in an interior relationship to this light of revelation. Therefore, many aspects
> of what in non-Christian spheres is called the "religious a priori" and is described
> in religious experience must, in fact, be shot through with elements of grace.[6]

Through the theological a priori, God's unmerited gracious self-communication invites
and enables all human beings to enter into a relationship with the Trinity.[7]

In the course of examining his criticisms of Rahner we saw that Balthasar's main
objection to modern philosophy - and specifically to the Cartesian-Kantian influence
on scholars such as Blondel, Scheuer, Maréchal and Rousselot - is that it blurs the
vital distinction which must be posited between the religious a priori and the
theological a priori and does not emphasise sufficiently that these exist for the sake
of the objective, a posteriori vision of Jesus' form.[8] The result is that the human
relation with God becomes limited almost entirely to the a priori desire for the
absolute. Kay draws the consequences:

> Jesus' form does not verify itself by virtue of the evidence contained in its beauty
> but by its ability to satisfy a person's present understanding of his drive towards
> transcendence. Christ is not believed primarily for his own sake but for the
> believer's sake...The form of Christ cannot be verified on the basis of any a priori
> evidence but must verify itself. The form of Christ makes a new revelation with its
> own evidence, which no insight into human dynamism can anticipate or verify.
> There is no need in man that can explain and verify Christ's words and acts
> throughout history. Likewise man has no a priori insight into the dynamism of God
> that could explain or verify Christ's words and deeds. The only sufficiently clear
> and credible explanation for what Christ does and teaches throughout history lies
> in the form of Christ itself. Christian faith is based radically on the a posteriori
> evidence of Christ's historical form and not primarily on ahistorical, a priori
> evidence that has been awakened or mediated to itself on the occasion of a

---

[5]The Glory of the Lord 1, 167.

[6]loc.cit.

[7]Cf. The Glory of the Lord 1, 155ff.

[8]The Glory of the Lord 1, 149. Cf. further J. Kay, Aesthetics and a posteriori evidence in
Balthasar's theological method, Communio Winter 1975, 191.

posteriori experience.[9]

A theological aesthetics such as Balthasar's, however, "avoids reducing the God of Christ to the dimensions of human need and thus robbing Christ of his credibility"[10]. Balthasar is quite right to insist on the importance of the distinction which must be posited between the religious a priori and the theological a priori if the gratuitousness of grace is not to be compromised. However, as we have shown, the claim that such a distinction does not exist in Rahner's theology must be rejected.[11] We saw that Rahner distinguishes between what Balthasar refers to as religious and theological a priori by postulating the state of "pure nature", which is ontic, not ontological, and which is only hypothetically postulated to protect the gratuitousness of grace. In such a state the human being would be subject only to what Balthasar refers to as the religious a priori. But for both Balthasar and Rahner, the human being never exists in a state in which he or she is subject only to a religious a priori. For Balthasar the theological a priori - a transcendental presupposition of all human knowledge drawing the human being into relationship with the Trinity - is co-extensive with the religious a priori.[12] Just as, according to Rahner, the human being's obediential potency is supernaturally enhanced in the ontological state in which the human being always finds himself or herself, Balthasar considers the religious a priori always to be similarly transformed. Therefore when Rahner claims that the (ontic) state of pure nature never existed in history but is a necessary valid hypothetical proposition to protect the gratuitousness of grace, he is making the very same point as Balthasar when the latter claims that the religious a priori never exists without the theological a priori but that the distinction must be posited in order to account for the gratuitousness of grace. For Balthasar as well as for Rahner the notion of a religious a priori existing without a theological a priori is purely hypothetical.

When we examine Balthasar's definition of the theological a priori given above it becomes very difficult to see where this differs critically from Rahner's understanding of the supernatural existential. The theological a priori represents the ontological and

---

[9]J. Kay, art.cit., 293, 296.

[10]art. cit., 299.

[11]For example, "The Cartesian-Kantian influence on theology has led numerous theologians to lose sight... of the distinction between the religious and theological a priori. Among the illustrious contemporary examples of this tendency are Barth, Rahner, Bultmann, Ebeling, Lonergan and Jung" (J. Kay, art.cit., 291).

[12]Cf. Spiritus Creator, 37, 241.

epistemological elevation of the religious a priori through grace, just as the
supernatural existential represents God's permanent influence enhancing or modifying
the creature's obediential potency, revealing to the creature the ultimate meaning of
human existence, which is God himself, and inviting the creature to commit himself
or herself to this meaning. Balthasar is quite prepared to admit that as a consequence
of his understanding of the theological a priori non-Christians are secretly (he could
have said "anonymously") placed by God's grace in an interior relationship to
revelation.[13] This corresponds precisely to the essential meaning of the theory of the
anonymous Christian. Therefore Rahner is right when he says that

> the critical evaluations of my interpretation (cf. H.U. von Balthasar, Cordula oder
> der Ernstfall...) simply overlook the fact that this 'Christianhood' of man, which
> is already present as a concomitant of grace, is precisely the condition for any
> proclamation of truth on the part of the Church, while conversely this grace itself
> only achieves its full consummation and becomes fully apprehensible as a historical
> phenomenon when it achieves and sustains an explicitly Christian creed, and a state
> in which it is embodied in the social life of the Church. Furthermore, such an
> authority as Balthasar himself puts forward the very same doctrine as that which
> he disputes in my interpretation.[14]

Rahner does not lose sight of the distinction which exists between the religious and
theological a priori, and his position is closer to Balthasar's than the latter seems to
recognise.

Up until now this point we have stressed the similarities which exist between the
manner in which both Rahner and Balthasar organise the human being's pre-
comprehension of God. The difference is that Balthasar is more aware than Rahner
of the danger of a relativisation of biblical revelation if the human being is presented
as already having within himself or herself the evidence necessary to verify the
historical form of Jesus. This is why Balthasar tries to play down the effectiveness
of the pre-comprehension. But surely if not only Rahner's supernatural existential but
also Balthasar's theological a priori are to serve any purpose at all, they must provide
some meaningful and valid pre-comprehension?[15] Balthasar himself claims that the
theological a priori has an effect such that through it "all are placed by God's grace
in an interior relationship to this light of revelation".[16] There is no reduction or
relativisation involved if it is on account of God's grace that one is able to recognise

---

[13]The Glory of the Lord 1, 167.

[14]Theological investigations 11, 39, n.15.

[15]As already pointed out, a real dynamism must have a real goal as its term.

[16]The Glory of the Lord 1, 167.

the historical form of Jesus of Nazareth. It is the same Jesus Christ who addresses the human being transcendentally and invites the human being to enter into a relationship with him. The presence both of a religious a priori and a theological a priori in the individual, the latter being a graced presence and all grace being the grace of Jesus Christ, must somehow serve to verify or authenticate the a posteriori manifestation of Christ.

Ultimately, Rahner and Balthasar are not in dispute about the presence of God's salvific grace in the life of the non-Christian. They disagree regarding what they consider to be the priority for theology today. Their disagreement is rooted in two different understandings of how the Church should address what is happening to Christian faith in the contemporary world.

Both Balthasar and Rahner see it as critical that theology should not only make statements of truth, but should also interpret them for each generation. But they disagree regarding how this interpretation should be done. According to Rahner, theology's most urgent task is to provide credible answers to the most urgent questions which people are asking.[17] The contemporary systematic theologian must also be an apologist. This is why, in Williams's words, Rahner's Christ is an answer to the human question.[18]

The danger, however, is that Christ might be presented only as the answer to the human question. On the other hand,

> Balthasar's Christ remains a question to all human answers, and to all attempts at metaphysical or theological closure.[19]

The theologian is challenged by Balthasar to present salvation as the most adequate, fulfilling and appropriate response possible to the human condition, and at the same time to point beyond this, to "the God of the ever-more"[20]. The value of Balthasar's work is that it is a constant reminder that God's gift of self is not merely proportional to human need. As we have already seen Balthasar himself says,

---

[17]Rahner's understanding of the purpose of theology is close to that of Paul Tillich: "(Theology) tries to correlate the questions implied in the situation with the answers implied in the message. It does not derive the answers from the questions as a self-defying apologetic theology does. Nor does it elaborate answers without relating them to the questions as a self-defying kerygmatic theology does. It correlates questions and answers, situation and message, human existence and divine manifestation" (Systematic theology, 1, 3).

[18]R. Williams, Balthasar and Rahner. In: J. Riches, ed., The analogy of beauty, 34.

[19]R. Williams, loc. cit.

[20]Cf. H. Heinz, Der Gott des Je-mehr. Der christologische Ansatz Hans Urs von Balthasars.

> It might be true that from the very beginning man was created to be disposed
> towards God's revelation, so that with God's grace even the sinner can accept all
> revelation. Gratia supponit naturam. But when God sends his own living Word to
> his creatures, he does so, not to instruct them about the mysteries of the world, nor
> primarily to fulfil their deepest needs and yearnings. Rather he communicates and
> actively demonstrates such unheard-of things that man feels not satisfied but
> awestruck by a love which he never could have hoped to experience. For who
> would dare to have described God as love, without having first received the
> revelation of the Trinity in the acceptance of the cross by the Son.[21]

The importance of Balthasar's criticisms of Rahner is that they alert us to a double
danger within this whole approach to doing theology. There is the danger first, that
we would come to understand God's gift of self merely as a response to human need,
and second, that the motivation for our love of God would be little more than a
selfish desire for self-fulfilment. There is a danger that God would be loved not for
his own, but for the lover's sake.

But is it not true that at least our initial interest in God is awakened because of a
perceived need, because of some experience which we have had which we cannot
otherwise satisfactorily account for? And further, when compared with divine love,
is it not inevitable that human love would appear relatively selfish and limited? Is it
really possible for a human being to love Christ other than primarily for the human
being's own sake? Should we not simply recognise the poverty of our ability to love,
the imperfection of human love and the infinite divide which exists between the nature
of human love for the divine and divine love for humanity? While recognising and
taking into account the infralapsarian creature's frailty, Balthasar nevertheless
challenges us not to surrender too easily. Above all he alerts us to the danger that we
might begin to think of divine love in terms of human love, i.e. that we might begin
to think that God loves us as imperfectly as we love him. Balthasar warns us not to
confuse our relationship with God - which is a real relationship with a living Being -
with our acceptance of an ideology or a code of conduct. This is a real danger today,
in a world in which it is increasingly more difficult to experience God's presence.[22]
However, in order to alert us to these dangers, Balthasar runs the risk of
undervaluing the human being's pre-comprehension of God. Balthasar's criticism not
just of Rahner but of this whole anthropological approach within theology must be
understood as a reaction, and, as with any reaction, it can be subject to distortion.
From an examination and confrontation of Balthasar's and Rahner's approaches an

---

[21]Current trends in Catholic theology and the responsibility of the Christian, Communio 5,
Spring 1978, 77-85.

[22]This point will be taken up in the final section of this chapter.

important and indispensable balance within contemporary fundamental theology can be struck. Rahner articulates the relationship between nature and grace in such a way that we can understand how God's love for us, which takes the form of a divine will to save all of humankind, can be effective. Balthasar reminds us that God's loving will to save humankind is infinitely deeper than our understanding of it, and that the poverty of our understanding is enriched only in the cross of Jesus Christ. One of the strengths of Balthasar's theology is that he stresses that the only sufficiently clear and credible explanation for what God does throughout history lies in the form of Christ itself. Though this cannot be the focal point for Rahner in the way it is for Balthasar, we have seen that Rahner nevertheless clearly accepts that:

> Not until the full and unsurpassable event of the historical self-objectification of God's self-communication to the world in Jesus Christ do we have an event which, as an eschatological event, fundamentally and absolutely precludes any historical corruption or any distorted interpretation in the further history of categorical revelation and of false religion.[23]

For both Balthasar and Rahner it is in and through the form of the historical Christ that we recognise God's activity throughout the world authoritatively. The history of the world is only understood in the light of salvation history.[24]

Rahner challenges the theologian to present theology in such a way that it is a credible mediation of the mystery of Christian faith in the light of contemporary human experience. Neither is it Balthasar's intention that theology would be insensitive to human experience. Balthasar challenges the theologian to mediate Christian faith credibly without at the same time making human experience the ultimate measure of the divine mystery. This would also be entirely unacceptable to Rahner.

---

[23]Foundations of Christian faith, 157.

[24]We must dispute Kay's further claim (art. cit., 291) that Rahner loses sight of the fact that the a priori exists for the sake of the objective, a posteriori vision of Jesus' form. With Balthasar, Rahner sees the objective a priori vision of Jesus' form as the "recognition and homecoming of everything in the way of truth and love which exists or could exist anywhere else" (Theological investigations 5, 9). We have already shown that Rahner's understanding of Jesus Christ, and especially the cross of Jesus Christ, as the Ursakrament (i.e. as the primary sign and instrument of salvation), his understanding of sacrament as symbol, and his (Thomistic) interpretation of the relationship between cause and effect - these endorse his claim that transcendental a priori revelation in a real sense exists for categorical a posteriori revelation (Section 3, Chapter 2). The claim that Rahner limits the human relation with God almost entirely to the a priori desire for the absolute is to be rejected as a failure to appreciate the innermost unity which must be considered to exist between transcendental a priori revelation and categorical a posteriori revelation. Like Balthasar, Rahner also recognises that the a priori desire for the absolute exists always and everywhere as an a priori which is supernaturally elevated by the grace of Christ. Compare H. U. von Balthasar, The Glory of the Lord 1, 167, and K. Rahner, Foundations of Christian faith, 153; Theological investigations 16, 215.

Anonymous Christianity and the missionary task of the Church today
Systematic Theology concerns itself with the contemporary questions asked by the Church and put to the Church: it does not have complete control over its agenda.[25] The greatest challenge facing the Church in a secularised and secularist Western Europe is to re-evangelise. It would be difficult for a Western European to claim to hear about Christianity for the first time. An increasing number of people in Western Europe are rejecting Christianity as it has been presented to them and as they have come to understand it.[26] The missionary in Western Europe finds that he or she is likely to be addressing people who have been baptised, have been educated in a school where at least some Christian doctrine was taught, and have grown up in a family in which Christian values had some importance. The missionary finds that many people accept aspects of the Church's teaching but do not see themselves as being in any way actively involved in the Church and do not see that the Church has any right to make demands on them, even if they are baptised. Some people accept without apology the cliché "Christ, yes; Church, no!" as descriptive of themselves. Others are hostile or just indifferent both to Christ and Church. The missionary in Europe today discovers many anomalies and contradictions in people's attitudes to Christianity and in their understanding of Church.

The theologian must offer some understanding of how these people can experience God's grace and make a positive response to God's grace even if their relationship to Christianity and the Church appears on the surface to be seriously flawed. Can the theory of the anonymous Christian be helpful in this context?

Rahner developed the theory of the anonymous Christian for application primarily in the context of widespread atheism. In 1968 he said,

> In the future it may be presumed that atheism of the explicit kind will be extremely widespread (though of course there will be very many different shades and degrees of this) ranging from an atheism of irresponsiveness and indifference towards religion as a matter of living practice to one that is very thoroughly worked out at the theoretical level, and in fact a militant atheism (...an atheism of this kind, as it exists in the concrete individual, is under certain circumstances perfectly compatible with an implicit and anonymous theism).[27]

The kind of atheism which the Christian missionary in Europe encounters today is better described as an indifference toward religion as a matter of living practice than

---

[25]W. Kasper, The methods of dogmatic theology, 30.

[26]Cf. F. Wetter ed., Kirche in Europa, 9-42, 139-159, 185-194.

[27]K. Rahner, Theological investigations 11, 177.

as a systematic atheism.[28] Atheism is defined broadly enough by the Second Vatican Council to include both extremes.[29] According to Gaudium et Spes, the term "atheist" is not meant to define only those who subscribe to atheism as a system which seeks to realise the human desire for autonomy, but also those, for example, who have a faulty notion of God and who have such an exalted concept of human existence that their faith languishes as a result. Therefore it can be argued that what the Council has to say about atheists may also be applied, and is more appropriately applied today, to those whose attitude to religious belief is more a matter of indifference than of systematic rejection.

We noted a development in the Council's understanding regarding the possibility of long-term inculpable atheism.[30] We found that even a most cautious interpretation of Gaudium et Spes and Lumen Gentium leaves open the possibility of long-term inculpable atheism. The one difficulty about applying this in the context of religious indifference in Europe is that inculpability refers to "those who, through no fault of their own, do not know the Gospel of Christ or his Church". Can one claim that even some baptised people, through no fault of their own, do not know the Gospel of Christ and the Church? We must admit the possibility of failure in previous efforts to evangelise. The Council included among atheists those who

> have such a faulty notion of God that when they disown this product of the imagination their denial has no reference to the God of the Gospels.[31]

Rahner also recognises the possibility that atheists who believe that they are rejecting God are really rejecting a false image of God:

but the moment we put the question seriously to ourselves of what part this concept of God effectively played in the lives of very many of these earlier 'theists' both inside and outside Christendom, then surely we can justifiably ask whether precisely this idea of God really had so very much to do with the true, living, and inconceivable God as he really is.[32]

---

[28] A recent German synod commented: "We shall survive our intellectual doubters more easily than the inarticulate doubts of the poor and insignificant and their memory of the Church's failure" (In: W. Kasper, Faith and the future, 25).

[29] Cf. Gaudium et Spes 19 - 21.

[30] See Chapter 1. The relevant conciliar statements are: Gaudium et Spes nn. 19-22, Lumen Gentium n. 16 and Ad Gentes. For K. Rahner's interpretation see Theological investigations 9, 146-148; Theological investigations 6, 297.

[31] Gaudium et Spes n. 19.

[32] Theological investigations 11, 179.

We can take it, therefore, that among those who are baptised and who grew up in an environment which was more or less Christian, there are people whose attitude to the Church and to explicit Christian faith is now inculpably a matter of hostility or indifference.

At the same time, of course, it must be asserted as a possibility that there are those whose rejection of Christianity and the Church is the result of a decision made in all freedom and with full knowledge. The teaching of the Council also makes their situation quite clear:

> Without doubt those who wilfully try to drive God from the heart and to avoid all questions about religion, not following the biddings of their conscience, are not free from blame.[33]

In the context of clarifying the relationship between the Christian and the anonymous Christian, Rahner also said that there is an incarnational order such that grace of its very nature seeks its historical embodiment in the word and above all in the sacrament, and this means that this grace itself would be denied if an individual sought in principle to frustrate the incarnational dynamism inherent in grace itself.[34] However there are many factors in modern society outside the control of the individual which frustrate this incarnational dynamism, as Rahner calls it. This would seem to be accepted also by the Council when it said that

> Modern civilisation itself, though not of its very nature but because it is too engrossed in the concerns of the world, can often make it harder to approach God.[35]

In individual cases one cannot and should not judge. However bearing in mind Christian conviction regarding the salvific will of God to save all humankind, one cannot but hope with confidence that God's grace is not only offered but more often than not also received and acted upon by many of those baptised whose attitude to explicit Christianity is indifference or even rejection.[36]

We know that God's grace is present at least as an offer to each human being, baptised or not baptised. Because God is the ultimate meaning of human existence, God's gracious self-offer reveals to the human being his or her ultimate meaning which is God alone. God's self-offer enables and necessitates the assuming of an

---

[33]Gaudium et Spes n.19

[34]Cf. the previous chapter. Cf. further Theological investigations 12, 173-174.

[35]Gaudium et Spes n.19.

[36]Cf. Theological investigations 6, 391-398. Compare H. U. von Balthasar, Dare we hope "that all men be saved"? 171-176.

attitude of ultimate acceptance or rejection of God.[37] It is a consequence both of Rahner's understanding of the supernatural existential, and arguably also of Balthasar's concept of the theological a priori, that a refusal of God's self-offer involves one in a contradiction with oneself. Such a refusal is not only a rejection of God but also a rejection of one's own supernaturally exalted nature. However, we cannot but believe - and in this we are given theological grounds by both Balthasar and Rahner - that there are many who are saved because they accept God's gracious self-offer in the innermost depths of their transcendental existence, but, baptised or not and for one reason or another for which they are not personally responsible, who fail to give their positive response to God's grace its proper categorical expression in explicit Christianity and the Church.

At this point it is important to say a word on the significant difference which baptism makes. At baptism, after a confession of faith one is united with Christ and formed into God's people. One receives the dignity of being an adopted child of God. Even if Christians later cease to respect or express their baptismal commitment in any obvious way, a commitment which, for the vast majority, was made in infancy, they are still in a permanent relationship to Christ and the Church through baptism. Therefore the missionary task with regard to these people is to re-awaken and re-activate an explicit response and commitment already made. In the following of their consciences, in their devotion to their day-to-day duties, in their kindness and compassion to those whom they encounter, these so-called "non-practising" Christians are expressing categorically the commitment to God's grace which they have already made in their hearts and explicitly at their baptism even though they do not recognise it and perhaps do not wish to.

In the lives of many of these people the Christian virtue of charity shines clearly. Many of these people make sacrifices daily for their brothers and sisters. The fact that they themselves do not see the manner in which they live their lives as a response to the commitment undertaken at their baptism, nor as a share in the communal work of the Church to build up Christ's body and infuse Christ's presence in the world, is a tragedy and a cause of shame for the Church. It weakens the Church in its effort to be the greatest possible radiance of the healing and compassion of Jesus Christ.

It may well be disputed that it is useful to relate the concept of anonymous Christians to what might be called nominal or non-practising Christians. The aim in so doing is

---

[37]Cf Chapter 1 for an account of Rahner's supernatural existential, and earlier this chapter (for an account of Balthasar's understanding of the theological a priori). Cf. further Theological investigations 5, 191; Glory of the Lord 1, 167.

to clarify the Church's self-understanding and its missionary task.

With regard to the Church's self-understanding, clearly there is no reason why so-called non-practising Christians should make practising Christians feel insecure or threatened. Through the doctrine of the anonymous Christian we can give grounds for our hope that so-called non-practising Christians who follow their consciences are indeed responding implicitly to God's grace even if on the categorical level they claim to deny this. Further, we can give such grounds for hope without at the same time rendering our own ecclesial activity superfluous. We understand that our belonging to the Church and our activity as members of Christ's body are not an   optional extra: it is the correct categorical realisation of an implicit positive response which we believe and hope we have made to God's self-offer transcendentally. The non-practising Christian is lacking the ultimate and objectively valid categorical expression of the response he or she has already implicitly made and at one stage in his or her life explicitly accepted in baptism. Though we can never be too sure that even our own response is adequate - aware of our sinfulness and guilt we cannot even pass judgement on our own state of justification - we nevertheless believe that in our active belonging to Christ's body we are attempting with God's grace to give expression to a decision which has been made following an encounter with the grace of Christ in our deepest selves, and were we to renege on expressing our transcendental acceptance of God's grace in this way, we believe we would be drawing our own very existence into the deepest contradiction imaginable.

Recognising the very real possibility which so-called non-practising Christians have of achieving salvation does not undermine the Church in its ministry. Rather it challenges the Church to consider the beginning of its missionary task as enabling these people to recognise God's grace already active in their lives. As missionaries we affirm the many aspects of these people's lives which are shot through with God's grace.[38] We challenge these people to cast aside false or inadequate images of Christianity and Church. We enable them to overcome past hurtful experiences which they may have had and by the witness of our own lives we invite them to recognise their true dignity and become what they already are in their hearts and through their baptism.[39]

---

[38]The Glory of the Lord 1, 167.

[39]Kasper reminds us of the nature of baptism as a standing invitation to all the baptised to become what they already are in Christ: "Die Taufe ist also das Eingangstor und die Grundlage des Christseins. Sie ist ein beständiger Anruf: Christ, erkenne deine Würde und werde, was du bist!" (W. Kasper, Von der Würde des Christseins, Hirtenbrief an die Gemeinden der Diözese Rottenburg-

Already it is clear that the advantage of applying the theory of the anonymous Christian along the lines suggested here is that it can give the Church confidence in its own identity and sense of purpose, and offer missionaries a sense of direction.

From the point of view of the Church's credibility it is absolutely necessary that we provide an explanation which is theologically sound of how so-called non-practising Christians can be saved. The Church claims that all salvation comes through Christ and that God wishes to save all humankind. When an increasing number of Christians adopt an attitude of ambivalence and indifference to the Church, and when the number of Christians actively involved in and committed to the Church decreases, the credibility of this claim is called into question. Theology has the responsibility to articulate this claim:

> a theology is not really ecclesial if it simply maintains its theses within the solidarity of the believing community. That is a necessary presupposition, but it is not the ultimate goal. A theology is truly ecclesial only when it realises its solidarity with unbelievers as well, when it regards their questions as questions directed towards its own faith.[40]

To summarise then: the doctrine of the anonymous Christian as developed by Rahner enables us to account theologically for the salvation of all those who, through no fault of their own, fail to give proper explicit expression to the acceptance of grace which they have already made implicitly.[41] People can be baptised and through no fault of their own still not know the Gospel of Christ and the Church. The missionary's task is to enable these people to recognise fully what they already are. Responding to this challenge is not an optional extra.

Conclusion

We began by observing that the most serious problem facing the Church today is to articulate the most profound of Christian truths: God wills the salvation of all humankind through Jesus Christ, who is the Saviour of the world, and the Church. We identified that the challenge facing the theologian is to provide a credible account of how all people can experience and respond to God's grace, and at the same time to proclaim the unique role of the incarnation and cross of Jesus Christ and of the Church in the mediation of salvation to all. In the course of examining Balthasar's

---

Stuttgart zur österlichen Bußzeit 1991.

[40]W. Kasper, The methods of dogmatic theology, 30.

[41]We cannot go into a discussion here on the efficacy of the grace of baptism among non-practising Christians.

criticisms of Karl Rahner's theory of the anonymous Christian, we have come to an understanding of how both Balthasar and Rahner account for the salvation of the world through Christ and the Church.

We saw that Rahner's real theological starting-point is his conviction that God wishes everyone to be saved and reach full knowledge of the truth (1Tim. 2:4). For Rahner, God's salvific will is the key: God so loved the world that he gave his Son (Jn 3:16). Balthasar does not dispute this. However, he believes it is a matter of urgency to proclaim how God's salvific will became effective: God reconciled the world to himself in Christ (2 Cor. 5:19). Concretely, we have identified that the challenge is to account credibly for the salvation of those who do not express their faith within Christianity, without undermining the Church's mission to the world.

In this chapter it has already been suggested that the theory of the anonymous Christian can be helpful in enabling us to identify the missionary task facing the Church today. In this concluding section we suggest how the contemporary faith situation requires an understanding of the efficacy of God's grace, such as Rahner offers, as well as an appreciation of the urgency of the Church's mission and ministry, which is characteristic of Balthasar's theology.

Christian faith must survive today in a Europe which is increasingly materialistic and consumerist. The difficulty is that a materialistic or consumerist attitude which initially manifests itself in regard to objects can overflow into how one relates to other people, the environment, and even to oneself. This dehumanising circle spirals into a kind of consumerist attitude to God. The dehumanising influences, particularly in Western European society, can mean that, for many, Augustine's cor inquietum is simply by-passed. More and more come to see the Church as marketing just one brand of meaning to life, and there are many others, better marketed, on the shelf.[42] The situation of the Church in mainland Western Europe, at the moment, reflected upon carefully, gives us at least a glimpse of how the situation within the Church in Ireland might develop over the next few decades. We cannot expect that the situation will be identical: disillusionment with the Church among younger generations in Ireland is coming much later in time than in mainland Europe and it would seem to be accompanied by at least a partial disillusionment with much of what has replaced the Church there. In Ireland the opportunity of a materially better lifestyle has been accompanied by, for example, changes in family life, migration to urban centres,

---

[42]W. Kasper comments that even in a so-called post-atheistic society, more and more people claim to be living happy and fulfilled human lives without belief in God. Cf. W. Kasper, An introduction to Christian faith, 19.

widespread unemployment and emigration. Many in Ireland find the Church increasingly unacceptable, or acceptable only on their own terms. For others it is largely irrelevant or just uninteresting. But at least as of now there is no one alternative indigenous value system offering itself coherently as a substitute. Indifference to the Church is stronger than hostility, and arguably, more hopeless. If hostility rather than indifference still characterises the reaction of many Irish people to the Church, perhaps it is a sign of a relationship gone wrong but not beyond rescue.[43]

Drawing on the reflections on secularisation by A. McIntyre (the author of After Virtue), M. P. Gallagher alerts the Irish Church to one of the most important consequences of the contemporary shift from the experience of authority to the authority of experience: emotivism.[44] Gallagher points to the danger that today many people might make serious moral judgements entirely on the basis of their emotions. Everyday experience would seem to support his theory: some teachers, for example, note that their insight and wisdom, as distinct from their technical knowledge, is accepted by young people as just one opinion among many, and evaluated on the basis of whether it makes them feel good or bad.

It is not surprising that contemporary religious indifference masks a type of atheism which is emotionally rather than rationally based. The crisis of facts which dominated the Enlightenment and fed a rationalistic kind of atheism has been replaced in the post-Enlightenment world by a new crisis of meaning. This is largely due to people's awareness of and disappointment with the limitations of science. The Enlightenment world was certain of its facts, but was dull and impoverished. The human capacity

---

[43]The following books and articles give us some insight into what is currently happening vis-à-vis faith in Ireland: M. Clarke et al, Mustard seeds, Dublin: Veritas, 1985; M. P. Gallagher, Help my unbelief, Dublin: Veritas, 1983; M. P. Gallagher, Struggles of faith, Dublin: Columba Press, 1990; T. Inglis, Moral monopoly: the Catholic Church in modern Irish society, Dublin: Gill and Macmillan, 1987; J. McDermott, Voices in the wilderness, Dublin: Columba Press, 1987; B. McMahon, Listening to youth, Dublin: Dominican Publications, 1987; D. Medcalf, ed., Challenge for young Ireland, National Youth Council of Ireland, Dublin, 1980; D. Murray, The future of the faith, Dublin: Veritas, 1985; M. Warren, Youth and the future of the Church, New York: Seabury Press, 1982; G. Daly, Faith and imagination, Doctrine and Life XLIX, 1982, 73-77; M. Liostún, The Church and young people, The Furrow 36, 1985; D. Neary, Changing patterns in youth ministry, Doctrine and Life XLII, 1985; R. Nowell, Parents and lapsing children, Doctrine and Life XLIX, 1982; D. Regan, Ireland: a Church in need of conversion, Doctrine and Life XLII, 1985.

[44]Cf. Struggles of faith, 51. On the implications of a crisis in authority for the Church see W. Kasper, An introduction to Christian faith, 10, 146-152. For an account of attitudes towards Church authority in Ireland see K. Byrne, Power to empower. In: J. McDermott, ed., Voices in the wilderness, 53.

for imagination and wonder suffered grievously. People are now disillusioned with being disillusioned and are inclined to ask not so much "Does God exist?" or "Did the resurrection of Jesus happen?" but rather "What does God's existence mean for me?" and "How does the death and resurrection of Jesus make a difference to my life?".

In his reaction against historical criticism Balthasar certainly responds to the new hunger for meaning. Arguing that our approach to scripture must be post-critical, as Kay points out, he makes the distinction between demythologisation and demythicisation encouraged by Paul Ricouer. We can survive without mythologies, but not without myths. A post-Enlightenment world aware of the shortcomings both of the human and the natural sciences is far less critical of myth and symbol and wants to "pass beyond the desert of criticism to this second naiveté".[45]

If it is true that today Christian faith must be mediated in a Europe in which there is a crisis of meaning, rather than of facts, and in which the authority of one's personal experience is in danger of collapsing into a kind of emotivism, then the area of dispute which we have been examining between Rahner and Balthasar is entirely relevant.

What is happening generally in society would seem to be what Balthasar identified as the logical outcome of the anthropological turn in philosophy, which began when Descartes presented God's existence as proportionate to the cogito and reached its climax when Feuerbach recognised that the divinity's role had become purely relative and advised that God be dispensed with. Even though Balthasar's criticisms of a reduction within Rahner's theological method cannot be validated, as already remarked earlier in this chapter, Balthasar rightly warns theology against contributing to an impoverishment in our understanding of God and consequently of humanity which would seem to be gaining ground in a materialistic and consumerist society.

An emotivist kind of atheism shows itself in a consumerist attitude to God rather than in blatant rejection. The idea of a personal God is acceptable or unacceptable on the basis of how it matches up to one's personal experience. While God's gift of self must be understood as the greatest possible fulfilment of the individual's poverty and

---

[45]J. Kay, Hans Urs von Balthasar, a Post-critical Theologian?, Concilium 7, 1981, 85. While the limitations of historical criticism cannot be denied, however, a post-critical approach to scripture cannot be uncritical, and while Balthasar cannot be regarded as entirely uncritical in his approach, he does not always integrate the findings of historical criticism satisfactorily into his work. Kay (art. cit., 88) admits that Balthasar's symbolic use of scripture is not without difficulties and takes the example of Balthasar's attitude to the role of women in the Church and his argument against women being ordained priests. On Balthasar's attitude to historical criticism see J. Riches, Today's word for Today IV, Hans Urs von Balthasar, Expository Times, 203-204.

need, at the same time, because of the importance given to personal experience, the danger would seem to be greater than ever that God's free and gracious self-giving would be made entirely subservient to human experience. Perhaps our first step towards tackling the dehumanising elements in contemporary society is to remind ourselves of what it means to say that God is present in the world. If we do not experience God, or if we experience God only as silent or absent, we have to accept that we have changed: somehow we have plugged ourselves out. God still loves the world. God still wishes everyone to be saved and to reach full knowledge of the truth.

The challenge facing the contemporary Church is that it must present the Christian faith in such a way that it is credible and enables the individual to make sense of his or her experience of life, and at the same time, that it must avoid reducing God to human experience. But human experience cannot be by-passed. A Christian cannot be expected to live solely off second-hand experiences of God, however authoritatively mediated. If the only authority which is respected today is the authority of personal experience, it is more urgent than ever to enable people to experience God personally, and this is the real crisis in contemporary faith.

The most tragic consequence of the inability to experience God personally at the categorical level is how it affects our ability to love. Without an experience of being loved by God, we cannot love God, others, our planet, even ourselves. We urgently need effective signs that genuine love is possible. This is why the Church can never be relativised.

The Church is the sacrament of Christ's love and its most urgent and obvious task today is, as Balthasar insists, to become the greatest possible radiance of Christ by the closest possible following of him. Those of us who are aware of God's mysterious loving presence in our lives must find the confidence and the courage to put this experience at the disposal of others. According to Rahner, prophets are none other than believers who can express their transcendental experience of God correctly.[46] Prophets put their own experience of God at the disposal of others in such a way that they can see faith in God as the purest and most profound expression of their own experience of life. Jesus was prophetic in precisely this sense: his obedient listening to God, whom he experienced as Father, expressed itself in word and action, and immediately enabled those who encountered him to make sense of their own experiences in a way which they could never have hoped or dreamed of. Though many were threatened and ran away from him, many others were liberated. The latter

---

[46]Foundations of Christian faith, 159.

recognised that Jesus spoke with no authority other than his own (Mk. 1: 21-28). Jesus did not impose an alien authority upon people's experiences from outside. He simply spoke the truth and it was self-authenticating. In Jesus authority and experience were one.

The Church cannot successfully teach any differently: Didache cannot be separated from Kerygma. Catholic truths can make but little sense without the experience of God's loving and forgiving presence.

As both Rahner and Balthasar have made clear, there is no substitute for Christian witness in enabling people to experience God's presence.[47] In a materialistic world this witness must be unambiguous, and if the consumerist attitude to objects, to people and ultimately to God is to be checked before it destroys both us and our environment, we need to learn again what it means to live simply: to love tenderly, to act justly and to walk humbly with our God (Mic. 6:8).

In Pope John Paul II's eighth encyclical, Redemptoris missio, published only recently, we read that

> It is necessary to keep these two truths together, namely, the real possibility of salvation in Christ for all mankind and the necessity of the Church for salvation. Both these truths help us to understand the one mystery of salvation, so that we can come to know God's mercy and our own responsibility.[48]

It is hoped that this dissertation has made some contribution towards demonstrating just how this might be achieved.

---

[47]Cf. for example K. Rahner, Theological observations on the concept of witness, Theological investigations 13, 152-168; H.U. von Balthasar, The moment of Christian witness. Cf. also John Paul II's encyclical Redemptoris missio, especially Chapter V, n. 42 where it is stressed that the primary form of evangelisation is witness.

[48]Redemptoris Missio, n. 9.

BIBLIOGRAPHY

1. BOOKS BY HANS URS VON BALTHASAR

Balthasar, H.U. von, The Christian state of life, San Francisco: Ignatius Press, 1985.

Balthasar, H.U. von, Convergences: to the source of Christian mystery, San Francisco: Ignatius Press, 1983.

Balthasar, H.U. von, Cordula oder der Ernstfall, Einsiedeln: Johannes Verlag, 1987 (English translation of 1967 edition: The moment of Christian witness, New Jersey: Newman Press, 1969).

Balthasar, H.U. von, Dare we hope "that all men may be saved", San Francisco: Ignatius Press, 1986.

Balthasar, H.U. von, Does Jesus know us - do we know him?, San Francisco: Ignatius Press, 1983.

Balthasar, H.U. von, Elucidations, London: SPCK, 1975.

Balthasar, H.U. von, First glance at Adrienne von Speyr, San Francisco: Ignatius Press, 1981.

Balthasar, H.U. von, The glory of the Lord 1, Edinburgh: T. and T. Clark, 1982.

Balthasar, H.U. von, The glory of the Lord 2, Edinburgh: T. and T. Clark, 1984.

Balthasar, H.U. von, The glory of the Lord 3, Edinburgh: T. and T. Clark, 1986.

Balthasar, H.U. von, The God question and modern man, New York: Herder and Herder, 1967 (English translation of Die Gottesfrage des heutigen Menschen, Wien: Verlag Herold, 1956).

Balthasar, H.U. von, Karl Barth, Darstellung und Deutung seiner Theologie, Olten: Hegner Bucherei im Summa Verlag, 1951.

Balthasar, H.U. von, Love alone: the way of revelation, London: Sheed and Ward, 1968.

Balthasar, H.U. von, Man in history: a theological study, London: Sheed and Ward, 1968.

Balthasar, H.U. von, New Elucidations, San Francisco: Ignatius Press, 1986.

Balthasar, H.U. von, Rechenschaft 1965, mit einer Bibliographie der Veröffentlichungen Hans Urs von Balthasars zusammengestellt von Berthe Widmer, Einsiedeln: Johannes Verlag, 1965.

Balthasar, H.U. von, Schleifung der Bastionen, Einsiedeln: Johannesverlag, 1952.

Balthasar, H.U. von, Science, religion and Christianity, London: Burns and Oates, 1958.

Balthasar, H.U. von, Test everything - hold fast to what is good, San Francisco: Ignatius Press, 1989.

Balthasar, H.U. von, Theodramatik Bd. 2, Einsiedeln: Johannesverlag, 1978.

Balthasar, H.U. von, Theodramatik Bd. 3, Einsiedeln: Johannesverlag, 1980.

Balthasar, H.U. von, Truth is symphonic: aspects of Christian pluralism, San Francisco: Ignatius Press, 1987.

Balthasar, H.U. von, Wer ist ein Christ?, Einsiedeln: Johannes Verlag, 1965 (English translation: Who is a Christian?, London: Burns and Oates, 1968).

Balthasar, H.U. von, Word and revelation, New York: Herder and Herder, 1965.

2. ARTICLES BY HANS URS VON BALTHASAR

Balthasar, H.U. von, Apologia pro Cordula sua, Civitas 22, 1966/67, 441-442.

Balthasar, H.U. von, A résumé of my thought, Communio, Winter 1988, 468-473.

Balthasar, H.U. von, Catholicism and the communion of saints, Communio, Summer 1988, 163-168.

Balthasar, H.U. von, Catholicism and the religions, Communio 5, 1978, 6-14.

Balthasar, H.U. von, Christian prayer, Communio 5, 1978, 14-22.

Balthasar, H.U. von, Creation and trinity, Communio, Fall 1988, 285-293.

Balthasar, H.U. von, Current trends in Catholic theology, Communio 5, 1978, 76-85.

Balthasar, H.U. von, Geist und Feuer, Herder-Korrespondenz 30, 1976, 30.

Balthasar, H.U. von, Grösse und Last der Theologie heute: einige grundsätzliche Gedanken zu zwei Aufsatzbänden Karl Rahners, Wort und Wahrheit 10, 1955, 531-533.

Balthasar, H.U. von, In retrospect, Communio 12, 1975, 198-220.

Balthasar, H.U. von, Karl Rahner zum 60. Geburtstag, Christliche Kultur, Beilage zu Neue Zürcher Nachrichten 28, Nr. 9., 1964.

Balthasar, H.U. von, Meeting God in today's world, Concilium 6 (1), 1965, 23-39.

Balthasar, H.U. von, Raser les Bastions, Dieu Vivant 25, 1953, 17-32.

Balthasar, H.U. von, Response to my critics, Communio 5, 1978, 69-76.

Balthasar, H.U. von, review of Rahner's Geist in Welt, Zeitschrift für Katholische Theologie 63, 1939, 371-379.

Balthasar, H.U. von, Von der Aufgaben der katholischen Philosophie in der Zeit, Annalen der Philosophischen Gesellschaft Innerschweiz, 3 Jahrgang Nr. 2/3, Dez./Jan. 1946/47, 1-38.

Balthasar, H.U. von, Wer ist ein Laie?, Communio 14, 1985, 109-123.

Balthasar, H.U. von, Wer ist ein Christ?, Schweizer Rundschau 64, 1965, 90-97.

Balthasar, H.U. von, and Gutwenger, E., Der Begriff der Natur in der Theologie, Zeitschrift für Katholische Theologie 75, 1953, 452-464.

3. BOOKS BY KARL RAHNER

Rahner, K., The Christian and the future, New York: Herder and Herder, 1967.

Rahner, K., The Christian commitment, New York: Sheed and Ward, 1963.

Rahner, K., The Church and the sacraments, Freiburg: Herder, 1963.

Rahner, K., Concerning Vatican Council II, New York: Seabury Press, 1974.

Rahner, K., Everyday Faith, New York: Herder & Herder, 1968.

Rahner, K., Experience of the spirit: source of theology, London: DLT, 1979

Rahner, K., Faith and ministry, London: DLT, 1983.

Rahner, K., Foundations of Christian faith, London: DLT, 1978.

Rahner, K., Further theology of the spiritual life, London: DLT, 1971.

Rahner, K., Geist in Welt: zur Metaphysik der endlichen Erkenntnis bei Thomas Aquino, München: Kosel, 1957.

Rahner, K., Glaube, der die Erde liebt: Christliche Besinnung im Alltag der Welt, Freiburg: Herder, 1966.

Rahner, K., God and revelation, London: DLT, 1983.

Rahner, K., God, Christ, Mary and grace, Baltimore: Helicon, 1961.

Rahner, K., Handbuch der Pastoraltheologie, II, 2, Freiburg: Herder, 1966.

Rahner, K. Hearers of the word, (trans. J. Donceel), New York: Seabury Press, 1969.

Rahner, K., Hominisation: the evolutionary origin of man as a theological problem, Freiburg: Herder, 1965.

Rahner, K., Jesus, man and the Church, London: DLT, 1968.

Rahner, K., Lexikon für Theologie und Kirche, Freiburg: Herder, 1957-1965.

Rahner, K., The love of Jesus and the love of neighbour, Slough: St. Paul Publications, 1983.

Rahner, K., Man in the Church, Baltimore: Helicon, 1963.

Rahner, K., Mary, mother of the Lord, Wheathampstead: Clark, 1974.

Rahner, K., Meditations on freedom and the spirit, London: Burns and Oates, 1977.

Rahner, K., Mission and grace: essays in pastoral theology, London: Sheed and Ward, 1963.

Rahner, K., The mystery of man and the foundation of a theological system, London: Sheed and Ward, 1985.
Rahner, K., On heresy, Freiburg: Herder, 1964.

Rahner, K., On the theology of death, Freiburg: Herder, 1961.

Rahner, K. and Weger, K. H., Our Christian faith, London: Burns and Oates, 1980.

Rahner, K., Penance in the early Church, London: DLT, 1983.

Rahner, K., The priest of today, Dublin: Veritas, 1977.

Rahner, K., The religious life today, London: Burns and Oates, 1976.

Rahner, K., Spirit in the world, London: Sheed and Ward, 1968.

Rahner, K., Studies in modern theology, Freiburg: Herder, 1965.

Rahner, K., The theology of the spiritual life, New York: Seabury, 1967.

Rahner, K., Theological investigations 1: God, Christ, Mary, and Grace, London: Darton, Longman and Todd, 1961.

Rahner, K., Theological investigations 2: man in the Church, London: Darton, Longman and Todd, 1963.

Rahner, K., Theological investigations 3: theology of the spiritual life, London: Darton, Longman and Todd, 1967.

Rahner, K., Theological investigations 4: more recent writings, London: Darton, Longman and Todd, 1966.

Rahner, K., Theological investigations 5: later writings, London: Darton, Longman and Todd, 1966.

Rahner, K., Theological investigations 6: concerning Vatican Council II, London: Darton, Longman and Todd, 1969.

Rahner, K., Theological investigations 7: further theology of the spiritual life, London: Darton, Longman and Todd, 1971.

Rahner, K., Theological investigations 8: further theology of the spiritual life ii, London: Darton, Longman and Todd, 1971.

Rahner, K., Theological investigations 9: writings of 1965-7 I, London: Darton, Longman and Todd, 1972.

Rahner, K., Theological investigations 10: writings of 1965-7 II, London: Darton, Longman and Todd, 1973.

Rahner, K., Theological investigations 11: confrontations, London: Darton, Longman and Todd, 1974.

Rahner, K., Theological investigations 12: confrontations 2, London: Darton, Longman and Todd, 1974.

Rahner, K., Theological investigations 13: theology, anthropology, Christology, London: Darton, Longman and Todd, 1975.

Rahner, K., Theological investigations 14: ecclesiology, questions in the church, the church in the world, London: Darton, Longman and Todd, 1976.

Rahner, K., Theological investigations 16: experience of the spirit, source of theology, London: Darton, Longman and Todd, 1979.

Rahner, K., Theological investigations 17: Jesus, man and the church, London: Darton, Longman and Todd, 1981.

Rahner, K., Theological investigations 18: God and revelation, London: Darton Longman and Todd, 1983.

Rahner, K., Theological investigations 19: faith and ministry, London: Darton, Longman and Todd, 1984.

Rahner, K., Theological investigations 20: concern for the church, London: Darton, Longman and Todd, 1981.

Rahner, K., Theological investigations 21: science and theology, London: Darton, Longman and Todd, 1988.

Rahner, K., Theology, anthropology and christology, London: DLT, 1975.

Rahner, K., The Trinity, London: Burns and Oates, 1975.

Rahner, K. and Häussling, A., The celebration of the eucharist, London: Burns and Oates, 1968.

Rahner, K. and Metz, J.B., The courage to pray, New York: Crossroad, 1981.

Rahner, K., and Ratzinger, J., Revelation and tradition, Freiburg, 1966.

Rahner, K., and Thüsing, W., Christologie-systematisch und exegetisch, Freiburg, 1972.

Rahner, K. and Vorgrimler, H., Concise theological dictionary, London: Burns and Oates, 1981.

4. ARTICLES BY KARL RAHNER

Rahner, K., Gnade als Mitte menschlicher Existenz, Herder-Korrrespondenz 28, 1974, 77-92 (ET Interview with Karl Rahner, The Month 1974 n.s., 637-645).

Rahner, K., Hans Urs von Balthasar, Civitas 20, 1964, 602.

Rahner, K., Die heidnischen Christen und die Christlichen Heiden - Matt. 8, 1-13, in Rahner, K., Glaube, der die Erde liebt: Christliche Besinnung im Alltag der Welt, Freiburg: Herder, 1966.

Rahner, K., Introduction au concept de philosophie existentiale chez Heidegger, Recherches de Science Reliegieuse 30, 1940, 152-171 (ET The concept of existential philosophy in Heidegger, Philosophy Today 13, 1969, 126-137).

Rahner, K., The teaching of the Second Vatican Council on atheism, Concilium 3, 1967, 5-13.

Rahner, K., Transcendentale Methode, Geist und Leben 1, Jan/Feb 1987, 1-2.

Rahner, K., Über das Verhältnis des Naturgesetztes zur übernatürlichen Gnadenordnung, Orient 20, 1956, 8 - 11.

Rahner, K., Über die Verkündigungstheologie, Pazmanita Tudósító XVL, 1941-1942, 3-10.

5. SECONDARY LITERATURE: BOOKS

Barth, K., Kirchliche Dogmatik IV/3 Zollikon: Zürich 1959.

Bouillard, H., Blondel und das Christentum, Mainz, 1963.

Branick, V. P., An ontology of understanding: Karl Rahner's metaphysics of knowledge in the context of modern German hermeneutics, Saint Louis: Marianist, 1974.

Chapelle, A., Hegel et la religion. Volume 1: la problematique, Paris, 1963.

Clarke. M., et al, Mustard seeds, Dublin: Veritas, 1985.

Daniélou, J., Le mystère de salut des nations, Paris, 1948.

Donceel, J., The philosophy of Karl Rahner, Albany: Magi Books, 1969.

Dulles, A. A history of apologetics, New York: Corpus, 1971.

Dupuis, J., Jésus Christ à la rencontre des religions, Paris: Desclèe, 1989.

Eicher, P., Die anthropologische Wende, Karl Rahners philosophischer Weg vom Wesen des Menschen zur personalen Existenz, Freiburg Schweiz: Universitäts Verlag, 1970.

Fabro, C., La svolta antropologica di Karl Rahner, Milan: Rusconi, 1974.

Fischer, K., Der Mensch als Geheimnis. Die Anthropologie Karl Rahners. Freiburg, 1974.

Flannery, A., ed., Vatican Council II: the conciliar and post-conciliar documents, Dublin: Dominican Publications, 1975.

Gaboriau, F., Le tournant théologique aujourd'hui selon Karl Rahner, Paris, 1968.

Geffré, C., The risk of interpretation, New York: Paulist Press, 1987.

Gelpi, D., Life and light: a guide to the theology of Karl Rahner, New York: Sheed and Ward, 1966.

Grün, A., Erlösung durch das Kreuz. Karl Rahners Beitrag zu einem heutigen Erlösungsverständnis, Münsterschwarzach: Vier-Türme Verlag, 1975.

M. P. Gallagher, Help my unbelief, Dublin: Veritas, 1983.

M. P. Gallagher, Struggles of faith, Dublin: Columba Press, 1990.

Haight, R., The experience and language of grace, New York: Paulist, 1979.

Heidegger, M., Being and time, Oxford: Blackwell, 1962.

Heidegger, M., Was heißt Denken?, Tübingen, 1954.

Heijden, B. van der, Karl Rahner: Darstellung und Kritik seiner Grundpositionen, Einsiedeln: Johannes Verlag, 1973.

Heinrich, D., Der ontologische Gottesbeweis, Tübingen, 1960.

Heinz, H. Der Gott des Je-mehr. Der christologische Ansatz Hans Urs von Balthasars Frankfurt/Bern: Lang, 1975.

Heislbetz, J., Theologische Gründe der nichtchristlichen Religionen (Quaestiones Disputatae 33), Freiburg: Herder, 1967.

Holz, H., Tranzendental-philosophie und Metaphysik, Mainz, 1966.

Imhof, P., and Biallowons, H., ed., Karl Rahner Im Gespräch, Band I: 1964-1977, Band 2: 1978-1982, München: Kösel Verlag, 1982.

Inglis, T., Moral monopoly: the Catholic Church in modern Irish society, Dublin: Gill and Macmillan, 1987.

Jüngel, E., The doctrine of the trinity, Edinburgh: Scottish Academic Press, 1976.

Jüngel, E., God as the mystery of the world, Edinburgh: T. and T. Clark, 1983.

Kasper, W., Faith and the future, Kent: Burns and Oates, 1986.

Kasper, W., The God of Jesus Christ, London: SCM Press, 1984.

Kasper, W. An introduction to Christian faith, London: Burns and Oates, 1980.

Kasper, W., Jesus the Christ, London: Burns and Oates, 1976.

Kasper, W., The methods of dogmatic theology, Shannon: Ecclesia Press, 1969.

Kehl, M., Kirche als Institution, Frankfurt, 1976.

Kehl, M., and Löser, W., ed., The von Balthasar reader, Edinburgh: T. and T. Clark, 1982.

Kern, W., Ausserhalb der Kirche kein Heil?, Freiburg: Herder, 1979.

Klinger, E., Christentum innerhalb und ausserhalb der Kirche, Quaestiones Disputatae 73, Freiburg: Herder, 1976.

Komanchak, J.A. et al., ed., The new dictionary of theology, Dublin: Gill and Macmillan, 1987.

Kühn, U., Christentum außerhalb der Kirche? zum interkonfessionellen Gespräch über das Verständnis der Welt, in: Lell, J., ed. Erneuerung der einen Kirche. Arbeiten aus der Kirchengeschichte und Konfessionskunde, Göttingen, 1966.

Lane, D., Christ at the centre, Dublin: Veritas, 1990.

Lane, D., The reality of Jesus, Dublin: Veritas, 1975.

Latourelle, R. and O'Collins, G., ed., Problems and perspectives of fundamental theology, New York: Paulist Press, 1982.

Lehmann, K., ed. Vor dem Geheimnis Gottes den Menschen verstehen. Karl Rahner zum 80 Geburtstag, München: Schnell und Steiner, 1984.

Lehmann, K., and Raffelt, A., ed. Rechenschaft des Glaubens, Karl Rahner-Lesebuch Herder Freiburg: Herder, 1979.

Lehmann, K., and Kasper, W., ed., Hans Urs von Balthasar. Gestalt und Werk, Köln: Communio, 1989.

Lewis, C.S., Mere Christianity, Fontana Books (Collins), 1974.

Lochbrunner, M., Analogia Caritatis, Herder: Freiburg, 1981.

Lubac, H. de, Catholicisme: Les aspects sociaux du dogme, Paris: Les Éditions du Cerf, 1947.

Lubac, H. de, Paradoxe et mystère de l'Eglise, Paris, 1967.

Lubac, H. de, Katholizismus als Gemeinschaft, Einsiedeln: Benziger, 1943.

Mackey, J.P., The Church: its credibility today, New York: Bruce 1970.

Mackey, J.P., Modern theology - a sense of direction, Oxford: Oxford University Press, 1987.

Macquarrie, J., Existentialism, London: Penguin, 1973.

Macquarrie, J., An existentialist theology, S.C.M. Press, 1955.

McDermott, J., Voices in the wilderness, Dublin: The Columba Press, 1987.

McMahon, B., Listening to youth, Dublin: Dominican Publications, 1987.

Maréchal, J., Le point de départ de la metaphysique. Cahier I: de l'antiquité á la fin du moyen age, Paris: Librairie Félix Alcan, 1921.

Maréchal, J., Le point de départ de la metaphysique. Cahier II: Le conflit du rationalisme et de l'empirisme dans la philosophie moderne, avant Kant, Paris: Librairie Félix Alcan, 1923.

Marías, J., History of philosophy, New York: Dover publications, 1967.

McCool, G., A Rahner reader, London: DLT, 1975.

McDonagh, E., ed., Irish challenges to theology: papers of the Irish Theological Association Conference 1984, Dublin: Dominican Publications, 1986.

Medcalf, D., ed. Challenge for young Ireland, National Youth Council of Ireland, Dublin, 1980

Metz, J.B., Christliche Anthropozentrik. Über die denkform des Thomas von Aquin, München, 1962.

Moltmann, J., Trinity and the kingdom of God, London: SCM, 1981.

Mondin, E., La nuova teologia Cattolica da Karl Rahner a Urs von Balthasar, Roma: Edizioni Logos, 1978.

Muck, O., The transcendental method, New York, 1968.

Murray, D., The future of the faith, Dublin: Veritas, 1985.

Neufeld, K. H., Rahner-Register: ein Schlüssel zu Karl Rahners Schriften zur Theologie 1 - X und zu seinem Lexikonartikeln, Zürich: Benzigen Verlag, 1974.

Newman, J.H., The idea of a university, New York: Image Books, 1959.

O'Collins, G., Interpreting Jesus, London: Darton, Longman and Todd, 1983.

O'Donnell. J., The mystery of the triune God, London: Sheed and Ward, 1987.

O'Donohue, Noel D., Mystics for our time: Carmelite meditations for a new age, Edinburgh: T&T Clark, 1990.

Pöggeler, O., Der Denkweg Martin Heideggers, Tübingen: Neske, 1963.

Richardson, W., Heidegger: through phenomenology to thought,

Riches, J.K., ed., The analogy of beauty, Edinburgh: T. and T. Clark, 1986.

Röper, A., The anonymous Christian, New York: Sheed and Ward, 1966.

Saward, J., The mysteries of March, London: Collins, 1990.

Schleiermacher, F., On religion: speech to its Cultured Despisers

Schwerdtfeger, N., Gnade und Welt: zum Grundgefüge von Karl Rahners Theorie der "Anonymen Christen", Freiburg: Herder, 1982.

Siewerth, G., Das Schicksal der Metaphysik von Thomas zu Heidegger, Johannes Verlag: Einsedeln, 1959.

Tillich, P., Begnungen. Paul Tillich über sich selbst und andere, Gesammelte Werke Vol. 12, Stuttgart, 1971.

Tillich, P., Systematic theology, 1978.

Vass, G., A theologian in search of a philosophy, London: Sheed and Ward, 1985.

Vass, G., The mystery of man and the foundations of a theological system, London: Sheed and Ward, 1985.

Vorgrimler, H., Karl Rahner: his life, thought and works, London: Burns and Oates, 1963.

Vorgrimler, H., ed., "Wagnis"-Theologie: Erfahrungen mit der Theologie K. Rahners, Freiburg: Herder, 1979.

Warren, M., Youth and the future of the Church, New York: Seabury Press, 1982.

Weger, K. - H., Karl Rahner: an introduction to his theology, London: Burns and Oates, 1980.

6. SECONDARY LITERATURE: ARTICLES

Anon., A modern conception of salvation which hampers apostolic zeal according to Fr. Karl Rahner, Christ to the world 8, 1963, 421-428, 543-544.

Babini, E., Jesus Christ, form and norm of man, Communio, Fall 1989, 446-457.

Boutin, M., Anonymous Christianity: a paradigm for interreligious encounter?, Journal of Ecumenical Studies 20 (4), 1983, 602-629.

Bürkle, H., Der Glaube an Gott in Hinduismus und Christentum, Zeitschrift für Missionwissenschaft und Religionswissenschaft 61, 1977, 177-187.

Burns, R.M., The agent intellect in Rahner and Aquinas, Heythrop Journal XXIX, 1988, 423-449.

Chantraine, G., Exegesis and contemplation, Communio, Fall 1989, 366-383.

Cobb, J.B., A question for Hans Urs von Balthasar, Communio 5, 1978.

Connolly, G., Blondel, spiritual experience and fundamental theology today, Science et Esprit 36 (3), 1984, 323-339.

Daly, G., Faith and imagination, Doctrine and Life XLIX, 1982, 73-77.

D'Costa, G., Karl Rahner's Anonymous Christian - A Reappraisal, Modern Theology 1 (2), 1985, 131-148.

Danker, W.J., The anonymous Christian and christology: A response, Missiology: an International Review 6 (2), 1978, 235-241.

Darlap, A., Fundamental Theologie der Heilsgeschichte, Mysterium Salutis 1, 1965, 3-153.

Donceel, J., Rahner's argument for God, America 123, 1970, 340-342.

Dupré, L., The glory of the Lord, Communio, Fall 1989, 384-412.

Eberhard, K.D., Karl Rahner and the supernatural existential, Thought 46, 1971, 537-561.

Eicher, P. Immanenz oder Tranzendenz? Gespräch mit Karl Rahner, Freiburger Zeitschrift für Philosophie und Theologie 15, 1968, 29-62.

Elders, L., Die Taufe der Weltreligionen. Bemerkengungen zu einer Theorie Karl Rahners, Theologie und Glaube LV, 1965, 124-131.

Engelhardt, P., Zu den anthropologischen Grundlagen der Ethik des Thomas von Aquin, Die Enthüllung des massgebenden Lebenzieles durch das desiderium naturale, Sein und Ethos 1, 1963, 186-212.

Escobar, P., Hans Urs von Balthasar: Christo-theologian, Communio 12, 1975, 301-316.

Freyne, S., Theology 23: Sacrifice for sin, The Furrow 25, 4, Apr.1974, 193-212.

Galvin, J., Gnade und Welt, Theological Studies 44, 1983, 725-727.

Geffré, C., Recent developments in fundamental theology: an interpretation, Concilium 5, 1969, 4-14.

Hacker, P., The Christian attitude toward non-christian religions, Zeitschrift für Missionwissenschaft und Religionswissenschaft 55, 1971, 81-97.

Haight, R., The unfolding of modernism in France: Blondel, Laborthonniere, Le Roy, Theological Studies 35, 1974, 633-666.

Hardon, J., Review of K. Rahner's On the theology of death, Catholic Biblical Quarterly 24, 1962, 343-344.

Henrici, P., Hans Urs von Balthasar: a sketch of his life, Communio, Fall 1989, 306-350.

Horne, B.L., Today's word for today, VI. Karl Rahner, The Expository Times 92, 1980-81, 324-328.

Hurd, R., Being is Being-present-to-self: Rahner's key to Aquinas's metaphysics, Thomist 52, 1988, 63-78.

Hurd, R., Heidegger and Aquinas: a Rahnerian bridge, Philosophy Today, Summer, 1984, 105-137.

Janke, W. Ontotheologie und Methodik, Philosophische Rundschau 12, 1964, 179-217.

Jüngel, E., Extra Christum nulla salus - als Grundsatz natürlicher Theologie?, Zeitschrift für Theologie und Kirche 72, 1975, 337-352.

Kannengiesser, C., Listening to the Fathers, Communio, Fall 1989, 413-418.

Kay, J., Aesthetics and a posteriori evidence in Balthasar's theological method, Communio 12, 1975, 288-316.

Kay, J., Hans Urs von Balthasar: a post-critical theologian? Concilium 7, 1981, 84-89.

Keefe, D.J., A methodological critique of von Balthasar's theological aesthetics, Communio 5, 1978.

Kruse, H., Die "Anonymen Christen" exegetisch gesehen, Münchener Theologische Zeitschrift 18, 1967, 2-29.

Küng, H., Anonyme Christen - wozu?, Orientierung 39, 1975, 214-216.

Lehmann, K., Some ideas from pastoral theology on the proclamation of the Christian message to non-believers today, Concilium 3, 1967, 43-52

Liostún, M., The Church and young people, The Furrow 36, 1985.

Löser, W., Being interpreted as love, Communio, Fall 1989, 475-490.

Lubac, H. de, A witness of Christ in the Church: Hans Urs von Balthasar, Communio 12, 1975, 229-250.

MacKinnon, E., The transcendental turn: necessary but not sufficient, Continuum 6, 1968, 225-232.

Macquarrie, J., The essence of Rahner's theology, The Expository Times 90, 1978, 58-59.

Malevez, L., L'Esprit et le desir de Dieu, Nouvelle Revue Théologique LXIX, 1947, 3-31.

Malevez, P., Cordula oder der Ernstfall, Nouvelle Revue Thèologique 89, 1967, 1107.

Malevez, P., Présence de la théologie à Dieu et à l'homme, Nouvelle Revue Thèologique 90, 1968, 784-800.

Maloney, D., Rahner and the "anonymous" Christian, America, 1970, 348-350.

Mannerman, T., Eine falsche Interpretationstradition von K. Rahners Hörer des Wortes, Zeitschrift für Katholische Theologie 92, 1970, 204-209.

McCool, G., The concept of the human person in Karl Rahner's theology, Theological Studies 22, 1961, 537-562.

McDermott, B., Karl Rahner: Foundations of Christian faith, Theological Studies 41, 1988, 343-347.

Muck, O. Heidegger und Karl Rahner, text of a lecture delivered at a conference on "Heidegger and Theology" at the Trent Institute of Culture, 9 Feb. 1990 and made public in the Rahner Archives, Innsbruck.

Neary, D., Changing patterns in youth ministry, Doctrine and Life XLXII, 1985.

Nowell, R., Parents and lapsing children, Doctrine and Life XLIX, 1982.

O'Donnell, J., Hans Urs von Balthasar: The form of his theology, Communio, Fall 1989, 458-474.

O'Donovan, L., A changing ecclesiology in a changing Church: a symposium on development in the ecclesiology of Karl Rahner, Theological studies 38, 1977, 736-762.

O'Donovan, L., God's glory in time, Communio 12, 1975, 251-270.

O'Hanlon, G., Does God change? H.U. von Balthasar on the immutability of God, Irish theological quarterly 53, 1987, 161-183.

O'Hanlon, D.J., Hans Urs von Balthasar on non-Christian religions and meditation, Communio 5, 1978, 60-68.

Proterra, M., Hans Urs von Balthasar: theologian, Communio 12, 1975, 270-288.

Race, A., Christianity and other religions: is inclusivism enough?, Theology 1,2, 1983, 178-186.

Ratzinger, J., The ecclesiology of the Second Vatican Council, Communio 13, 1986.

Ratzinger, J., Homily at the funeral liturgy for Hans Urs von Balthasar, Communio, Winter 1988, 512-516.

Ratzinger, J., Vom Verstehen des Glaubens, Theologische Revue 74, 1978, 176-186.

Regan, D., Ireland: a Church in need of conversion, Doctrine and Life XLXII, 1985.

Riches, J.K., The theology of Hans Urs von Balthasar: 1, Theology LXXV, 1972, 562-571.

Riches, J.K., The theology of Hans Urs von Balthasar: 2, Theology LXXV, 1972, 648-654.

Riches, J.K., Today's word for today, The Expository Times 92, 1980-1981, 200-205.

Riesenhuber, K., Der anonyme Christ, nach Karl Rahner, Zeitschrift für Katholische Theologie LXXXVI, 1964, 286-303.

Roberts, L., The collision of Rahner and Balthasar, Continuum 5, 1968, 753-757.

Rooy, J.A. van, Christ and the religions: the issues at stake, Missionalia 13, 1985, 3-13.

Rosato, P., Spirit christology: ambiguity and promise, Theological Studies 38, 1977, 423-469.

Roten, J., The two halves of the moon, Communio, Fall 1989, 419-446.

Ruesche, F., review of Rahner's Geist in Welt, TG 32, 1940, 299.

Schindler, J. P., Christ and Church: a spectrum, Theological Studies 37, 1976, 545-566.

Schineller, J.P., Christ and Church: A spectrum of views, Theological Studies 37, 1976, 545-566.

Schmitz, K.L., Divine initiative and Christian praxis, Communio 5, 1978, 44-52.

Schönborn, C., Does the Church need philosophy?, Communio, Fall 1988, 335-349.

Schreiter, R., The anonymous Christian and christology, Occasional Bulletin of Missionary Research 2, 1978, 2-11.

Sesboüé, B., Karl Rahner et les chrétiens anonymes, Etudes 361, 1984, 521-536.

Sicari, A., Theology and holiness, Communio, Fall 1989, 351-365.

Sudbrack, J., Um den Stellenswort der Spiritualität im Gesamt der Theologie, Geist und Leben 37, 1964, 387-393.

Surlis, P., Rahner and Lonergan on method in theology (Part 1), Irish Theological Studies 39, 1972, 23-42.

Surlis, P., Rahner and Lonergan on method in theology (Part 2), Irish Theological Quarterly, 38, 1971, 187-201.

Tallon, A., Connaturality in Aquinas and Rahner, Philosophy Today, Summer, 1984, 138-147.

Vacek, J., Development within Rahner's theology, Irish Theological Quarterly 42, 1975, 36-49.

Vass, G., The faith needed for salvation - 1, The Month 1 (new series), 1970, 201-208.

Verestegegui, Christianisme et religions non-chrétiennes: Analyse de la 'tendance Daniélou', Euntes Docete 25, 1970, 227-229.

Vorgrimler, H., Uber die "anonymen Christen", Hochland 56, 1963/1964, 363-364.

Vorgrimler, H., Was hat er gegeben - was haben wir genommen? Orientierung 48, 1984, 31-35.

Vries, J. de, review of Rahner's Geist in Welt, Scholastik 15, 1940, 404-409.

Waldenfels, H., Theologische Akkomodation, Hochland 58, 1965/1966, 189-204.

Waldenfels, H., ...omnes homines vult salvos fieri...(1 Tim. 2:4). De sententia O. Caroli Rahner S.J. circa voluntatem salvificam Dei universalem, Shingaku Kenkyu 12, 1962.

Waldstein, M., Hans Urs von Balthasar's theological aesthetics, Communio 9, 1984, 12-27.

Willens, B. A., Who belongs to the Church?, Concilium I/1, 1965, 62-71.

Zeller, H., review of Rahner's Geist in Welt, Gregorianum 209, 1939, 471-474.

7. SECONDARY LITERATURE: DISSERTATIONS

Heinz, H., Der Gott des Je-mehr. Der Christologische Ansatz Hans Urs von Balthasars, Frankfurt, 1975.

Sachs, J., The Pneumatology and Christian spirituality of Hans Urs von Balthasar, die Katholisch-theologische Fakultät, Tübingen, 1984.

Saldanha, C., Divine Pedagogy: a patristic view of non-Christian religions, Faculty of Theology, Pontifical University, Maynooth, 1978.

Scheurich, H., Halle-Wittenberg, reference in Theological Studies 44, 1983.

Shim, J. Glaube und Heil: Eine Untersuchung zur theorie von den "anonymen Christen" Karl Rahners, die Katholisch-theologische Fakultät, Tübingen, 1975.

Simons, E., Philosophie der Offenbarung, Stuttgart, 1966.

Striewe, H., "reditio subjecti in seipsum" - Der Einfluß Hegels, Kants und Fichtes auf die Religionsphilosophie Karl Rahners, die philosophische Fakültat, Freiburg-in-Bresgau, 1979.

Merrill Morse

Kosuke Koyama
A Model for Intercultural Theology

Frankfurt/M., Bern, New York, Paris, 1991. XIV, 317 pp.
Studien zur interkulturellen Geschichte des Christentums/Etudes
d'Histoire Interculturelle du Christianisme/ Studies in the Intercultural
History of Christianity. Begründet von /fondé par/founded by
Hans Jochen Margull †, Hamburg
Herausgegeben von/édité par/edited by Richard Friedli,
Walter J. Hollenweger, Theo Sundermeier. Vol. 71
ISBN 3-631-43962-8   pb. DM 89.--

The highly pluralistic, intercultural nature of the modern world
challenges Christiaity to reexamine its relationship to other religions
and to reconsider the nature of theology itself. No longer can theology
be grounded primarily in the methods and terminology of Western
culture. Kosuke Koyama illustrates an Asian approach to theological
methodology. He also models a uniquely Christocentric yet open-
ended approach to Christian encounters with the world's cultures and
religions.

Contents: Koyama's Biographical, Japanese, and Asian Context –
Koyama's Hermeneutical Core: Crucified Mind, Neighbourology –
Narrative and Theoretical Language in Theology

Verlag Peter Lang Frankfurt a.M. · Berlin · Bern · New York · Paris · Wien
Auslieferung: Verlag Peter Lang AG, Jupiterstr. 15, CH-3000 Bern 15
Telefon (004131) 9411122, Telefax (004131) 9411131
- Preisänderungen vorbehalten -